PRAISE FOR THE FINANCIAL AID HANDBOOK

"With this book, Carol and Ruth have done the impossible...they have provided essential information about financing a college education, the language with which to have difficult conversations about college cost, and they have made this complex topic easy to understand...and even fun! This book is a necessary reference for any family beginning a college search. Loaded with information about financing a college education, readers will come away with indispensable 'behind the scenes' understanding about how it all works."

—Sara Kyle, associate director of college counseling, The Blake School

"The timing of this book could not be better! Sorting college options according to what you can afford...or 'who will fund you'....is practically revolutionary! It also demystifies a great deal of the admissions process. A boon to students and their families everywhere! This is a book aimed at young people making that momentous decision about college. The twist? Basing your college search on 'who will fund you' to attend their institution! So, it's also a book for families. This information will change the way you look at college admissions...and your own personal finances. This is information you will not find in your guidance office or those big fat college choice manuals. Carol and Ruth demystify financial aid and the admissions processes in a readable and 'no nonsense' voice. Read this before it's too late!"

—Mary A. Ackerman, director of external relations, Office of the President, Search Institute

"As someone involved in administering student financial assistance and enrollment management for over 35 years, I would strongly recommend this publication to students, parents, and any high school or college enrollment professional looking for a new, refreshing take on the essentials of financing higher education."

—David L. Pardieck, executive director, Office of Financial Assistance, Bradley University

THE
FINANCIAL AID
HANDBOOK

*GETTING THE EDUCATION YOU WANT
FOR THE PRICE YOU CAN AFFORD*

❖| CAROL STACK AND RUTH VEDVIK |❖

CAREER
PRESS

The Career Press, Inc.
Franklin Lakes, NJ

THE FINANCIAL AID HANDBOOK
EDITED BY JODI BRANDON
TYPESET BY GINA HOOGERHYDE
Cover design by Rob Johnson/Toprotype
Printed in the U.S.A.

To order this title, please call toll-free 1-800-CAREER-1 (NJ and Canada: 201-848-0310) to order using VISA or MasterCard, or for further information on books from Career Press.

CAREER
PRESS

The Career Press, Inc.
220 West Parkway, Unit 12
Pompton Plains, NJ 07444
www.careerpress.com

Library of Congress Cataloging-in-Publication Data

Stack, Carol.
    The financial aid handbook : getting the education you want for the price you can afford / by Carol Stack and Ruth Vedvik.
        p. cm.
    Includes bibliographical references and index.
    ISBN 978-1-60163-166-4 -- ISBN 978-1-60163-660-7 (ebook) 1. Student aid--United States--Handbooks, manuals, etc. 2.
Student loans--United States--Handbooks, manuals, etc. 3. College costs--
    United States--Handbooks, manuals, etc. I. Vedvik, Ruth. II. Title.

LB2337.4.S68 2011
378.30973--dc22

2010054606

High school students, we dedicate this book to you, the children who are (however trite it might sound) our future.

ACKNOWLEDGMENTS

Special thanks to Barbara Cleveland, our secret weapon and without whom this book would not have happened.

Lots of love to David, Craig, and Ian for their patience and support.

We'd like to extend a heartfelt thank you to our agent, Joelle Delbourgo, and authors Chris Farrell and Jessica Bruder for providing critical early feedback and assistance.

We'd also like to thank our colleagues who aided us enormously in this process—either by reading, critiquing, or just plain listening—in no particular order: Dave Pardieck, Sandy Douglas, Mary Ackerman, Kate Taylor, Dave Busse, Tom Weede, Dan Walls, Sarah Kyle, Michael Kyle, Sally Daniels, Ray Brown, Herald Johnson, Kim Johnson, Al McIvor, Betty Hackett, Mona Bowe, Jon McGee, Jim Day, and the entire staff of Hardwick-Day. You are all brilliant, helpful, and kind. Thank you for your help, your conversation, and your friendship.

This book couldn't exist without all of the students, parents, and guidance counselors we have had the privilege of serving throughout the years.

CONTENTS

PREFACE FOR PARENTS

It's finally here: time to send your baby off to college. We recommend kick-starting the process with two books: ours (more below) and *Letting Go: A Parent's Guide to Understanding the College Years* by Karen Levin Coburn and Madge Lawrence Treeger (a fabulous and insightful description of what it really means when your child goes off to college).

You can't help but notice that we've addressed this book to students. Our reasoning for that is simple. Even though we know that the decision to select a particular college or university is usually a family decision, the process itself—ranging from the first request for information to the application, essay, letters of reference, and many of the financial aid forms—is for the student to complete. It is vital that students take ownership of the process—with the best information possible. Like you, we know the difficulty of engaging the attention of a high school student in a confusing process overlaid with information that is boring at best. Our goal for this book is to help students understand the convergence of roles (theirs and yours) in college choice and payment. We know not only because we've both worked in the world of college admission and financial aid for more than 35 years, we've each coached our own children through the process—sometimes kicking and screaming.

There are more than 4,400 colleges and universities in the United States. This book will help your student find a great college, maybe one you've not even heard of, that will value her academic ability, or talent, or special characteristics (embraces being green, a commitment to Amnesty International, or Ultimate Frisbee) and will *fund* her education. Really, that's how it works.

In the chapters of this book we detail the "what's," "how's," and "why's" of the financial aid process in clear language that we hope will connect with students—and with you. We also describe a process for students to use to identify those colleges and universities that will fund their study, explain to them the realities of college costs, and suggest ways in which they begin the process and discussion with you about those costs and their management. And we've included a bonus: a chapter directed to you to help you begin and structure those awkward conversations about money for college and your own financial situation.

So, buy this book, read it, and have your student sit down and read it. You'll notice we not only directed the book to students, but also wrote in language that will resonate with them. After all, when was the last time your student read something written to or for you? Never? Probably. We know you'll read and hopefully enjoy the language of the teen world. We had fun with it, maybe even periodically went a little over the top, but we're desperate to get their attention. Doing a college search the way we recommend will change their lives. Really, it will. For you, following our advice will help to keep you from assuming astronomic amounts of debt or to pay any more out of your pocket than really, truly necessary to get your student a great education at a place that values him enough to pay him to attend.

This is how it works. We hope you enjoy the book, we hope it changes your student's life, and we can practically guarantee that if you and your student do things our way you'll save money.

INTRODUCTION

There is a thought that may have already occurred to you, high school students. If not, it's coming soon.

You'll think to yourself, "If only I had a disability."

You'll look at your toes and think, "I could lose a toe."

If it would give you an edge in the college admissions process, you would gladly lose a toe. "That could be an interesting essay," you'll think: "My Life Without Toe(s)."

Or, better yet: If only you were really, really poor; if only you were an orphan; if only you had survived cancer, or somehow overcome an enormous adversity like the "Homeless to Harvard" girl who, you think to yourself, *got into Harvard*. If only you had been a runaway, lived on a train, gotten an experience that could distinguish you, lost the aforementioned toe. You'll have a moment where you are actually jealous of your classmates that are in foster care or have children of their own or are physically disabled or ran away from their abusive parents to live with a distant relative.

You might feel like a nerd, like a nothing, like a perfectly Plain Jane who has nothing interesting to offer, who has never taken any chances, and who doesn't have anything to show for the safe and middle-class life you've led. You'll think you should have made some tragic problem for yourself and then risen above it in a demonstrable, essay-friendly manner. Sadly, you did not. You stayed home, went to school, did your homework, practiced the piano, and slowly, througout time, morphed into the perfect candidate to get rejected from Amherst on the basis that "we have too many like her already." Or even worse, accepted—and then asked to take out a home mortgage's worth of loans to cover your tuition.

That might not sound worse to you, to get accepted at a little Ivy like Amherst. "Worse?" you think. "How on earth could that possibly be worse than getting rejected?" Getting rejected is humiliating, especially if one of your friends gets in. Your entire high school career has been filled—been overflowing—with people telling you that you should go to the best college you can possibly get into and that everything you do is important "for college" and for "when you apply to college." Every single thing you do is something that "colleges like to see" or "colleges don't like to see."

College—and where people go to college—is where we, as a society, begin to split the wheat from the chaff. Thanks to ratings boards, we can actually define colleges in a straight and linear hierarchy: good, better, best. People who go to Harvard and Yale are the smartest (how many times have you heard "So-and-so went to Harvard. He's a really bright guy."), and everyone else is slightly dumber than that. You want to go to the best school possible, because that is what everyone will approve of, and where you go to college affects the rest of your life. If you don't get into the right school, you won't be able to get a good job, and then you'll be poor and sad and dumb to boot for the rest of your entire life.

Let us just say this: That kind of thinking is bananas. It is crazy. It is nuts. It makes no sense. Because here is the thing, the thing that is so important: *College costs money. A lot of money.* We'll repeat it one more time: College costs a lot of money.

Seriously, *a lot* of money—anywhere between $80 and $180 *thousand* dollars. That's $80,000–$180,000, with all of the zeroes attached.

With $180,000 you could buy, according to our expert Googling:

√ *One Lamborghini.*

√ *A one-bedroom condo in suburban Boulder, Colorado.*

√ *A three-bedroom house in Idaho.*

√ *18 horses (trail horses).*

√ *One racehorse (champion thoroughbred).*

There is a secret to financial aid that no one has ever, and probably will never, tell you (at least before you graduate). Before we get into it, let us explain why: It is not a secret to anyone who truly understands capitalism. There is no secret admission and financial aid cabal, and no Skull & Bones in underground meeting rooms. The secret, or rather the facts of financial aid, are simply a function of the American market. When it comes to telling students, not only do the people who understand this assume that that *you're* not smart enough to understand it, but colleges (and admission officers, and financial aid officers) need you to be ignorant of the fact, in order to drive up their application numbers, and thus increase their selectivity. This is both a function of your age, and the accessibility you likely have to at least two mid-career incomes (read: You are young, and therefore dumb, and your parents have more money than someone who is 25).

We'll try to describe this as simply as possible, because you probably haven't had very much actual, on-the-ground experience with running a business (not because you're dumb, but because you're not really allowed by law). Colleges gain income from tuition, from donors, from the U.S. government, and from endowments, the holding of wealth that they invest on the open market, in stocks, bonds, CDs, and other accounts. Money, in capitalism, essentially begets more money. Colleges improve their money-earning potential by climbing up a scale of selectivity, much in the same way that one would assume that someone who graduates from Harvard would make more money (or have the opportunities to make more money) than someone who graduates from the local community college. Elitism and status beget more elitism and status, as colleges, through time, whittle their student bodies down to Olympic-level packs of the best and the brightest.

Tuition dollars are used, essentially, as leverage to acquire the kind of students that a school wants in order to increase their status and selectivity. All tuition dollars forfeited (read: scholarships given to students) are dollars that must be spent by the college, and are only barely offset by the tuition payments made in full by non-scholarship students.

If this sounds cold, that's because, well, it is. Universities are businesses, just like everything else, not an altruistic force that exists solely to spread the "life of the mind." A university is not the secular, or non-religious, version of a church; it is much more like the intellectual equivalent of Google: millions of users, or consumers, whose needs and search terms dictate what the Internet will produce. The more people Google "Britney Spears" or "Tila Tequila," the more popular they become; the more students request programs such as Microsoft certification, the more schools will offer it, and the more that schools with proven employment for their graduates can attract students.

Universities, however, are not above their devotion to their product, that "life of the mind" we mentioned earlier. Just because it's not free doesn't mean it isn't there. There is, essentially, a hierarchy that holds the top schools (Ivies) above the almost-top schools ("Little" and "Public" Ivies) above a competitive upper-middle of small privates, and then a solid middle of publics and *really* small privates. Somewhere after the Ivies and Little Ivies are schools whose alumni are not so wealthy, and need to be enticed to donate with things besides status. For example, you might not get your name on the library, but you will be invited to a rock opera. Those schools are the creative and thoughtful places that are, you might say, actually less burdened by the status and selectivity needs of their alumni and students than colleges with more money than the country of Belgium. Those schools might have less stuff and less cash (for example, they won't pay to send you on spring break or give you a state-of-the-art gym in every dorm) but nonetheless, they are wonderful places to learn and grow into an adult.

But why? Why would you want to go to a place that has less stuff and less of a status name? The reason is simple. It's the important thing we told you about before: money.

College costs a lot of money.

And chances are, you have neither a 4.0, perfect SATs and a hundred extracurriculars, or wealthy parents who can afford to shell out the entire cost of attendance. You are most likely an interesting person with pretty good grades and a family that might be doing okay, but not making a lot of money. Your family's income may not be low enough (we're talking *really* low: less than $30,000 a year for your entire household) to qualify you for a huge need-based aid package. Chances are, you will have to take out loans, and under no circumstances will the name brand of your alma mater outweigh the burden of that debt. If you have a $700 monthly loan payment, *it does not matter where you went to college,* you will not be able to move to, say New York City or Los Angeles, and take the unpaid internship; you will *absolutely* need to get a better job. The world has changed. Very few employers hire people straight out of college with no work experience; there are simply too many people who have both a degree and relevant work experience under their belt at the age of 21.

So what does this mean for you, you might ask? How on earth can you take this information and get into college, much less pay for it?

This entire book is devoted to helping you answer that question. The first thing you need to do is understand that you may end up at a school you have never heard of; we're going to ask you to do research and to expose yourself to the hundreds of marvelous schools that use the market to their advantage (read: will pay for you to be there, because they can and they want a student like you).

We need you to let go of all the crap everyone has thrown at you, let go of the status ambitions, let go of the ego, and let go of the admission pressure. Let go of the voice in your head that says you won't get anywhere if you don't climb the social ladder. You're already doing great, just as you are. For starters, you're reading this book, which shows that you're already interested in taking responsibility for the events in your own life. You will become a successful and intellectually satisfied person in life, even if you don't go to your reach school (the school you probably can't get into, but you're going to try). The world is an amazing and wonderful place, filled with problems to solve and abstract intellectual equations to ponder—at your job, on the subway, or playing cards with friends in a dimly lit kitchen, listening to music.

Life is an adventure, and college has something to offer that no one can take away from you: It's the first time in your life when your life will really, truly be your own. It won't belong to anyone else—not your parents, not even your professors (after all, it's up to you to go to class). When you graduate from high school, the world will suddenly come into being and become yours to explore.

If you keep reading, and try to do what we ask, we promise that we will help you get into and pay for the right school for you, and graduate with a reasonable amount of debt.

This isn't a manual of academic tricks. We are explaining the market; this is not a game-the-system book, in the sense that we're going to teach you how to put one over on colleges and universities. Rather, we're giving you the tools to make an intelligent (and extraordinarily expensive) purchase in a market that will affect you after you graduate. You will not graduate from college into a fantasyland with fat salaries and job security; that has all changed with the recession that began in 2007, and closing your eyes for four years and racking up debt will not change that.

You might be wondering *why* we would tell you this. Will it affect our careers? Hardly—at least, we hope not. As an industry, we need to figure out a better way to run the business of higher education. Paying full tuition is not financially feasible for most of the people in our country, and the way in which our economy is developing requires a new economic resource: intelligent and educated minds who can produce America's only remaining and inimitable resource, that of culture. Culture includes popular culture, architecture, design, art, music and sounds (did you know Brian Eno, from the band Roxy Music, created the Microsoft "turning on" noise?), novels, history books, and even political speeches.

Culture is what comes from the mind, not the ground; other countries have surpassed us in manufacturing and natural resources, and only by figuring out how to work with them intelligently and ethically will we be able to have a true and prosperous form of globalization. Without that—without the people who ask "Should I?" or "Is there a better way?" instead of "Can I?"—our world will turn into a futuristic, sci-fi nightmare where technology is used for its worst purposes against a helpless proletariat of worker bees.

Okay, okay. We realize that *might* be a little dramatic. But what we're trying to tell you is that we care. We care about students individually, and we care very deeply about our country's educational system. We've devoted our lives to it—more than 70 years between the two of us. And now, after all this time, we've decided to pass on what we know. No one else, as far as we know, has gathered all the resources that we have between the covers of this book—and there's more on our website at *thefinancialaid-handbook.com*. Grab a cup of coffee, settle down in your favorite chair, and—please—turn off your cell phone. It's time to get real about college.

The Seven Biggest Myths About Paying for College

If you're like most people, you will apply to five to 10 schools that you like, fill out your FAFSA, then cross your fingers and see who gives you the best offer. Then you will beg and plead with your parents, take out loans, and head off for college in the fall after your senior year. You may already have some idea of your family's finances; you're certainly going to apply for financial aid, if you've already picked up this book. Maybe you're planning on taking out some loans; but you'll figure all of it out *after* you've applied.

Perhaps you've *already* applied, and the FAFSA deadline is coming up—and you just want to know how to get the most money out of the government. ("Hand over the tricks, ladies! Give me some charts and instructions, and let's be done with it!")

Well, kid, we're sorry, but we can't do that. Like anything worth learning in college, you've got to listen to some old person drone on for a while. In your case that old person is the two of us, Carol and Ruth.

If you've already applied to colleges, and you're just trying to use this book to figure out your FAFSA (Free Application for Federal Student Aid) or apply for private scholarships, we have something terrible to tell you: You might not get a significant amount of aid.

The biggest scholarships and financial aid you can get—the kind that really matter—come from colleges themselves, and in order to get them, you've got to apply to the right kind of place. If it's already too late, and you're looking at taking on huge student loans, please turn immediately to Chapter 11. How much is *too* much to take out in student loans? Well, we consider anything over $32,000 total, or $8,000 per year, to be unacceptable; see Chapter 3.

You might be thinking, "Why? Why does it matter how much I pay for college? College is an *investment*; I'll be able to pay it back if I get a good job. And the better the college I go to, the better the job I'll be able to get."

Unfortunately, that's not always true. But it's incredibly difficult to understand why that's not true; you're never given the opportunity to question it. *Socrates is a man; all men are mortal; therefore Socrates is mortal.* The more you pay for something, the more valuable it is; the more expensive the college, the better the education and the better the opportunities that follow. You've never been *asked* to question that kind of logic; it seems as natural as Socrates's conclusion that he is mortal. And you are an American teenager—going to college will happen no matter what. It's the new high school diploma. It is a foregone conclusion—an absolute must, a compulsory, mandatory event in your life. Here is your circumstance: You will turn 18, graduate from high school, and head off to college. Going to college does not feel like a choice. But it is a choice. *Going to college, and where you go to college, is a choice.* The reason that it is a choice—and not mandatory—is because college is not free. It must be paid for. And because it must be paid for, you are a consumer, the same as someone selecting a new pair of jeans at the local mall.

When you think about colleges, there is a hierarchy in your brain of what is okay, what is pretty good, what is better, and what is best. There are a couple of assumptions you're going to make about college:

1. *The more selective a college is, the better the college.*

2. *The more expensive the college is, the better the college.*

These two things aren't necessarily true. You've got to question both of these assumptions.

We're going to spend the rest of this book explaining to you that much of what you *think* you know about colleges and universities is, in many ways, untrue. The most basic thing that we need you to understand is this:

Colleges are a business, and you are their target market.

But this doesn't make you helpless. You're a consumer of education; you have the right to choose how you spend your money. The marketing of education, though intoxicating, is nowhere near as potent as tobacco marketing, for example. How many people have you met who are "addicted to learning" (other than scarily enthusiastic, middle-aged teachers with embroidered cat sweaters and "History Is Fun!" pins)? Education marketing isn't nearly as potent, but nonetheless, the effect is the same: You and your peers are under the impression that the "better" the college you attend, the "better" the job you get will be.

This is reinforced by successful people with degrees from elite colleges. Maybe you know them, or you read about them in the newspaper or in books or whatever. You might think that they're successful because of where they went to school, and that may be partially true. Going to school—any school—is important. A great education is extremely helpful in life, not in the least because it opens up your mind to all the possibilities of the world. But successful people are generally successful for two main reasons:

1. *They don't give up. Even when they fail, they pick themselves up and try something new. They are dogged and determined and have thick skins like elephants.*

2. *They're good at getting other people to trust them. Whether they are money managers, editors-in-chief, CEOs, or famous authors, they are trustworthy in some way or another.*

Those are not qualities that one can purchase; those are personal traits that one earns, you might say, through a lifetime of hurling yourself into experiences and thinking that "life is an adventure in the great unknown." No college can *teach* you that, although many, many colleges—easily 1,000 out of the 4,400 schools in the United States—will give you opportunities and experiences to figure that out on your own.

But again, college isn't free; colleges are businesses that need to charge you for their services. And their services are kind of strange: They're going to sell you a product (a diploma) that also comes with an experience (four years of reading and talking and studying). The idea is that the product (the diploma) will help you get a good, well-paying job, and that the experience (the four years of reading and talking and studying) is the cherry on top—at least, that is the easiest, most saleable idea.

The reality, of course, is that the brand name of the diploma has little to no value without the skills and experiences you have in the classroom. Those four years of reading and writing and talking and studying and failing and succeeding and picking yourself back up again and trying something new are what give you those two qualities of successful people:

1. *You learn to persevere.*

2. *You learn not to try and sell anything you don't really have (in other words, you become trustworthy; you discover the value of integrity).*

But because that is nearly impossible to sell (and they can't guarantee that you'll come out with either #1 *or* #2), it's difficult to distill into a marketing campaign, into a slogan, or onto a brochure. So colleges try to sell the diploma instead of the experience—to sell, in short, their brand.

Yes! Colleges have brand identities, just like the Swiffer sweeper, just like Mercedes-Benz, just like Bloomingdale's. They've all got a "brand" and an "identity" and they all spend *a lot* of money on marketing. All the images you have of "college" and "what college means" are part of the rhetoric, the intentional language, of college marketing: ivy leaves crawling up brick walls and snowy-bearded professors spouting Keats to dreamy-eyed undergrads in perfectly preppy ensembles. That means sororities and fraternities; fresh notebooks and acceptance letters on linen paper; exclusive clubs and first-class tickets to the next echelon of society. College is the golden stamp of the upwardly mobile, just as cigarettes, once upon a time, were the hallmark of the teenage rebel.

You might think that colleges and tobacco companies are different, because tobacco is "evil" and learning is "good." But at the end of the day, they're not that different: They are selling a product. Just as someone standing in a deli, waiting to buy a soda, or a magazine, or sugary candy does, when you shop for colleges you have been the target of millions of dollars in marketing campaigns. Those campaigns are reinforced by rankings lists such as *U.S. News & World Report.* It doesn't *seem* to be the same as soda or magazine or candy marketing because we, as a society, have accepted that learning is "good." Don't get us wrong: Learning *is* good. But at what cost? At what point does paying for education become a bourgeois vice, a trap of intellectual vanity, instead of a legitimately useful thing?

One of our favorite stories about the trap of higher education comes from a *New York Times* article from May 29, 2010. In an article entitled "Placing the Blame as Students Are Buried in Debt," the paper profiled a recent graduate of New York University, a 26-year-old woman who took on just less than $100,000 in private student loans in order to finance an undergraduate degree in women's and religious studies. Cortney [sic] Munna now makes $22 an hour as a photographer's assistant, a position that hardly requires a college degree. Her monthly payments, once she stops deferring them (she's currently taking night school classes for another degree), will be roughly $700 per month.

"I don't want to spend the rest of my life slaving away to pay for an education I got for four years and would happily give back," she said. "It feels wrong to me."

Well, of course she doesn't. But what prevented her from using basic algebra—the kind that a high school sophomore would understand—to determine how much her education was going to cost her?

The answer is simple: She was blinded by her perception of NYU's brand. She and her mother are both quoted in the article as stating that NYU was a "good" school, and because it was a "good" school, it was worth paying for with money they didn't have to spend. *Is* NYU a good school? It's certainly as good a place as any other well-funded research institution to get a good education. But the logic that is implied with "good" is that NYU's degree would help this young woman get a "good" job, a well-paying job, no matter what her chosen field of study. Does she have one? Absolutely not—at least not one that has anything at all do with her college education. The job she has might be "good" in that it is intellectually and creatively stimulating, but it's not well-paying and she certainly didn't need a college degree to get it. And now, Ms. Munna will have to figure out how to make a $700 per month loan payment, on top her other bills (such as rent, food, and transportation—easily $1,500–2,000 a month on their own). Forget about travel, about new clothes, and about going out; Ms. Munna will have to make a base salary of at least $45,000 a year (if she wants to live on beans and rice) just to make her monthly bills.

Maybe Ms. Munna is a fluke, you might think—NYU *is* a good school. But how do you know that? If high graduate salaries mean that one school is "better" than another, then NYU fails; the highest reported salary for NYU graduates in a recent study by payscale.com is for students who became high school teachers, with an average annual salary between $46,387 and $71,280, making NYU's graduates solidly middle-class. Yet, NYU *costs* as much as Harvard, whose highest reported salaries for graduates in the same survey are for students who became CEOs, and make between $99,159 and $287,152 per year.

That does, in a sense, make Harvard "worth" paying for—but not NYU, even though its cost of attendance is actually higher ($55,559 annually at NYU, versus $53,950 at Harvard).

So what does this tell us? Well, hopefully, you understand that, although NYU might be a good place to get a good, or quality, education, it's certainly not a place that can calculate a significant return on investment, the way Harvard does. In other words, NYU—and hundreds of other "good" schools just like it—cannot statistically demonstrate that their graduates make more money than graduates of many other schools.

There are about 20 colleges that can prove, year after year, that their graduates make *a lot* of money. Ever hear the phrase *starving engineer*? Yeah, us neither. Unsurprisingly, these places, these 20 schools that provide a significant return on investment, are engineering schools and the eight original Ivy League colleges—Harvard et al. So if you're going to major in engineering, math, or one of the hard sciences—and you know you're going to be good at it and stick with it—then everything you already know about college probably *does* make sense. Go ahead and apply to the best engineering school you can get into; take out crazy loans and work your butt off. Statistically, you will likely be rewarded with a high-paying job. But as for the rest of you? Everyone who doesn't know what their major is going to be, or what they'll be doing in 10 years? Sorry, but you've got to keep reading. We've got seven major myths about college to break down for you.

MYTH #1: YOU GET WHAT YOU PAY FOR

To be honest, when we started to come up with our myths, we could have gone on for hours. Heck, we could come up with a hundred—and not just about college. We can come up with money myths for just about anything, but we wanted to keep it simple. So let's start with the simplest myth of all: that you "get what you pay for." You've surely heard that expression, which implies that cost, the *actual dollar cost of anything*, has a direct correlation to the value you're going to receive.

What does that mean? Well, it means that we live in a capitalist economy, with a system of exchange known as the free market. The market is known as "free" because anyone, anywhere, can dictate the retail price for their own product. You might be familiar with Etsy, the online marketplace for handmade goods. Let's pretend Ruth has suddenly taken up knitting and decided to sell her chunky yarn scarves on Etsy. She can charge whatever she wants for them; in the free market, the government cannot step in and say, "Hey Ruth! The scarves you're selling on Etsy are too expensive. They should only cost $25." Ruth can go online and set up her page and charge $125 a scarf, if she so desires. She is "free" to set the cost of her goods at any number she likes, and neither the government nor the theoretical buyer of her scarves can do a darn thing about it. The only thing the consumer can do is not buy a scarf. So the consumer *can*, in essence, exert some kind of price control by *not buying any of Ruth's scarves*. After a week of no sales, Ruth might think, "Maybe these scarves are too darned expensive." And then, perhaps, she'll lower the price.

So the rules that govern the free market dictate that *demand* is the control mechanism of price—simply put, that the market will not support a cost that is higher than the generally agreed-upon value for any given thing. This means that it's nigh-impossible to sell, for example, a Honda Civic, generally a $20,000 car, for $60,000, unless that Civic has some kind of additional value—Barack Obama campaigned for Senate in it, for example. You'd still have to be willing to shell out another $40K for the privilege of driving to work in a "piece of history," though; if you didn't care about Obama, Illinois, or the 2006 Senate race, you'd only have to pay $20K at any dealership in the country for *the same exact car*. The accepted value for that Honda Civic is $20,000, and presumably, a car whose basic cost is *always* $60,000—such as a brand-new Mercedes Benz—is going to be a "better," or "nicer" car.

When it comes to college, value is a tricky thing. What do you get out of college, exactly? What is the primary reason to even go to college—other than the simple joy of learning? Is it to discover who you are? Is it to make friends? No. These are important to be sure, but they're much, much harder to put a price tag on. The point, to be blunt, is to get a good job. You want to go to college and come out on the other side with a good job, a better—in other words, higher-paying—job than you could get with just a high school diploma.

College graduates *do* make more money than people with just a high school diploma. On average, college graduates make anywhere from $280,000 to $800,000 more throughout the course of their lifetimes, depending on who you ask.[1] But graduates from where? From what college?

If a college education has, on average, an additional lifetime value of at least $280,000, then it stands to reason that the "best" college educations have a larger lifetime value—more than $800,000 dollars. And what are the "best" colleges? What constitutes a school whose diploma can really, truly increase your lifetime earning potential?

The answer to that one is simple: The 20 or so colleges we mentioned earlier, the ones that provide the highest dollar amount of lifetime earnings, are the eight original Ivy League colleges and a slew of engineering schools such as Harvey Mudd, RPI, MIT, WPI CalTech, Lehigh, and Union College. You can also throw in Notre Dame, Georgetown, Duke, Amherst, Colgate, and Carnegie Mellon, according to research done earlier this year by payscale.com, a website that tracks compensation data. The unfortunate thing about that particular list—which you can find online at that site and our site—is that it doesn't break down the numbers by major. But looking at it, we can tell you flat out that their data is likely heavily skewed by people who majored in math and the sciences: by engineers and bankers.

We'd like to tell you something about ourselves: We did not go to college thinking that we would make a lot of money someday. And we don't make a lot of money—but we do really, really love our jobs. Carol majored in literature at Macalester College in St. Paul, Minnesota, and Ruth majored in psychology and elementary education at Augsburg College in Minneapolis, Minnesota—both small, private liberal arts colleges that did not cost a lot of money at the time. Frankly, women of our generation were often expected to go to college to get our "Mrs." Degree: to find a husband (we suppose that's another kind of "earning potential," albeit one that kind of stinks). Making a lot of money wasn't something that women like us actively thought about doing, unless it was making out like a bandit in a divorce settlement. It wasn't something our mothers encouraged us or even expected us to do; although they expected us to know how to support ourselves, bringing home the bacon was not "women's work." And college was inexpensive enough that the idea of paying back student loans (neither of us had any) was of literally no concern to us. We wanted to go to college, get away from our parents, learn something, pierce our ears, grow our hair long, meet guys, and change who we were—that was the privilege of the 1970s. Did we "get what we paid for," back then? Absolutely. We learned as much we could and we grew up. What we paid, in the early 1970s, was *peanuts* compared to what college costs now—even though earnings for college graduates haven't risen significantly (about 1 percent per year) since 1975, the first year we entered the job market.[2]

Although your parents probably graduated at least a decade after we did, college costs didn't change as dramatically as they have in the last 10 years. In 1980, the average four-year private college charged just $3,225 per academic year, and a four-year public college charged just $738, on average (in today's dollars).[3] So just like us, your parents probably feel that they "got what they paid for"; the cost of college was not, for them, prohibitively expensive, and the idea that a more expensive college could provide a better education was much closer to the truth than it is now.

The cost of college has risen nearly tenfold since then. The average private four-year college now charges $27,293; the average public four-year charges $7,605. That might sound low to you; it certainly sounds low to us. Based on our experiences with the schools we work for, we'd ballpark an average figure somewhere around $35,000 per year; looking at elite colleges (and pretenders to the elite throne) we would say the average cost of attendance is around $50,000 per year.

But how many people actually pay that full $26,000, $35,000, or even $50,000 dollars?

What would you guess?

Do you think everyone pays the same price?

They don't. Students and families pay wildly different prices to attend the same schools, take the exact same classes, and get the same diploma. And that's where the idea that "you get what you pay for" falls apart. If you can buy a car for $60,000, but everyone else is paying only $20,000 for it, does that make it more valuable? Absolutely not—and the same is true for college. If you pay an extra 10, 30, or even 100 thousand dollars more for your education, does that make it a better education? You can't ever re-sell your diploma, the bank can't repossess it, and you can't take out a loan on it, so why would you pay more than anyone else does for it? If you were really thinking about it, you would pay as little as you possibly could.

Cost, when it comes to college, is totally mutable—it is changeable and based solely on how much the college *thinks* you're willing or able to pay. This is a practice known as "tuition discounting." It allows colleges to change the price around for students they really want. Everybody does it—private colleges, big state schools, and even community colleges.

That means that if you apply to a college where you are in the top 25 percent of the incoming class, there is a very good chance that the advertised price—whatever it says on the website and admission materials about "how much it costs"—will be heavily discounted, just for you, regardless of your family's financial situation. We would say, in our experience, that students who are in the top 25 percent of the incoming class almost always get a scholarship of some kind—frequently half-tuition or higher.

MYTH #2: IF YOU GET INTO YOUR REACH SCHOOL, YOU SHOULD GO THERE

If the school you're dreaming of attending is a "reach" for you, then *you absolutely should not go there*, unless your family can afford to pay for it out of pocket. A "reach" school means that you'll be in the academic bottom of the incoming freshman class, and you won't get enough merit aid (that is, a scholarship) to make up for the high cost of tuition. Essentially, when it comes to admission, the bottom half of the class pays for the top half of the class. Andrew Manshel, the former CFO for Barnard College, stated in an opinion piece for the *Wall Street Journal* on April 7, 2010, that colleges charge as much as they do *because they can*: "There are qualified paying customers lined up at the door." Who is the most willing to pay that price? The student or parent who never dreamed that little Fanny or Freddy was "good enough" to get into an elite, or *perceived elite*, school. Fanny and Freddy are the most susceptible consumers for the college, the ones who are willing to take on loans and sell property in order to move up a level—in order to "be accepted" by what they perceive as a place that is "better" than who they already are.

And from the college's perspective? Why admit students who aren't as "good" as the other students? Truth be told, Fanny or Freddy was admitted to her or his reach school solely because the school predicted that the student's family would be so thrilled that they'd move mountains just to pay full price. When Fanny or Freddy—or anyone else in the bottom of the incoming class, who can define acceptance into that college as a "reach"—are accepted, the school can then turn around and offer an enhanced scholarship to a Maxine or Martin, who has incredible test scores, has through-the-roof-recommendations, and is being vied for by 12 other colleges. Fanny and Freddy have the money for tuition—but Maxine and Martin have the statistical advantages that will help the college move up in the ratings to secure more Fannies and Freddies who will pay more to be at a "better" school. Both kinds of students provide income to the college: Fannies and Freddies through direct payment of tuition, and Maxine and Martin as Fanny-and-Freddy bait. Believe us, you'd much rather be a Maxine than a Fanny: Maxine doesn't pay a lot, and Fanny does.

This might not make any sense to you. An important thing to know about tuition costs is that they are often determined on an entirely different balance sheet from the rest of university costs; in other words, how much a college costs does not directly reflect how much it costs the college to enroll a student. Tuition and overhead are, in essence, often very different things, and actual tuition—the real price of college—is determined on a student-by-student basis. *Your tuition costs are all about how much the college thinks it has to discount (or not discount, in many cases) the sticker price in order to get you, and your money or your grades, to go there.*

Our friend Jon McGee, who works at Saint John's University and the College of Saint Benedict in Minnesota, has a wonderful phrase he uses to explain college tuition to friends and family: "In no other business can someone ask, 'How much does it cost?' and the response is, 'Well, give me a copy of your tax return and a transcript, and I'll let you know.'"

That process is of enormous value to colleges; it allows them to learn all about you before they determine whether or not they're going to admit you, and for how much.

From now on, you're not going to use the words *safety* and *reach*. Those words are bad. Wipe them from your consciousness. There are two new words on the horizon: *funded* and *unfunded*.

You're going to start, right now, thinking about college the exact same way that people think about graduate school: Where can you get funded? It's no longer about getting in—it's about getting funded. For graduate school, there's no shame in going to whatever school will fund you; any prospective graduate student will tell you that he'd rather go to the University of Illinois or the University of Minnesota as a funded student than to Harvard as an unfunded student. And now colleges—all 4,400 of the degree-granting colleges and universities in the United States—are going to part like the Red Sea into two categories in your mind: funded and unfunded. There is no more safety; there is no more reach. Now there are only two kinds of schools: the kind that will fund you and give you a sizeable scholarship, and the kind that won't.

Promise us, through the pages of this book, that you will not go, under any circumstances, to an unfunded school. Let's make a pact here and now to only *apply* to schools that you can think of as "funded." Why should you promise us that? Well, this book is called *The Financial Aid Handbook*. If you were rolling in dough, you wouldn't have bought it; you wouldn't be reading this paragraph right now. You'd be out on a yacht in St. Tropez, throwing gold krugerands in the air—well, maybe you would still be in high school, but you wouldn't be thinking about how to pay for college.

We know what you've been told. You're supposed to go to the best college that you can get into—go to your reach school, if you can get in. Then, after you get in, you're supposed to figure out how to pay for it. But that is backward: To that, young man or woman, we say "no way." You're going to figure out what schools will fund you—and then you'll apply.

MYTH #3: I'LL WAIT UNTIL AFTER I'M ACCEPTED TO FIGURE OUT HOW TO PAY

For as long as we've been working in college admission (more than 70 years between the two of us), students have started the college search by finding schools they *could* love—and then falling *crazy* in love with one final choice. The standard college application cycle is about 18 months long; it begins when you take the PSAT or ACT Plan as a junior, then ends when you set foot on campus a year and a half later. After you take the PSAT or ACT Plan, you'll get all sorts of colorful brochures in the mail, and get bombarded with e-mails, too. Those mailers scream "Look at us! Love us! We're the college for you!"

You're getting those brochures in the mail because of your test scores. The colleges sending you these multicolored, high-resolution love letters have looked at your scores, and determined that you're a likely candidate for admission—that you've got at the very least, the lowest test scores they're willing to accept. Despite what you might think, those colleges don't have *any* access to information about your family's financial situation; they have no idea if you are capable of paying to go there, or not. To be frank, they don't *want* to know; colleges don't generally want to shock you by talking about money (how gauche!). Colleges want to lure you in with the perfect first date (or campus visit); they want *you* to fall in love with *them*. As to whether or not they'll love you back, that remains to be seen—after you've applied and sent in your transcripts and FAFSA. At that point, you've splayed yourself upon the altar of love; you've declared, "I love you, college." And that's when you're the most vulnerable: when you're desperate, to be loved back. That's the moment when you're most likely to say to yourself "I didn't get a scholarship, but it's only $20,000 in loans per year. That's worth it, right?"

Let's go back to what our friend Jon says about college tuition. You may have forgotten it already; that's all right. We'll just repeat it. Jon says, "In no other business can someone ask, 'How much does it cost?' and the response is, 'Well, give me a copy of your tax return and a transcript, and I'll let you know.'"

It's true. Can you think of any other product that requires you to submit to an in-depth review before you can purchase it? Other than country club memberships and co-op apartment buildings, there are virtually no other products (*you're buying it, so education is a product*) where someone gets to extensively review and judge you before you're allowed to buy. It's kind of a humiliating thing, if you think about it; the retailer (the college) gets to know all about you, your hopes and dreams, the last four years of your life, and your parents' assets, before it will even *deign* to tell you how much its product (your education) will cost you.

And that process of reviewing you, of holding power over you, is how colleges get you to that point where you say "It's only $20,000 in loans per year." And then you become a Cortney Munna from earlier in the chapter: someone with all the best intentions, tons of debt, and no job.

Before you apply, though, it is possible to predict how much each school is going to charge you—by analyzing yourself the same way that colleges and universities do. That process is detailed in our MAP, or Merit Aid Profile, in Chapter 6.

You've also got to figure out how much you and your family can afford to pay. After you do that, you can find schools you like, determine whether or not you have a good chance of getting funded there and then, finally, visit and apply.

MYTH #4: IF MY PARENTS SAY THEY WON'T PAY, I'LL GET MORE AID

There are lots of word-of-mouth stories that become persistent urban myths. Someone hears from someone that "so-and-so got more money from a school because their parents wouldn't fill out the FAFSA," or "so-and-so became legally independent (legally emancipated) from their family and got a full scholarship."

Unfortunately, these stories are almost always just that: stories. One of the fundamental tenets of financial aid—which is funded and supported by the U.S. government and its taxpayers—is that your parents are fully responsible for your college education. The FAFSA is used to determine how much money your family has available to pay for college. Simply because your parents don't *want* to pay does not excuse them from the responsibility to do so. In order for your family to be absolved of all responsibility to pay, you would have to qualify as an independent. To qualify, you would have to meet at least one of the following criteria:

√ *Are you an orphan, are you in foster care, or have you been a ward of the court at any time since your 13th birthday?*

√ *Are you an emancipated minor or in legal guardianship as determined by the court?*

√ *Are you a verified unaccompanied youth who is either homeless or at risk for homelessness?*

√ *Were you born before January 1, 1989 (for entrance in fall 2012)?*

√ *Were you married as of the date of your application for aid?*

√ *At the beginning of the school year will you be enrolled in graduate or professional school?*

√ *Are you currently serving in the active military or a veteran?*

√ *Do you have children who receive more than half their support from you?*

√ *Do you have other dependents who receive more than half their support from you?*

If you can say yes to any of those questions, you can be treated as an independent student. If not, your parents must fill out the FAFSA in order for you to receive any aid.

In some circumstances—especially with divorce and blended families—one or more of your parents may absolutely refuse to pay or provide you with their financial information. If this is the case, please see Chapter 4.

If your parents are reading this with you right now, please make sure they read the following paragraph:

Parents: When you graduated from high school, you may have been able to make your way through the world without a college diploma. That is no longer the case. If you've brought children into this world, you have the responsibility to help them through it. That doesn't mean they have to go to the most expensive college (if you've read even *one page* of our book so far, you'll know we'd never advocate for that), but it does mean that in order for them to receive any financial aid, you must fill out the FAFSA and help your children in any way you can. College is not only a wonderful experience, but it has become as necessary as high school. Please don't let your own experiences in the world allow you to make judgments about what your children should or should not have. Please trust us when we say that they ought to go to college for many good and sound reasons, and if you don't at least help them by filling out the FAFSA, the federal government won't be able to give your children *any aid at all*. You will be punishing your children and handicapping them financially if you do not fill out the FAFSA (or PROFILE). For more information, please take a look at Chapter 5, written just for you.

Whew. There, we've said it. If your parents aren't convinced by our pleas, turn to Chapter 4 and try some of our other tactics.

MYTH #5: ONLY THE VERY POOREST WILL GET ANY FINANCIAL AID

You don't have to be poor to get financial aid. The popular press often focuses only on the Pell Grant program (which generally gives grants to low-income students) whenever financial aid is mentioned; this leads many, many students to believe that financial aid is only for poor people. But the Pell Grant isn't the only form of financial aid that comes out of the FAFSA or PROFILE; there are numerous kinds of grants (money you never have to pay back), loans (money you do have to pay back), and work-study (money you earn while in school) that you become eligible for by filling out the FAFSA or PROFILE.

We'll give you more detail in Chapter 2, but here are the bare-bones statistics on how your eligibility for financial aid is determined:

The FAFSA is the Free Application for Federal Student Aid. It's a series of forms you fill out (in print or online) that details your parents' assets: their income, their savings, their dependents (including older relatives), and the number of children that will attend college. It also details your, the student's, assets (although you probably don't have much). All the numbers you put down get crunched through a standard formula that determines something called your EFC: your expected family contribution. The EFC is the amount of money in actual cash that your family is expected to contribute each year (anywhere from $0 to $99,999), and filling out your FAFSA also makes you eligible for federal fixed-rate student loans. You can also get a loan from a bank at a high interest rate, but that's a terrible idea. Turn to Chapter 3 for more about loans and debt.

Most recipients of Pell Grants have a household income of less than $50,000 annually, but the more children or dependents your family has, the less the actual income amount matters. Although it's not common, families with incomes of more than $100,000 per year *do* receive the Pell Grant and other forms of need-based aid[4]; it just depends on how your family has to spend their money. According to the federal government's FAFSA calculation, taking care of an elderly relative is a reasonable expenditure that lowers your EFC, but making payments on a yacht is not; same with sending four kids to college (low EFC!) versus buying four new cars (high EFC!).

The best thing about the FAFSA is the FAFSA4caster, which allows you to estimate what your EFC will be, anytime you want—even if you're in seventh or eighth grade. This helps to give families a realistic starting place for the discussion about college costs, and we think it's one of the smartest things the Department of Education has ever done. It's online and it takes just about half an hour. Go to *fafsa4caster.ed.gov* to fill it out!

MYTH #6: I CAN PAY SOMEONE $99 TO FIND SCHOLARSHIPS FOR ME

Anyone who charges you to find scholarships for you is scamming you. They're taking advantage of your fear, your youth, and your parents' desire to get you into college. An enormous amount of free information is out there about private scholarships (the kind you find on lists, on websites, or in books in your library); we're big fans of FastWeb (full disclosure: Ruth used to be on the board), a free online service that will match you to scholarships that are a good fit (and sometimes to school-specific scholarships). (Check our website at *thefinancialaidhandbook.com* for the addresses for FastWeb and other sources we recommend.)

The confusing thing about "scholarships" is that the word has two uses. One is for "private" scholarships, the kind you can read about on the Internet or in books. Private scholarships come from Coca-Cola, from the 4-H club, from the Bertha Carruthers Institute for Proper Young Ladies, and from the Doug Douggleston Memorial Golf Foundation. They come from veterans organizations, from the PTA, from your local Gambler's Anonymous club; they come from anywhere and anyone. They *don't* come from individual colleges.

The other use of the word *scholarship* is for the other kind, the kind that come only from the college. They're known as "institutional" scholarships, or *merit aid.* You're going to read the words *merit aid* a lot in this book—get used to it! Merit aid only comes from the college itself, and you become eligible simply by applying. Merit aid is the same as tuition discounting. It's the same as an institutional scholarship, and it's part of—gasp!—financial aid. We know. It's confusing. Essentially, merit aid is never advertised in books or on websites other than the college's own. To find out about what kind of merit aid is available at the college of your choice, you'll have to do some research. We cover this in Chapter 6.

Never, ever pay for scholarships—and limit the amount of time you spend applying to private scholarships. It can be a huge drain of your time and energy, and although all of those books on the shelf at Barnes & Noble tell you there are "Thousands of scholarships inside!!!" and "Billions of dollars in free money!!!" what they neglect to tell you is that there are currently 17 million college students in the United States, and many of them are applying for the exact same scholarships. If you're going to spend time and energy sending off scholarship application after scholarship application, please be judicious about it and use a free service such as FastWeb or cappex.com to narrow down the best options.

MYTH #7: MY STATE SCHOOL WILL BE THE CHEAPEST FOR ME

Other than tuition, the basic costs of education—room and board, books, travel, and other expenses—are generally the same at any kind of school, be it public or private. Unless you plan on living at home, you won't be saving much on anything except tuition, and even then you may not save much.

The main problem with public universities is their graduation rates; the chances of graduating in four years are significantly higher at a private school. Public schools often have unwieldy core curricula that make it difficult to change majors (which students almost always do), and your chances of graduating in five years—instead of four—at a public are nearly 50 percent.[5] It's best to graduate in four years, if you can; otherwise you lose two or more years on the job market (or hey, bumming around Europe, or teaching English in Japan).

Although the average cost of tuition at a public university is about one third less than the average cost of tuition at a private school, your chances of getting a scholarship are generally slimmer. We're not saying that you *shouldn't* apply to your local state school—we think you should!—but it can't be the *only* place you apply. There are plenty of private colleges that will welcome you into their open arms and discount their tuition (ahem, we mean give you a merit aid scholarship) enough to be quite price competitive with your local public.

That's all for myths, folks. We hope you've enjoyed this eye-opening trek into the world of college admission and tuition! And if you didn't, we sincerely hope that it has been at least useful. For the advanced (or more literal-minded) among you, Chapter 2 concerns the basic nuts and bolts of financial aid. If you're just beginning to learn about money and don't care to bore yourself with the details just yet, please turn to Chapter 3, where we talk about student loans, debt, and life after graduation.

THE BASICS

No matter where you're thinking about going, you ought to apply for financial aid. You might not think that you "need" financial aid, or suspect you're not eligible for it, but you absolutely should apply for it anyway.

The cornerstone of every financial aid process is the FAFSA, or the Free Application for Federal Student Aid. It's the very first thing you fill out, and you'll have to fill it out each year while you're in school. The FAFSA determines your "need," or how much your family should pay for college. Your "need" has two components:

1. *How much your family should pay in actual cash each year, also known as your EFC (expected family contribution).*

2. *Whether or not you're eligible for federally funded grants (money you don't have to pay back) or loans (money you do have to pay back).*

You can file the FAFSA as soon as January 1st, so you'll need to get your parents to file their taxes for the previous year as early as they can. Trust us, the sooner they can file their taxes, the sooner this process will be over with. Don't put it off; it will just become more of a headache.

The FAFSA is provided by the U.S. Department of Education, part of the federal government. We didn't always have the FAFSA; your parents probably didn't use it, because it only came into being in 1992.

You might wonder, "Why do we even have financial aid?" Furthermore, "Who is paying for me to go to college? Why would they do that? What do they gain? Why is the government involved in what is often a private enterprise? And really, what is 'need?'"

Need: noun. A necessary duty, or obligation; a lack of something requisite, desirable, or useful; a condition requiring supply or relief; or the lack of the means of subsistence (poverty).

In your case, "need" is your lack of something requisite, desirable, or useful: money.

But how do colleges define need? How do they determine who needs money, and who doesn't? You might think that it's a simple process, but for such a tiny word, with such a seemingly simple definition, it manages to confuse nearly everyone who is wondering how to finance a college education.

You might think that colleges define need with a simple set of definitions—with a chart, perhaps. That chart you're thinking of might look something like this:

Income Level	Financial Aid Award
Lower-lower income	Full tuition
Middle-lower income	$25K per year
Upper-lower income	$20K per year
Lower-middle income	$15K per year
Middle-middle income	$10K per year
Upper-middle income	$5K per year

Lower-upper income	Bupkis
Middle-upper income	We're insulted you even asked
Upper-upper income	Yes, colleges will take gold bricks in payment

Unfortunately, we made that chart up. No such chart exists; if there was such a thing, you wouldn't need this book, and we'd be out of a job.

So if colleges aren't using a chart like that, how do they do it? Is it consistent? Who makes the guidelines?

Well, defining need happens on a case-by-case, or individual, basis, and takes into account both your financial information, your grades, and sometimes your demographic information. But because finances are complicated, there is an overarching set of guidelines, or a methodology, that defines *how* we define need. That's the FAFSA.

NEED DICTIONARY: THE TOP 25 WORDS AND PHRASES YOU "NEED" TO KNOW

FAFSA: The Free Application for Federal Student Aid is the form you fill out to share your financial information with colleges, so they can determine how much you can afford to pay. The FAFSA's federal methodology determines your EFC, and the results are forwarded to your choice of colleges. You may file for the FAFSA on January 1st of the year you plan to enroll in college. That means if I want to go to Ruth's Pretty Good College in the fall of 2013, I'll submit my FAFSA on January 1, 2013. FAFSA is a noun, in case you were wondering, but you may also use it as a shorthand verb (Have you FAFSA-ed?) by conjugating it in the usual manner.

EFC (expected family contribution): This is the amount of money that you, and your family, are expected to spend on your college education, annually, as calculated by the federal methodology used in the FAFSA.

COA (cost of attendance): Every college and university calculates its own cost of attendance, which includes tuition, fees, housing, food, books, personal supplies, and transportation. *Also called a "budget" when calculating* *your financial aid package; the college will subtract your EFC from the COA to arrive at your "need."*

Net Price Calculator: As of October 2011, all colleges and universities are required to display a Net Price Calculator (NPC) on their websites. The calculator must provide cost of attendance and grant and scholarship aid, broken down by EFC range, housing type, and tuition.

FAFSA4caster: We *love* FAFSA4caster. This is a quick (30 minutes or so) "pretend FAFSA" that you can use online at fafsa4caster.ed.gov, anytime, day or night, to get a good idea of what your EFC will be, in the months and even years (if your household income is consistent) leading up to the January of your senior year of high school.

CSS PROFILE: The FAFSA is free, but the PROFILE is not. It costs $25 for the first college, and $16 for each subsequent college. It's often required from students by colleges that want to determine how they hand out non-federal money (read: the college's own funds) to students, and is a much more detailed form than the FAFSA. It requires both parents, custodial and non-custodial, to fill it out; it takes into account home equity, and it's tied to the consumer price index, which the FAFSA is not. The CSS PROFILE is administered by a private nonprofit, the College Board. To access the PROFILE and for a list of colleges that require or accept it, go to *profile.collegeboard.com*. Most schools require financial aid applicants to file the PROFILE if they are applying early decision.

Methodology: This simply means "formula," as in all the formulas you learned in algebra. The "federal methodology" is the FAFSA system for taking the financial data from everyone who wants to apply for financial aid, and using a standardized system—a methodology—to determine how much discretionary income they have for education. An "Institutional Methodology" is used in the PROFILE.

Institution: Colleges love this word. This does not mean a mental hospital, prison, or sanitarium. *Institution* refers simply to any one body of post-secondary education (you know, after high school). An institution can be a community college, a private college, a university, or a trade school. They're all defined by the Department of Education as "Higher Education Institutions," or HEIs for short. When a college is giving its own money for a scholarship or grant, that money is called "institutional money" to distinguish it from that which comes from state or federal governments, or any other outside scholarship organization.

Dependents: Anyone who depends on your parents, including you. This is a frequently misunderstood question in the FAFSA. Count yourself as a dependent. You will likely be claimed as a dependent through all four years of college by your parents, even though you may file your own taxes.

Dependency Status: There is a worksheet to determine whether or not your parents can legally claim you as a dependent. It's not just a matter of declaring yourself independent; you have to pass a series of tests, online, at *fafsa.ed.gov*. Things including age, marital status, military employment, and level of education determine whether or not you are an independent. If you are an 18-year-old who is unmarried, not in the military, and living in your parents' house, you are probably dependent.

SAR (Student Aid Report): The Student Aid Report is the document (either paper or electronic) that lists the information you've reported on your FAFSA. Your EFC will be in the upper-right-hand corner of the front page. This is the form that gets sent out to colleges.

PIN (personal identification number): You use your PIN to sign into FAFSA online; if you don't have one, apply for one at *pin.ed.gov*. (To sign the FAFSA electronically, your custodial parent should also apply for a PIN of his or her own.)

Student Aid Eligibility: The period of time for which you are eligible for student aid, loans, or grants from the federal government. Eight total semesters for full-time undergraduate, non-consecutive. *Your student loan eligibility can be removed if you have, or acquire, a felony drug conviction.*

Loan: Any amount of money you have to borrow, then repay. Loans have interest, or a percentage of the total amount that you have to pay additionally to the holder of your loan. No one hands out money for nothing; expect, for example, on a $10,000 loan at 6.8 percent interest (the federal rate; a private bank will likely charge more) to repay a total of $13, 809.66, or an additional $3,809.66 on a 10-year term.

Term: The amount of time you have to repay a loan.

Parent: Who is considered a parent? Well, your biological, adopted, or step-parents are; but grandparents, foster parents, legal guardians, older siblings, uncles, or aunts are *not* considered parents unless they have legally adopted you. If your parents are divorced, the parent you have lived with most in the last 12 months is considered your parent for the purposes of the FAFSA. For PROFILE, both parents—custodial and non-custodial—will have to fill out forms. *If your divorced or widowed custodial parent has* *remarried, you must also provide information about his or her spouse on the FAFSA and PROFILE.* Note to parents who are looking to remarry: If you remarry, you will take on the financial burden of educating your new spouse's children, and they yours, in the eyes of the federal government. These are modern times. If you're not ready to unite your lives both emotionally *and financially*, please think long and hard about living in sin and what it can do for your pocketbook. It is important for you to understand that, although marriage can have its benefits, it can also have its federally determined flaws.

School Code: This is a number code for each college or university that you want to receive your FAFSA information. Search for it on the FAFSA website at *fafsa.ed.gov*. Be forewarned: If you misspell the name of the school, you won't find it. This may be confusing because it's not "College Code," but the federal government uses "School" interchangeably for K–12 and higher education institutions.

DRN (Data Release Number): This is the four-digit number that will be assigned to your individual FAFSA. It's on the upper-right-hand corner of your electronic SAR, is printed on your paper SAR, and also appears on your confirmation page. This number gives you access to all of your FAFSA information, so don't give it to anyone that you don't want to see your FAFSA. You'll need this number to change your permanent mailing address, e-mail address, telephone, school number codes, or housing plans.

Signature Page: If you don't use a PIN to sign your FAFSA electronically, you (and your parents, if you're a dependent, which you probably are) will have to physically sign, with pen and ink, a signature page and send it off in the mail. The address to which you will send it is printed on the signature page itself. Just as when you sign with a PIN, you agree to the following conditions, from the U.S. Department of Education:

√ *You will use federal student aid funds received during the award year covered by this application solely for educational expenses related to attendance during that year at the institution of higher education that determined eligibility for those funds;*

√ *You are not in default on a Title IV educational loan, or have repaid or made satisfactory arrangements to repay the loan if you are in default;*

√ You do not owe an overpayment on a Title IV educational grant, or you have made satisfactory arrangements to repay that overpayment;

√ You will notify your school if you do owe an overpayment or are in default; and

√ You understand that the Secretary of Education has the authority to verify income reported on this application with the Internal Revenue Service and other federal agencies.

If you purposely give false or misleading information, you may be fined $20,000, sent to prison, or both.

Confirmation Number: Even though you might think that having a DRN, an SSN, and a transaction number is enough, the federal government disagrees with you. The last page of FAFSA on the Web will include a confirmation page, with—you guessed it—a confirmation number. They don't tell you how you might need to use it, but they do ask you to keep it for your records, just in case. And hey, you're keeping track of all the other numbers anyway—what's one more to add to the list?

Database Mismatches, or "Flags": When you complete the FAFSA, you need to follow the directions to the letter, and complete all the information carefully and correctly. Some of the information on the FAFSA is cross-referenced with other federal databases, such as your Social Security number, name, and birth date; these need to match your Social Security records. Even though I might like to go by "Carolita Stack," my given name is Carol Ann Stack, so if I were filing the FAFSA, Carol Ann Stack would be the name on the form. If there is a "database mismatch," your application will be *flagged* for correction and verification. This slows everything down, so be extra careful and double-check every piece of info on your FAFSA.

Verification: As any good moneylender does, the federal government reserves the right to verify, or double-check the truthfulness, of the information you've put in your FAFSA. They can also require colleges and universities to double-check your information before anyone hands you a dime. So don't lie.

FAA: Not the Federal Aviation Administration, but the designation for the Financial Aid Administrator at your college of choice. They're responsible for awarding aid and for ensuring compliance with state and federal regulations—in short, they're in charge. Never tick off your FAA; never try to bribe him or her, either. This is a person with whom you may have a good many conversations in the years to come (especially if you come from a non-traditional household with multiple divorces, children, and so on), so try to just be cool with them.

Supplemental or Institutional Application: A form designed by individual colleges to collect additional financial information. It's free for the student, and different at every school. Not all schools require this.

FAFSA Transaction: Every time you file a FAFSA, or make corrections to your existing FAFSA, it's referred to as a "transaction," and a "transaction number" and new SAR are created. So, when you speak with the financial aid office at your school, they may refer to a change you made in "transaction 3" or "transaction 5."

DEFINING NEED, ONE MORE TIME

At the beginning of the chapter, we couldn't define need beyond the dictionary definition. It's on a case-by-case basis, we said. That's still true, but now that you've so thoughtfully and thoroughly read our Need Dictionary, you'll understand when we say that defining actual need happens by:

taking a college's COA (Cost of Attendance) and subtracting your EFC.

That means, for example, if Carol's Pretty Good College has a COA of $45,000 (which includes tuition, books, housing, food, transportation, personal supplies, and so on) and the FAFSA determines Ruth's EFC to be $10,000, then Ruth's need is $45,000 – $10,000 = $35,000. This is how much Ruth can conceivably get from the federal government and the college itself in both loans and grants.

Bear in mind that actual need can be $35,000 at one college, and only $15,000 at another. Actual need changes based on the COA of the college in question.

Let's pretend that Carol's husband, David, opens up a college of his own. He decides to charge less than his beautiful wife does. So, at David's Wonderful College for Young People, the COA is $35,000; Ruth's EFC, as determined by the FAFSA, is still $10,000. So Ruth's "actual need" at David's Wonderful College for Young People is $35,000 – $10,000 = $25,000. That's how much the college could conceivably help her get in federal loans and grants.

Even though the "actual need" changes, the EFC is still $10,000, and that number is difficult to change or adjust. Whatever your EFC is determined to be is how much your family *should* be paying in cash annually, but that number often sounds extremely high to families. That's where "perceived need" comes in: Your parents may think that you have more need than you actually do, based on their spending habits. Often, families have more in debt that they do in assets. Consumer debt—things such as car payments, mortgages, and credit card debt—won't take your family off the hook when calculating your EFC. The federal methodology simply looks at how much money you have coming in, *not how you spend it.* Many families look at their EFC and think, "How am I going to come up with that kind of money? What am I supposed to do, sell my house?"

Well, you could take out a home equity loan, or you could start changing your lifestyle. We cover ways to do that in Chapter 5. The EFC is not an unreasonable formula, as much as it might seem to be. Keep reading, and we'll explain it more in-depth.

THE EXPECTED FAMILY CONTRIBUTION: LET'S GET (RIGHT) DOWN TO THE REAL NITTY-GRITTY

Although Gladys Knight and her Pips never attended college, we bet that if confronted with the EFC, they would have broken out into "Nitty-Gritty" right there in the financial aid office and demanded some answers. Don't get the Gladys Knight reference? Well, your parents will. They'd probably like to read this chapter, too, so once you're done with it, hand it over to them.

How on earth do they calculate the EFC? Gosh, Gladys, we're so glad you asked. Well, for a dependent student, which 99.9 percent of you high school students are, there are two components to the EFC:

1. *The parents' contribution from income, and from assets.*

2. *The student's contribution from income, and from assets.*

For starters, all the financial information used is from what's known as the "base year," or the taxable year that precedes enrollment. For a student starting college in the fall of 2013, the base year would be 2012. To calculate the parental contribution from income, first the methodology takes account of the taxable income earned in the base year, and adds directly to that the amount of untaxed income earned in the base year. All of this information has been reported on your FAFSA. Then, any income that can be excluded is subtracted; that includes education tax credits, child support, certain kinds of earnings received by the parent (if the parent is a student, for example, and earned federal work study funding). The final number is the parents' total income for the base year.

From the total income, allowances are subtracted for:

√ *Paid federal income tax.*

√ *State and other taxes.*

√ *Social Security tax (FICA).*

√ *An "Income Protection Allowance." Known as the IPA, this accounts for basic living expenses needed to maintain the family as a whole. The IPA recognizes that certain expenses must be met, before a family can even begin to think about paying for college. The IPA is a benchmark (read: set number) based on an income level below which a household is assumed to have no discretionary income (read: extra spending money). The amount of the allowance, which varies by family size and number of children enrolled in college, is adjusted each year according to changes in the Consumer Price Index. The IPA has the following breakdown:*

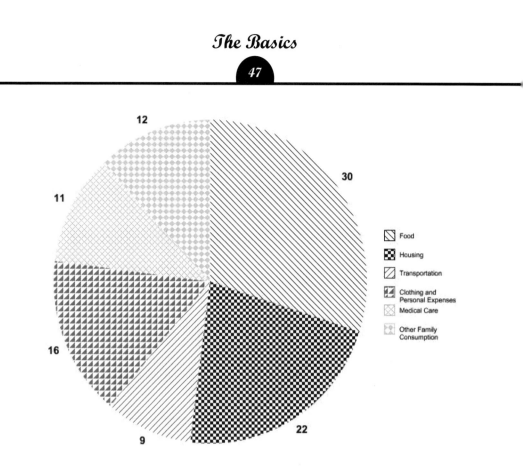

- *The IPA is helpful, but it's not a huge amount. For a family of four, with one child in college, the income protection allowance is $24,970 (for the 20011–12 fiscal year). That's not very much.*

- *There's also a subtraction for employment expenses. That allowance is 35 percent of the lesser of the two earned incomes (if there are two working parents), or of the earned income of a single parent, capped at $3,100. Earned income is important; it's not the same as a taxable asset. So, onto assets we go!*

ASSETS

The calculation of your parents' total assets is again taken from information that you've reported on your FAFSA. The information used to calculate this are:

√ *Cash, checking, and savings.*

√ *Net worth of current investments. This includes real estate (but not the family's primary residence), trust funds, money market accounts, certificates of deposit, stocks, stock options, bonds, 529 plans, commodities, and more.*

√ *Net worth of a business or investment farm, unless it has 100 or fewer employees.*

All of those things are added together, and then an education savings and asset protection allowance is deducted from this to protect the parents' assets. You might be thinking "What would they want to spend money on besides my college education?" Well, there are a lot of things: retirement, emergencies, other family members, education for themselves or any siblings you might have, that busted water heater, turning your room into a gym, and so forth.

After the education saving and asset protection allowance is deducted, the remainder is considered to be a "discretionary net worth," or an amount of liquid cash ripe for the spending. However, not all of it is assumed to be available for education; a 12 percent asset conversion rate is applied to the discretionary net worth, and that finally results in your parents' contribution from assets. If the number is negative, it's reset to zero.

At last. We've calculated both the contribution from income, and the contribution from assets.

After this, the process starts over, with the student's income and assets. The process is essentially the same, except for a few important differences:

√ *The Income Protection Allowance for the student is set at $5,250.*

√ *No adjustment is made to the net worth of a dependent's business or farm. (Parents: This means that putting shell corporations in the name of your children to hide your own assets will not help you.)*

√ *There is no asset protection allowance for a student's assets.*

√ *The contribution is assessed at a flat rate of 20 percent (no sliding scale).*

√ The student contribution is the sum that comes from adding the student's income and assets.

√ The EFC (expected family contribution) is the sum of the parents' contribution and the student's contribution.

There is, however, a simplified version of the EFC that disregards assets. A dependent student qualifies for this simplified calculation if:

√ The parents' combined adjusted gross income (or income earned from work) was less than $50,000, and either:

- The parents were not required to file an IRS form 1040,

- One of them is a dislocated worker, as defined in the Workforce Investment Act of 1988, or

- Anyone counted in their household size received a means-tested federal benefit, such as welfare.

There's also an automatic zero EFC (yes, you read that right: an automatic zero, as in no dollars) if, and only if:

√ The parents' combined adjusted gross income (or combined income earned from work) is $30,000 or less, and either:

- The parents were not required to file an IRS form 1040,

- One of them is a dislocated worker, as defined in the Workforce Investment Act of 1988, or

- Anyone counted in their household size received a means-tested federal benefit, such as welfare, during any of the three previous years.

You've probably heard about the zero EFC before. It's often known as a "full ride." But kids, here is the thing: If you suspect that you qualify for an EFC of zero, *you still have to fill out the FAFSA, correctly and on time.* If you don't do that, colleges won't be able to help you. If your parents can't help you fill out the form, contact your school's guidance counselor, and tell him or her you suspect you qualify for a zero EFC and you'd like help in filling out the FAFSA. He or she should set aside at least an hour to make sure that you get the form filled out correctly. There's nothing embarrassing or wrong about asking for help, and we've noticed often in households that do qualify for a zero EFC, the parents are usually working multiple jobs, or working at night. They simply don't have the time to help you figure this out, so asking a guidance counselor is a great way to get it done without causing discord at home between you and your already-stressed parent(s).

WHAT DOES ALL OF THIS TELL YOU?

Well, it means that we've tried to create a formula to assess need, but, as with any other formula, in many ways, it's pretty arbitrary. While the final analysis is probably pretty darn good at separating those with no ability to pay (zero EFC) from those with a great capability to pay (an EFC of greater than $90,000), it isn't particularly good about the shades of gray in between, where most families fall. And though it might seem tempting to shift assets from a parent to a child to try and hide those funds from the government, in the end, the asset rate—up to 12 percent for parents and a set 20 percent for children—makes shifting assets (read: moving money around) a lose-lose.

You will likely fall into the middle, into a gray area, where your EFC doesn't compute and you don't think you can live up to paying it outright. The lower your EFC, the higher your aid award from any given college. Although there are a number of strategies out there for adjusting your EFC (pushing taxable income into the next fiscal year, for example), in the end, it won't make much difference. Pushing income into the next year will only come back and bite you in the rear when you fill out the FAFSA again (yes, you have to fill it out every year), so the best thing to do is to look at your spending and try to adjust. For extenuating circumstances—for example, if one or both of your parents recently lost their jobs, a problem that is increasingly common for college freshmen—you'll have to negotiate directly with the aid office. You can't appeal your EFC, but you can explain it to the FAA (Financial Aid Administrator) at your college of choice.

For a good idea of what your EFC will be, use the FAFSA4caster, anytime, day or night, in the months or years leading up to January 1st of you senior year. It's online at *fafsa4caster.ed.gov*, and it's a great way to start planning for your college costs during your sophomore and junior years (if you expect income to remain consistent).

THE CSS PROFILE

It's different from the FAFSA, and it's mandatory at many schools.

Is it helpful? Yes! Is it a pain? Yes.

You may have to fill out the CSS PROFILE, which is administered by the College Board (a private organization) in addition to the FAFSA. Why? It seems crazy! What else do they want from you? How many times can you possibly write out your Social Security number and calculate your income? Well, just like the government, colleges are stingy about giving away their money, and in many cases—especially with divorced families—it's easier to hide assets from the FAFSA than it is from the PROFILE.

Let's get to a basic explanation of the PROFILE. The PROFILE takes into account the equity of the home you live in. Colleges that use the PROFILE often make assumptions or demands that the FAFSA does not; for example, they may ask each family to have an additional contribution from assets based on the family's home equity situation, or expect from each student a summer earning contribution of a specified amount. It's different at every school, so if you've already narrowed down your list, and you know for sure that some of those schools require the PROFILE, request from their financial aid office an explanation of how they use the PROFILE to determine aid. This might be a helpful way to anticipate your aid award. Why is this helpful? Because it may be that the college in which you are the most interested assumes each student will have $3,500 from summer earnings or that her family will be able to obtain financing from home equity. Knowing what the assumptions from the college are will mean that you will be able to consider, and counter, when the time comes.

A quick note for all you students with Deadbeat Dads and Moms: If one of your parents is punishing an ex-spouse by denying you financial support for your college education, and *has the means to pay for your education* (read: has money), the PROFILE may not be your friend. The PROFILE requires both custodial *and* non-custodial parents to submit their financial information; the FAFSA only requires the parent you reside with the most to fill it out. So if you have one wealthy parent, who you don't live with and who is refusing to pay for your education, and he or she fills out the PROFILE, your aid award from the college will *not* be consistent with your EFC. It'll be much lower than it would be if you only turned in a FAFSA. So if you have a Deadbeat Dad or Mom (and parents, you know who you are), contact each college you're applying to that requires the PROFILE and request a waiver of non-custodial information. It'll be painful, and you'll have to spell out exactly what is so disharmonious about your family life to a total stranger over the phone, but financially it's worth it. Dry your tears, because if you have Deadbeat Dad or Mom and you're attending a school that requires the PROFILE, you might have to do this annually.

On a personal experience note, this is actually pretty common. During our careers, we've handed out countless tissues and had hundreds of phone calls with students who are in a sticky divorce situation, and don't know what to do. They were embarrassed and hurt and confused, but they were all pretty pleased to discover that the colleges we worked for (and every single college or university you will apply to) had a protocol for Deadbeat Dads and Moms. It's ugly and it's hurtful, but it's a common thing, and you can't adjust your aid award or get the non-custodial form waived unless you contact the financial aid office at the colleges you're applying to and simply lay it all out there.

The PROFILE is an online form that can be found at *profileonline. collegeboard.com*.

AFTER THE EFC: NEED-AWARE AND NEED-BLIND

When it comes to need, colleges and universities fall into one of two categories: need-aware, and need-blind. Let's start off with need-blind, the more common of the two need categories.

The Ivies, and other schools with buckets of money, describe themselves as need-blind and say that they "promise to meet full need." This means that they can admit anyone who fits their academic profile, regardless of their ability to pay, and that they'll meet the student's full demonstrated need. Translation: They'll pay for the gap between your COA and EFC.

Three important things about these schools: They have very large endowments, they have an incredibly strong brand presence in the market (which means they might be a "reach," or "unfunded" for you), and their students have out-of-this world academic credentials. A typical student admitted to a need-blind school that meets full need has high test scores, has a high GPA, speaks multiple languages, plays two instruments, lettered in multiple sports, and makes Mother Teresa look like Snooki from *Jersey Shore* when it comes to community service. Statistically, there's only one thing that correlates with all of those attributes: family income. The wealthier your parents, the more likely you are to score high (thanks to extra tutoring), play sports (costly equipment and time), and volunteer (no need to work after school for money)—so when you really break down the incoming freshman class of most need-blind schools, there really isn't much economic diversity there.

Another permutation of need-blind is to be need-blind for admission, but not to meet the full need of everyone who applied for assistance (or to meet that need in different packages for different students). This is often called "admit-deny": admit to the college, but deny for full aid. This can get kind of ugly, but not all schools have the money to fund everyone, or they may offer aid packages that are less attractive to some students. This approach is fairly common. At Carol's Pretty Good College, for example, we really value students who are in the top 10 percent of their graduating class. So, we award our aid on a "matrix basis" (and many, many colleges publish their matrices, something we talk about in Chapter 6, which is what you'll use to search for your match), where a student in the top 10 percent of his class will get a need-based aid package with a higher percentage of his need met with "Gift Assistance" (a merit aid scholarship) than a student who is only in the top 25 percent of his class. The student of lesser value to the college will get a package that has more loan and work, and less scholarship money, or he may not get any institutional money (merit aid) at all. Remember that you can have need and still get a package of the state and federal funds you might be entitled to, but it won't meet your full need—it won't fund you.

Need-aware is the other kind of admission policy. It means that if you apply, and you can't afford to pay and they don't care to fund you, they won't bother admitting you. It sounds unethical, but it's not. From their perspective, why admit-deny? What's the point? If they genuinely don't think that you have the money to pay, and they can't find an excuse to pay for you—either a financial excuse (you really can't afford it) or a merit excuse (you're a star and they want you)—why waste your time with an offer of acceptance? This is an important thing to remember when you start to get your acceptances and rejections in the mail. You might have been qualified for entrance to a certain college, but if they really didn't think you could or would pay, then you didn't get admitted. It also helps to explain why some of your classmates with weaker credentials could be admitted to places you weren't: They simply might have more money. It's unfair, and it stinks, but at least you don't have to feel rejected on the basis of your academic credentials alone.

One interesting variation on this is Reed College in Portland, Oregon, which has a policy called "come anyway." Reed College is need-aware, and meets full need if it does accept you. Every year, Reed College has more students it really wants than it has money for, so Reed says to some of these students, essentially, "Tell you what: Come anyway. We don't have aid for you in your first year, but if you come anyway, we promise to meet your full need for your remaining three years."

Reed is an interesting example, in that it's totally unique—and everyone's individual aid offer is, at the end of the day, unique. There's no "always" when it comes to aid; there's just "more likely" and "less likely." That's why in Chapter 6, we put so much emphasis on doing the research: You've already come up with a list of schools that match your credentials and put you in the "more likely" category, before you've even applied. If you get accepted, it's up to you to compare your offers and eventually figure out the right place for you (which, in an ideal universe, is a college you'd love to go).

THE GAP

Finally, we come to the crux of the need issue: the Gap. No matter where you get in, there's likely going to be a gap between the merit aid offer you get from the school, and what you still have to pay out. The Gap looks like this:

1. COA – EFC = *Actual Need*

2. *Actual Need – Aid Offer From the College of Your Choice = The Gap*

If you can't pay your full EFC, you can also add the difference between the full EFC and the amount you can actually pay (known as your actual EFC) to the Gap, which brings you to the total amount of money you have to come up with. If that math looks weird to you, or you don't understand it, try making a quick worksheet that looks like this:

Direct Costs	College A	College B
Tuition	22,000	17,000
Fees	150	2,500
Room and Board	8,500	9,500
TOTAL COSTS	30,650	29,000
Scholarships/Grants	12,000	8,000
Balance	17,650	21,000
Your EFC (use fafsa4caster!)	10,000	10,000
The Gap:	7,650	11,000

The ideal college is one that has the smallest possible Gap, and the best emotional and intellectual fit. In the previous scenario described, College A wins out, by a neat $3,350 per year, or $13,400 over four years. Please note that scholarships/grants do not include work-study or loans.

HOW ARE YOU SUPPOSED TO FILL THE GAP?

You'll fill the Gap with grants (money you don't have to repay, if you're eligible), federal student loans, work-study, and need-based and/or merit-based aid. We get into student loans extensively in the next chapter, but our rule for student debt is simple: Don't take on more than $32,000 total in loans, or roughly $8K per year, in student loan debt—federal loans, never private. If your loans exceed that, you might not be able to pay them back, and live the life you'd like to. To think about it another way, don't take on more in loans than you expect to make your first year out of college. According to Liz Pulliam Weston, the financial planner at MSN Money, the average starting salary for college graduates is just $30,000 per year; CNBC estimates the same starting salary at just over $48,000, a rather optimistic amount. But considering the state of the economy as we write this book—where only one in four students who graduated from college in 2010 who applied for a job actually have one—we think it's best to err on the side of caution. And the Project on Student Debt (*projectonstudentdebt.org*), a nonprofit independent research and policy group (and as smart and thoughtful an organization as we've ever seen), considers the national average in 2008, the most recent year for which such data is available, of $23,200 in student debt to be too high. So keep your loans as low as you can.

GRANTS

Grants, however, are wonderful. Take as many of those as you possibly can. Grants can come from the state government, federal government, or nongovernmental sources, and you never have to pay them back.

PELL GRANTS

Pell Grants are probably one of the most well-known federal grant programs. They originated in 1972 as the "Basic Educational Opportunity Grant Program," but were renamed for Senator Clayton Pell of Rhode Island in 1980. Pell Grants are targeted to the neediest of the college-going population. *Both U.S. citizens and eligible non-citizens can receive a Pell Grant.* For information about Pell Grant eligibility, go to *studentaid.ed.gov*.

Pell is a pretty large program, awarding roughly $18 billion dollars annually in grants to more than 5.5 million students. Generally, to receive a Pell Grant, you must have an EFC of less than $5,274. The best thing about Pell is that it's what's known as an "entitlement" grant; that means it's yours to take with you no matter where you want to study. The maximum annual award for a Pell Grant is, as of publication, $5,500 per student per year. The FAFSA will determine whether or not you're eligible for a Pell.

SEOGs (Supplemental Educational Opportunity Grants)

SEOGs come from the federal government. As do Pell Grants, SEOGs go to the neediest students, generally students with an EFC of $4,500 or lower. The very neediest students (likely those with an EFC of 0) will be considered *first* for SEOGs. The primary difference between SEOGs and Pell Grants is that a Pell gets paid directly to you, but an SEOG will go directly to your school, which is required to give it to you, either by crediting your account, paying you directly, or both, at least twice per academic year. The maximum SEOG is $4,000 per student, per year. SEOGs have been routinely underfunded in recent years, so they generally go only to the very neediest students.

TEACH Grants

If you're already a junior or senior in college and you're looking for more federal grants, check out the TEACH grant. TEACH grants are for students who agree to teach full-time in schools that serve low-income students for at least four years in the eight years following graduation. Basically, if you know you're going to teach in either an underserved population or subject, or both, a TEACH grant will net you roughly $4,000 per year. If you don't teach, it reverts to a low-interest loan. For more information, go to *studentaid.ed.gov*.

State Grants

State grants are generally only awarded to students who are going to stay *within* that state for college; in other words, Minnesota will not give Minnesota state grant money to a student who goes to study in California. But not all states have a large variety of options for your college education; Wyoming, Alaska, and New Mexico all have limited numbers of colleges, and have some grant monies that may be taken out of state for qualified applicants. State grant awards vary widely. For example, the Cal Grant award was $9,708 for tuition and fees for a student who attends a private college in California, whereas the "Access Missouri Grant" has a maximum of $4,600 for students who wish to study at private colleges in Missouri. For an extended list of state grants and more, please visit our website at *thefinancialaidhandbook.com*.

Work- Study

At most colleges, students with need are usually awarded a work-study contract. This is, besides grants, probably our favorite kind of financial aid. Work-study means that you have to work an on-campus job (such as baking muffins in the cafeteria, working at the campus coffee shop, or shelving books in the library) in order to earn your money. After you've earned it, it's yours to do with what you want. Generally, a work-study award is about $3,000 per year, which means roughly 10–12 hours of work per week. On-campus work-study jobs are awesome. What other employer allows you to schedule your work around your classes and hang out with your classmates at the same time? You don't have to commute, because you're working on-campus. You don't have to have any work experience at all to get a work-study job (although experience can sometimes help you choose what job to do). The biggest benefit of all is a statistical one: Research over the years has shown that students who work 10–12 hours per week on campus are more likely to be successful.[1] That's because with a work-study job, you spend time, outside of class, with another set of adults, professors, or mentors who are interested in your ongoing success. If you've already gone through the application and aid process and you *haven't* been awarded work-study, call your financial aid office ask how you can get an on-campus job, or if they will reduce your loan amount with work-study.

Student Loans

Really, the only student loans you should ever become familiar with are Stafford Loans. Also known as the Direct Stafford Loan Program, Staffords are administered completely by the federal government. The amount you can borrow depends on your year in school (freshman, sophomore, and so on), and in some ways your need as determined by the FAFSA. Staffords fall into two types.

Stafford Subsidized Loans

Also known as "sub" loans, a subsidized loan is one for which the government pays the interest on the loan while you're still in school and for six months after you graduate. If you take on a sub Stafford loan after July 1st, 2011, the interest rate will be fixed at 3.4 percent. That's a great interest rate. There are, however, limits to how many sub loans you can take out:

$3500 your freshman year, $4500 your sophomore year, and $5,500 your junior and senior years. If you're going to take out that much each year, do so in *only* sub loans, if possible; they're the absolute cheapest loans you can get. You do not need a cosigner for a Stafford loan.

STAFFORD UNSUBSIDIZED LOANS

Also known as "unsub" loans, an unsubsidized loan is where the government doesn't pay the interest on the loan while you're in school. The loan will accrue interest from the very first day you take it out. Unsub loans are generally more expensive, because they carry an extra four (or more) years of interest. Unlike sub loans, the limits aren't staggered: You can take out up to $2,000 in unsub loans any year that you're in school—freshman, sophomore, junior, or senior. If your parents don't qualify for a PLUS loan (a kind of student loan for parents), you may take out up to $6,000 in unsub loans each year that you're enrolled in college.

The maximum amount of money you can take out in federal loans is $31,000. Our absolute maximum amount of *reasonable* student debt is $32,000; that gives you an extra $1,000 in wiggle room for credit-card debt, a state-based student loan, or a Perkins, or, in an absolute pinch, a private loan.

STATE LOANS

Some states offer student loans that are accessible for both state residents attending colleges out of state, and for non-residents coming in-state; the Minnesota SELF loan is a good example. Minnesota SELF offers something that private loans can't; there are no origination, guarantee, or processing fees, and it has a limit of up to $10,000 per year. Because it's not a state or federally guaranteed loan, though, these lenders often require a cosigner (just as with a private loan), and the payment of interest while the borrower (you) is in school. They also have variable interest rates, meaning that the interest can go up or change with the market. State loans, like private loans, are best only for real emergencies.

PRIVATE LOANS

Private loans come from banks. Banks such as Wells Fargo, Chase, Bank of America, Wachovia, and almost any other bank in the country offer student loans. Do not be confused by banks: They don't lend money to students because they're interested in helping you go to college. Banks want to make money off of you, plain and simple. They'll also try and paint federal loans as *bad*. If you go to a student loan or aid fair, they'll be there, handing out free popcorn, tote bags, or some other swag to try to get your attention. Private loans are the most expensive kind you can take out, and generally a truly terrible idea.

We hate private loans so much we could literally fill an entire book about them with horrible stories, but that wouldn't be very helpful. So here are the basics: When you take out a private loan, there are as many possible kinds of fees as there are colors in the spectrum, just like a mortgage or a car payment. Banks have no interest at all in lending money to you, someone with no employment or credit history, for a product they can never repossess. What would they do with your diploma? Put it on their wall? No. They can't do anything with it. The only real incentive to lend to you is that you can't ever declare bankruptcy, and they can charge you anything you agree to. As you can imagine, that fine print can be pretty darn fine. Interest rates on private loans are high, and they vary with the market. If you miss a payment, something bad will inevitably happen: Your credit will be affected, you'll get an extremely high fee tacked on, or, worst-case scenario, you could find that your debt has *actually doubled*. You'll also need a cosigner, so if you don't pay back the bank, you'll drag your cosigner into the muck with you. Most private loans aren't insured against death or disability, either. That means if you die or get into a horrific accident, your family will be stuck with your student loans in addition to your medical bills. We get into this much more in-depth in the next chapter, but bottom line: Do not take out private student loans. Ever.

If you don't follow our advice and you do take off a private loan, pay it off as fast as possible, and prioritize it the same way you would for any other high-interest debt.

SCHOLARSHIPS

MERIT AID

We touched briefly on merit aid, also known as scholarships, gift aid, or tuition discounting, in Chapter 1. Merit aid will be your best friend when it comes to filling the Gap, but you won't find out what your merit aid award is until *after* you've applied. (For more information about predicting your merit aid award, turn to Chapter 6, where we cover the basics of understanding your likelihood of receiving a scholarship.) Merit aid comes from the college itself; in other words, it's their own money. Merit aid often goes to the students who have the highest test scores, class rank, GPA, or community involvement (academic, extracurricular, athletic, or community leaders) of the incoming freshman class. That means at a school where your stats are *just good enough* to get you in the door, you won't get any merit aid—but at a school where you're the best and the brightest, you'll get half-tuition or more. Unlike need-based aid, colleges can give out merit aid to whomever they please; after all, it's their own cash. For sample merit aid awards, our MAP (merit aid profile) or more information about merit aid and tuition discounting, please turn to Chapter 6.

TALENT-BASED SCHOLARSHIPS

Talent-based colleges and universities are far from cultural wastelands. Instead, they reward talent *as well as* academics—music and theatre nerds, Quiz Bowl stars, debaters, and other kinds of special talents that they reward with scholarships—*if* that talent is important to the college or university. That "if" can be really important. If, for example, a school with a Scottish heritage has a bagpipe band on campus, then having that band at school events—homecoming, alumni, graduation, and so on—is a big priority. What do you need for a proper Scottish band? Bagpipe players! Odds are, that school has a "talent award" to reward and recruit bagpipe players—but they don't care a fig for students who play in a drum and bugle corps.

ATHLETIC SCHOLARSHIPS

If you're skilled enough in any given sport that your coach or athletic trainer has encouraged you to apply to a DI or DII school, go directly to the ncaa.org eligibility center online. Never, ever pay anyone to find an athletic scholarship for you; just like someone trying to sell you a bridge in Brooklyn, or an "inheritance" in Nigeria, anyone who charges for a scholarship is scamming you. *The Athletic Recruiting and Scholarship Guide* is a great resource for students and parents who are looking for an athletic scholarship. However, if you're just someone who loves to play—and plays well—DIII schools might be a better fit for you. But you won't get an athletic scholarship at a DIII school; they cannot and do not give athletic scholarships.

HOW MUCH FINANCIAL AID CAN I GET?

If you've read all of this straight through—without flipping to other chapters, forgetting about this book entirely, or pulling your hair out—we salute you. This is where is gets *really* complicated; it's different at every single school.

Our hard-and-fast rule for aid is this: *If you're in the top 25 percent of applicants, you'll get the most need- and merit-based aid possible.* Different schools all have different amounts of money to give out, so your offers may vary from place to place. But if you're in the top 25 percent, you'll likely get the best package that college can give. So if you really need those aid dollars, don't waste your time applying to colleges where you fall in the bottom 50 percent; you may get *some* aid, but it won't be enough.

For each school that you like—and that you think will fund you— you'll fill out our MAP chart (or heck, make your own; just copy it from Chapter 6 or download it from our website) and determine the likelihood of receiving enough in aid (grants, loans, and need-based and merit-based aid) to fill the Gap. And once you've decided on a school, applied, and been accepted, you'll have to fill out the FAFSA again every single year. The better you understand the language, the formulas, and the structure of financial aid, the higher your chances of being able to effectively negoti- ate your financial aid awards in the coming years. So although this chapter might have bored you to tears (or worse, scared the pants off of you), it's time to celebrate: The worst is over. This was absolutely the most foreign and confusing part of the book, and now you've got an incredible wealth of financial aid knowledge under your belt. It'll benefit you in the next four years, and if/when you apply to graduate school. Time to dog-ear the page, grab a soda, pass this chapter off to your parents, and go sit outside with your friends for an afternoon. Promise us you won't talk about college for even a minute.

3

LET'S TALK ABOUT DEBT

Who are you going to be when you graduate from college?

It's nearly impossible to know the answer. You might be interested in becoming a veterinarian; you might become a CPA; maybe you'll be chaining yourself to hundred-year-old redwoods and fighting for the rights of our planet. Whatever you do, you want who you are—essentially how you define yourself—to be about the things you do, about what you're interested in.

The magnificent freedom of a college education will allow you to decide that for yourself. You'll be able to learn about all avenues of life, and dream up scenarios of yourself walking down them: in a sharp suit, clutching a pair of drumsticks, wielding a paintbrush, or climbing a mountain. Trust us, you will want, and will love, to walk or *run* down those avenues. And the only thing that will hold you back are your student loans.

You can choose how to live after you graduate. If you want to spend your money on a fancy apartment, go ahead; if you want to share a house with eight other people so that you can go skiing every weekend, you can do that too. You can have a cell phone (or not). You can have a TV (or not). You

63

can choose how to spend your money in every single way except for one: your student loan payments.

When you take out student loans, you are agreeing to make a monthly payment for the next 10 or 20 years after you graduate from college—anywhere from $50 to $1,000 per month or more.

There's no two ways about it: Taking out a student loan means agreeing to a monthly payment that begins right after you graduate.

Your monthly student loan payments are something you'll choose well before you graduate from college. You will choose them the *instant* that you decide what college to go to, when you decide how much you'll need to borrow each year in order to graduate. The total amount you will borrow, on a particular loan term (either 10 or 20 years; we recommend 10), will be broken down into monthly payments, scheduled for the next 10 to 20 years after you graduate, from the moment you sign off on your first Direct Stafford.

Now, there's nothing *wrong* with taking out student loans; in fact, we encourage it. Taking on a reasonable amount of what is generally known as "good debt" can be a very positive thing. It'll raise your credit score and further enable you to take on other loans (like for graduate school, or a house) later in life. And from your family's perspective, it's *your* education; you should be responsible to pay for as much of it as you can. You've probably assumed, as well, that you are absolutely going to take out loans. Most of your friends will. But how much do you really know about loans? How much do you know about borrowing? Unless you've had a credit card that you're responsible for paying, we bet you don't know very much at all. Student loans are something you shouldn't walk into blindly, assuming that no matter how much you take out, it will pay off in the end. You need to think hard about it, do the math, plan for the future (in the worst-case, lowest-paying job scenario possible), and *then* take out a loan.

How much you will take on in student loans is *not* a mystery to be solved after you graduate. You will know, unequivocally, from the very first day of college, how much your monthly payments and total debt will be. Student loans, unlike a mortgage or a car loan, cannot be dissolved in bankruptcy. In fact, one of the few ways to get rid of them entirely (without paying them off, of course) is through *death*. Student loans will have, quite literally, a death grip on you.

This might seem incredibly unfair. Why can people buy million-dollar houses with money they don't have, and then get let off the hook in bankruptcy? You're borrowing for your *education*. It's not a Jaguar convertible; it's not a private plane; it is not a frivolous purchase. It is something that you genuinely need in order to move forward in life, so why are student loans so difficult to discharge?

A great deal of the difference lies in what you're purchasing: education. Let's start with the concept of *equity*. When you think about purchasing a house or a car with money you don't have, the bank that lends the money to you sees the house or the car as something called equity, which means the actual dollar value of the property. If you default on your loan payments for your mansion, yacht, or helicopter, the bank that loaned you the money to buy it in the first place becomes the actual owner. The bank can repossess—and most importantly—*resell* the mansion, yacht, or helicopter at any time. What on earth would a bank do with your college diploma? The lender can't do anything with it; it's illegal to sell on eBay, and the college certainly won't buy it back. It is of literally no value to anyone except *you*. So the lender—in this case the federal government—does have a vested interest in helping you repay the loan. The lender, in the case of what we'll call "educational equity," does the only thing it can to help you out: keep interest rates low and promise not to change (or "adjust," in the insidious language of banking) them before the end of the loan term (that is, the last day you have to pay it back—10 or 20 years into the future).

The other major problem with student loans is, quite frankly, *you*. What incentive does a bank possibly have to give tens of thousands of dollars, for the purchase of something they can never repossess or resell, to someone with no credit history or employment record? The bank has no guarantee, at all, that you'll repay the loan (other than a general statistical likelihood that college graduates have jobs). For actual banks—private lenders such as U.S. Bank and Wells Fargo—the problem of *you* is the biggest problem of all. Private banks will not only require a cosigner with a good credit history, but they'll keep your interest rates sky-high: 10 percent or more. We'll cover this again later, but student loans from private banks—from anyone except the federal government's Direct Stafford program—are a total rip-off that is absolutely, shamelessly designed to take your money. Never, ever, ever take them out.

Even federal loans can have their drawbacks if you take out too many, or don't plan for the future—if you don't think about how much it's going to cost you from *day one*. If you're not careful, your student loans will be the only thing that defines you; they can severely limit how you can live and what you can do with your life.

Debt even affects people who don't want to, or care about, making a lot of money. In fact, it often affects them the most.

Let's look at an example, a real person that we interviewed earlier this year whose life is not only affected, but has been completely altered by his student debt. Gray, a 35-year-old painter who lives in New York, attended a private arts college on and off for several years in his early 20s. He now lives under an assumed name in an attempt to avoid his student loan debt of roughly $66,000, which, thanks to mounting interest, grows larger each year. Gray lives in a tenement-style apartment building with a month-to-month lease. His credit rating has been destroyed by his inability to repay his student loans, so the prospect of finding a nicer (or safer) place to live is impossible without using someone else's real name on a credit check or lease application. His cell phone is registered under a girlfriend's name. He is currently unemployed; if he were to get a job using his real name, his wages would likely be garnished each month by a collection agency.

When Gray first started attending art school, he received financial help from his parents and, with their encouragement, took on loans. Although he presumably signed the student loan equivalent of a promissory note (something that says "I know I have to pay this back"), he doesn't remember it, or even seriously thinking about repayment. The math, he says, was optimistic:

> *I wasn't concerned about [repayment] when I took out the loans. I mean, all my friends were paying like $160 a month for their loans, and I [thought] okay, that's doable. My rent at that time was $450, I sell one painting a month, I had a $20 per hour part time job, I thought, I can do this…. But I wasn't concerned about [repaying the loans], really. I was more envious of the kids who were qualified to borrow so much money that they didn't have to work!*

Although his loans would eventually require a monthly payment of $355, more than double $160 per month, that amount of $160—what his friends were paying—stuck in his head. That was what he assumed his own loans would cost. He says of his first year in art school:

I got into school, I got the loans, my parents were excited. They said, "We'll pay your rent, just go to school, you can work a part-time job so you can have money for this and that." That lasted for two months. And then my dad lost his job.... And that was where it all started to unravel. I mean, I don't blame them. But I thought, this is bulls**t. Now I have to pay everything. I have to pay the rent, I have to pay for school. And then I started to get really pissed off and thought, I don't want to go to school anymore, this is a waste of money.

Gray left school after two years, and then returned after a few years and a period of unemployment. He attended classes for another year and a half, but was unable to graduate due to nonpayment.

He managed to avoid his loans for a few years. He nearly forgot about them; he pushed them into the corner of his mind where he could pretend they didn't exist. As far as he was concerned, he shouldn't have to repay loans for something that he never received (a BA). But one day, of course, his loans finally caught up with him. Gray walked into the office where he'd been working and discovered that his paycheck was nearly half of what it should have been. Confused and upset, he sought out the office manager, who informed him that she'd gotten a letter from the company overseeing his loans, and that the missing loan payments had been taken from his wages automatically. He called the company in question, which demanded $700 monthly loan payments; Gray eventually negotiated it down to $355 per month.

That humiliating and humbling moment, standing there with half a paycheck, was when Gray says that he finally realized he would actually have to repay his loans. Before that, his loans had been an abstract concept—something he tried not to think about. But when his student loans interfered with his job, Gray came back to earth. "It was like an anvil hitting me on the head. When I got that paycheck from my work, with half of it gone, and that was how I found out—and my work was so unsympathetic.... Welcome to reality. Really fast."

Perhaps $66,000 does not sound as if it's a lot of debt to you—but for someone like Gray, whose only goal is to become a successful working artist—it's become a nearly impossible amount of money to repay. Many artists work day jobs, but literally only to pay their rent, utilities, and materials; the fewer hours they can work, the better. Working more only increases the amount of time they *don't* spend doing what they love, be it painting, drawing, or sculpting. Many artists will tell you, as well, that their graduate programs were where they really grew as artists, and began to find commercial success. For someone like Gray, not only does his lack of a BA make graduate school nearly impossible, but he literally could not afford to go. Although Gray's situation is severe, his advice to young artists is certainly something worth thinking about:

> *I would tell some 18 year-old who maybe thought he was an art star in high school, to just go to a four-year, affordable university. If you want to be an artist, go to graduate school. That's where galleries pull from. They don't care about undergraduates.... No one will pay attention to undergraduates. Don't do your undergrad at art school.... If you're going to go into art, then always look at the most affordable ways to learn. It's usually through your friends. Just create a crew of other artists that you can pull from.*

If you can't relate to Gray—if you read his story and think, "I will never be like that; I will choose a lucrative major and career, graduate, and be able to pay back my student loans no matter what the cost," we've got news for you.

The recession that began at the end of 2007 has impacted the graduating classes of 2009 and 2010 so deeply that for students graduating from college in the last two years, only one out of every five students who applied for a job actually had one.[1] By the time you graduate in 2015, 2016, 2017, or 2018, the graduates who come before you might *still* be fighting for entry-level positions.[2] Even if the economy recovers so much that there is a large shortfall of college-educated workers (as much as 3 million in 2018, according to a recent study from Georgetown University[3]) the competition from previously unemployed recent college graduates—who have spent the intervening years of the recession acquiring more education, connections, and internships on their resumes—will be fierce.

We're not trying to make you depressed; we're just trying to be realistic. Even if you *can* get a job right after you graduate, the best jobs are often the lowest-paying ones: internships or low-level positions that allow you to acquire the connections and networks you'll need to move ahead in your career during later years. But if you've got an $800 monthly loan payment to repay, you literally *will not be able* to take an unpaid or minimum-wage internship at the Council on Foreign Relations or at *Vogue*—you'll have to take a higher-paying job, likely something *really boring*, just to make your monthly payments.

WHAT DOES TAKING ON A LOAN REALLY MEAN?

When you take on a loan, you have to take on a promissory note that functions as any other legal contract does: You agree to a set of terms. Those terms, according to the U.S. Department of Education, include the following (emphasis ours):

√ *Loan is to be used only for educational expenses.*

√ *Must be repaid including any fees and interest.*

√ *Must repay even if you do not complete your education.*

√ *Must repay within 10 years unless they are consolidated or select special repayment options.*

√ *Federal loans can be prepaid without penalty.*

√ *Minimum monthly payment will be at least $50.*

√ *Repayment will begin six months after leaving school or dropping to less than half time.*

√ *If I fail to repay a loan, I may be considered in default, and the following may result:*

   • *My default status may be reported to a national credit bureau and have a negative effect on my credit rating for seven years.*

   • *The entire unpaid amount of my loan, including interest, may become due and payable immediately.*

   • *I may lose deferment and repayment options.*

   • *My federal and state income-tax refunds and other federal payments may be withheld.*

   • *My wages may be garnished.*

   • *I may be assessed collection costs, including attorney's fees.*

- *I may be ineligible to receive any further federal or state financial aid.*

- *I may be ineligible to obtain a state professional license in my field.*

- *I may be sued.*

Those terms are serious. When you take out a student loan, you absolutely must repay it. As we described previously in this chapter, they're incredibly difficult to discharge, or get rid of.

If you can't repay your student loans, you'll find it very, very difficult to achieve your dreams, like Gray. And though you may not be an artist, you'll have something that drives you. What is it? Are you passionate about good nutrition for children? Are you an advocate for women's rights? Do you love being outside and active every day? Are you committed to activities at your church, temple, mosque, or other religious or community institution? Are you a political animal who wants to be in the thick of the local, state, or federal government?

Those questions could determine who you become, but if you can't repay your loans, the only question you'll be asking yourself is this: "How do I make enough money, and live cheaply enough, to pay off my loans?" Money, and the pursuit and redistribution of it, could become your only passion.

Although you might not see it, Gray is an excellent example of someone you *could be*: a person who knew who he was and what he wanted to do, but never, ever, sat down and did the simple math of what he was borrowing versus how much he might make. You could be the most ambitious, directed, and passionate student of all time, but if you don't do the math, you might borrow more than you can afford and wind up living in a tenement under an assumed name the way Gray does. We're serious! It can happen to anyone. So to really understand student loans, that's the first thing we're going to ask you to do: learn about the math.

MONEY, MONEY, MONEY

How much money do you think you'll make when you graduate?

Go ahead. Write it down: $_____

Well, because writing a book is sort of a one-way street, we have no idea what that number looks like. But we *can* bet that the number you wrote down is based on previous conversations you've had with other people, sort of like how Gray's assumption of his student loan payments ($160) came from what he knew his friends were paying (and had nothing to do with his own situation). So let's try and figure out an income for you that is all about *you*—and not about what you've heard from other people.

Open your computer's browser and head to payscale.com, a website that tracks compensation data. You'll be able to enter all types of information (education, location, what kind of job at what kind of company) without giving out your personal contact information. When you've finished, the calculator should give you an estimated salary.

We decided to research a couple of options. For example, according to Payscale's calculator, a graduate with a BA in accounting from Augsburg College in Minneapolis who moves to Chicago and gets a job as a CPA for an insurance company will earn an average starting salary of $46,727. Does that sound like a lot of money to you? It's less than you think (although it's still pretty good). Let's break it down.

WHAT DOES $46,000 GET YOU IN CHICAGO?

Each month you'll make about $3,896. You'll lose roughly $579 in federal income taxes, $242 in Social Security, $56 in Medicare, and $117 to the great state of Illinois. This leaves you with about $2,900 per month after taxes. Subtract another $200 for health insurance (and hey, that's if you can get it cheap—through your employer) and you're down to $2,700. But, you don't live in a box on the street; you'll need an apartment. According to apartments.com, you can rent an unfurnished studio apartment in Lincoln Park (a lovely little neighborhood in the city) for about $750 per month; throw in your utilities (cell phone, electricity, Internet, and cooking gas) at around another $200, transportation at $150 (that's for the subway and the occasional late-night cab ride; forget about buying a car just yet), and your monthly income is down to $1,600 per month, or $400 per week—from a paycheck that you estimated at nearly $3,900 per month. And that's if you're a CPA—a relatively high-paying job, and a good fit for someone who majored in math. Throw in a student loan of $32,000 on a 10-year repayment term ($8,000 per year, the federal maximum), and that monthly loan payment of $368.26 brings your disposable income down to just $307 per week for food, clothing, travel, and entertainment. Let's be real: You're not going to sit home and be a hermit. There are concerts to attend, and movies, weddings, and parties to go to. That's fairly manageable for a CPA who live in Chicago on about $43 per day; to someone who works in the arts (or someone like Gray, who barely works at all), that's a king's ransom.

If you've never heard of Augsburg, the college we used for this example, it's a mid-selectivity private liberal arts college in Minneapolis. Their sticker price for tuition is $37,812, but their average net price (the price that most students pay) is just $23,070, and the average grant received by students is $14,472. Their average annual student loan debt upon graduation is $7,892. Augsburg is also Ruth's alma mater.

But other kinds of majors—say, anyone in the humanities—might not be so lucky as our CPA. Let's look at a young friend of ours, Red. Red graduated from an elite college in the last five years with a bachelor's degree in history. During college, she worked at one of the school's museums as a security guard, making minimum wage. She got her first job at a major art museum, in the education department. Her income that year was just $21,000—and it was remarkable that she was paid at all, considering the legions of unpaid interns, some of whom had more education than she did (masters and PhDs), who worked for and with her. But, it was a fantastic job that allowed her to meet dozens of helpful, fascinating people and sit around all day looking at, and learning about, art. Red even met Robert Rauschenberg's turtle, and knows more about art (and the art industry) than many people we know. If that sounds like something you'd be interested in, read on.

WHAT DOES $21,000 GET YOU IN NEW YORK?

Our young friend Red lived in New York City—but not on the fashionable, expensive island of Manhattan (or even in uber-hip Brooklyn). She lived in Astoria, Queens (just across the bridge from Manhattan and her office) and split a tiny, one-bedroom apartment with her boyfriend. In NYC, housing is often the largest expenditure for young professionals (or indeed, anyone); her frugality and willingness to share her space brought her rent down to just $500 a month. (Unsurprisingly, the relationship didn't last.) After taxes, her monthly income was about $1,400; subtract that $500 rent and she was down to $900. Subtract a monthly $100 MetroCard for the subway (forget about cabs—no matter how high her heels were, she hoofed it) and another $100 for utilities (shared with the aforementioned boyfriend), and she had just $700 with which to feed and clothe herself—about $175 per week, or $25 per day. Subtract a student loan payment of $386.26 ($32,000 in total debt, or $8,000 per year) and that $750 a month gets cut in (more than) half: $314 per month, or $78 per week (or $11 per day) to feed, clothe, and entertain herself. How did she do it? Well, she ate a lot of rice and went to *a lot* of dinner parties, bringing handmade origami instead of a bottle of wine. She only saw movies in the park (where they were free). She didn't have health insurance that year, but luckily, she didn't break anything or get the flu, and her local Planed Parenthood took care of her birth control and annual OB/GYN visit. She rode her bicycle when she wasn't taking the subway, and she shopped in friends' closets (that is, borrowed) and at thrift stores. It was a brutal year, but the job was so amazing that she wouldn't have done it any other way. The punch that low-paying (but prestigious) arts job packed on her resume (Education Department, Major Art Museum) continues to help her to this day. It even factored into her recent admission into an Ivy League graduate school program. If her student loans had surpassed $32,000, there is *no way* she would have been able to take that important first job—and though she didn't live like a queen (or even like a middle-class person), it was worth it.

Not all humanities jobs lead to a life of dignified poverty. Let's think about other humanities jobs, in other cities. If you'd like to be a writer, Los Angeles is a great place to get your start. Hundreds of movies are being made each year. Someday, you could make a lucrative back-end deal and become the next Oscar-winning billionaire screenwriter—or you could get a salaried studio job and do (pretty) well for yourself. According to Payscale, a recent graduate who went to UCLA and majored in creative writing that gets a job as a script writer in L.A. could make $38,684 per year, on average.

WHAT DOES $38,000 GET YOU IN LOS ANGELES?

After taxes (which are high in California), your $38,684 goes down to about $29,772. That's $2,481 per month. According to apartments. com, a studio apartment in Silver Lake (a hip, amenity-rich neighborhood filled with young creative professionals) could cost an average of $1,000 per month. Subtract that $1,000, and you're down to $1,481. Take away another $150 for utilities (you'll need less electricity for heating and cooling in that perfect 75-degree LA weather) and you're down to $1,331. It's L.A., so you'll need a car. No subways for you. If you'd like to buy a new car, you can purchase a new Ford Fusion with a 72-month payment at 1.9 percent for $271 per month; that leaves you with $1,060 per month, or $265 per week. Take away $35 per week for gas (maybe more; this will depend on where you live and what you drive), another $20 per week for car insurance, and you're down to $210 per week, or about $30 per day, with which to feed, clothe, and entertain yourself—and pay your student loans or health insurance. What are you going to do? Well, we think you should move. If you can share a three-bedroom apartment in Silver Lake with some friends, your rent could come down to just $600 per month and your utilities down to $100 (more people use more electricity, and want things—especially in LA—such as cable TV or a cleaning service). That gives you an extra $450 per month, easily enough to cover your $368 student loan payment. You can put the remaining $100 away for either health insurance (if you can get it through your company) or as an emergency-health fund. Although it sounds risky, for young people, paying for full-coverage health insurance can often cost you much more than it's worth; you might want to get a cheaper plan, say at around that $100 per month, that covers catastrophes (like broken legs and car accidents), and pay out-of-pocket for a subsidized healthcare provider like Planned Parenthood that can give you an annual checkup and provide you with essentials like birth control and antibiotics.

If science is what interests you, you're in luck. The United States has a multi-trillion-dollar science economy, making everything from rockets and bombs to Viagra and solar panels. You're on the road to long hours in the lab and big payoffs at the bank. Let's pretend your favorite subject is chemistry and, for good measure, you're a southerner. According to Payscale, if you're a recent graduate of Berry College in Georgia who majored in chemical engineering, you could make an average of $59,966 as a chemical engineer working for a pharmaceutical company. Where would you go? If you're a good southern girl or boy, you'll head to Atlanta, the nearest big city. It's got a great music scene, tons of nightlife, and, more importantly, a large professional economy.

WHAT DOES $59,000 GET YOU IN ATLANTA?

Hotlanta is *hot*. If you're a southerner, you'll know that you can't live without central air-conditioning; if you're a Yankee, you'll know you need it as soon as you step off the plane. According to apartments.com, a one-bedroom apartment with central air could run you an average of $900 per month in East Atlanta, a young, walkable, and bohemian neighborhood. After taxes, your monthly take-home pay is $3,563; subtract your rent of $900, utilities at $200 (your A/C could run for six to eight months of the year), and a car payment of $271 per month and weekly overhead of $55 for insurance and gas, and you've got $1,972 left over to spend. Looks like you can afford health insurance ($200 per month) and a student loan of $32,000 ($368 per month) with cash to spare, leaving you with $1,404 monthly, or $351 per week for food, clothing, travel, and anything else you can dream up. You won't be taking a private plane anytime soon, but you'll be comfortable.

Unless you plan on a career in computer science, engineering, or complex mathematics, this range—$21,000 to $59,000—is a reasonable, likely salary range for your first job after graduation. Your first job is what can make or break your career—or even help you figure out what you *never* want to do for money.

Another young friend of ours, who we'll call Kelly, majored in "culture & politics" as an undergraduate at an elite university. He was financially independent from his family and thought that law school—and a cushy, high-paying job at a law firm—would be his ticket to happiness. His first year out of school was spent toiling away at a prestigious law firm—and counting the seconds, every day, until he could leave the office. The practice of law can be lucrative, but there's a cost: It can be boring, the hours are murder, and new lawyers can take decades to break into the real profit-sharing model of a firm (partnership). Kelly was unimpressed—in fact, *de*pressed—by the life he had always assumed would give him what he wanted: financial security. After a year, Kelly—who had *always* been concerned first and foremost about his financial future—decided to take a chance. He left the law firm and took a new path as a PhD student in the humanities. Financial security is still important to him, he says, but he's discovered that emotional and intellectual security—the kind that only a job you really love can provide—has trumped the notion that money buys happiness. Thankfully, Kelly's low undergraduate debt—around $25,000 total—meant that he didn't have to worry about large repayment sums, or borrowing additional amounts for graduate school. If Kelly had taken on any more student loans, he says, he would have had to stay in the law firm where he got his start, ticking away the hours, years, and then decades on the clock before he felt free enough to pursue what he really wanted. He would have lost the first half of his life to his student loans.

HOW MANY LOANS TO TAKE: THE $8K DEBT CHALLENGE

In all of our previous examples, you may have noticed that we used the exact same student loan payment for each theoretical graduate in each city. That's not because all student loans are the same, but because that is the absolute most—the worst-case scenario of student loans—that you should expect to take out. A $368-per-month payment is usual for a federal student loan of $8,000 per year on a 10-year term, or $32,000 total. That amount is the absolute *most* you should spend on student loans. Ideally, you wouldn't borrow anywhere close to that much, but the federal limits will allow you to. Why do we suggest a cap of $32,000? Well, we've got two great reasons:

#1: BORROWING FROM THE FEDERAL GOVERNMENT IS YOUR BEST (AND CHEAPEST) BET

A total of $32,000 will keep you in loans that come directly from the federal government. The most money you can take out in federal loans is $31,000: freshmen, $5,500, sophomores, $6,500, and juniors and seniors, $7,500. That's a total of $27,000 in Direct Staffords for four years, you're given an additional $4,000 in eligibility for summer tuition and other living expenses, should you require it or if it takes you more than four years to graduate. If your parents are not eligible for a PLUS Loan, your Direct Stafford eligibility skyrockets—but that doesn't mean you should take any more than we recommend. Your loans will be a mix of subsidized and unsubsidized loans. Subsidized loans have less interest than unsubsidized; for a "sub" loan, the government does not charge interest while you're still in school. We're giving you $1,000 for either a Perkins Loan or credit-card debt; that's enough to cover occasional incidentals, like travel costs for extracurricular activities, the loss of part-time income from taking an unpaid internship for one semester, or traveling while studying abroad. With $8,000 per year in loans, and income from a part-time job during the summer or on weekends, there's no need to take out any private loans (the kind with high interest that come from a private bank), ever. Federal loans are the absolute best kind of loans you can take, for the following reasons:

√ *With federal loans, interest rates are set. They don't change with LIBOR (the London Interbank Offered Rate, a scale to which many loans are pegged) rates, or adjust with the prime. That means that from the very beginning, you'll know exactly how much debt you're taking on. Remember that student loan debt isn't just the amount you borrow; it's also the interest you pay for borrowing the money. Federal student loans of $32,000 require repayment of at least an additional $12,190.70, bringing your total debt to $44,190.70 or more.*

√ *You don't need a cosigner with a federal loan. This is very important. A cosigner is someone who agrees to repay your loans if you cannot do so; he or she takes on the same responsibility for the loan that you do. If you don't pay, your cosigner has to. And that "has to" is an absolute.*

√ *You don't choose your payment program when you take out the loan. With most private student loans, you have to select the repayment terms when you take out the loan, and what might look "doable" during your freshman year of college may be completely unmanageable when you graduate. But then, you'll be stuck. If you don't pay your loans, your wages could be garnished and you could be sued.*

#2: TOTAL STUDENT LOAN DEBT SHOULD HAVE A 1:1 RATIO OR LESS TO YOUR FIRST YEAR OF INCOME

Most financial planners have different approaches to finances, but they all agree on one thing: Your total student loans should be *less than or equal to* your annual income your first year out of college. That means if you're going to major in the liberal arts—whose graduates have an average starting salary of $33, 540[4]—your total debt cannot be more than $33,540. From a monthly, not annual, perspective, this means that your monthly student loan payments should not exceed 10 to 15 percent of your monthly gross.

There are financial planners out there who suggest that if you go to an elite or Ivy League college, you can safely take on more debt. We are not those kinds of advisors. *We cannot find any statistical evidence anywhere that suggests taking on more debt for college is an intelligent thing to do.* Your undergraduate, or bachelor's degree, is not the same thing as a law or medical degree. It does not "pay back" in the same way that people think law school and med school does; an undergraduate degree is the new high school diploma. It's an essential—not a bargaining foothold in the payroll office.

Almost everyone you will ever work with in a professional environment (particularly a corporate one) will have gone to college. It's standard. Going to college, despite the oft-quoted statistic that "a college degree is worth an extra million dollars over one's lifetime," is not very lucrative anymore. Saying that it is is a completely dated idea that will not be true for your generation (unless inflation spikes and a million bucks is what you use to buy a loaf of bread, like in Zimbabwe); it's the equivalent of saying, "The Ford Model-T is the best car on the market!" Clearly, the Model-T is no longer the "best" car on the market; there are better cars (and better graduate degrees and resumes) out there. Don't be fooled by financial advisors who haven't realized what decade they live in. Spend as little as you can on the best education possible. Brand name will only be important insofar as a brand name *identifies* a community; how that community rallies around its members changes from school to school and has *absolutely nothing* to do with the ratings imposed on them by publications such as the *Princeton Review* and *U.S. News & World Report*.

MEETING THE $8K DEBT CHALLENGE

We challenge you, students and parents, to meet our $8K Debt Challenge. Don't take on a dime more than $8,000 per year, or $32,000 total, in loans. If the schools you're looking at will cost too much, *don't go there*. Find a different school, one that will value who you are as a student, and give you a scholarship. Believe us, $32,000 in loans—which means $32,000 more than you're *already paying out of pocket*—is enough for your college education. Spend any more and you begin to slide uncontrollably down the slippery slope of debt. *If you can't meet our challenge, your student loan payments will outweigh the benefits of your college education.*

To estimate whether or not you can meet our $8K Debt Challenge, turn to Chapter 7, and use our Cost-Conscious Search Chart. Once you've applied, been accepted, and received your final aid awards, use the three-step process we outline in Chapter 10.

THE DANGERS OF CREDIT CARDS

On the flip side, if you don't take on enough debt to support yourself while you're in college (and income from a part-time job isn't enough), you'll be tempted to head down the yellow brick road of credit cards. We know, *everyone* warns you against the dangers of credit cards; there's a reason for that. They're dangerous and, really, there's no good reason for you to have one. An "emergency" credit card quickly turns into a "just this once" repository for iTunes purchases, impulsive online shopping, trips to the bar, and so on. The deferred payments can really mess with your head, and before you know it, you wind up with a mountain of credit card debt.

If you come from an affluent family or community and you're used to having nice things whenever you'd like them, the shock of being what we call "college broke"—the genteel poverty of most college students, who live on ramen, dining hall food, and PBR—can send you tumbling down the rabbit hole into a bad credit trip that can last for years or even decades.

Clay, a young man we interviewed earlier this year, came from an affluent community where at least 90 percent of his peers went on to a four-year university. He describes his college experience as "an extension of high school." He grew up, he says, "never knowing the value of a dollar…. I was always in a bubble, and being taken care of. Nothing bad ever happened to me." He had credit cards from the age of 15 on. Clay always assumed his parents could pay for whatever debt he accrued, but their divorce and other financial difficulties prevented them from doing so. During college, Clay took out loans, worked multiple jobs, and racked up credit-card debts to support his financially reckless lifestyle, which included, he says, things like weekend plane trips to major cities "just to go to Abercrombie & Fitch." His mother has tried to help him pay off his credit card and student loan debts, which currently total around $85,000. In order to help him, she's extended the entire line of home equity credit on her home, and now owes the bank more than she paid for their family house 25 years ago. She has also had to take a second job, just to pay his debts. Clay says:

> *I'm ashamed of what I've actually done to my family…. I'm not saying the onus isn't completely on me—but a lot of it was my up-bringing. My parents did not structure my behavior and teach me the value of a dollar. And I'm so thankful for my mom, for coming in and bailing me out—but she's done it now five times. When is enough* enough? *And we're at a point now—my mom shares her finances 100% with me—you know,* there is no more money. We just went through all of the credit cards…. I owe my mom more than what she's given me. And it sucks.*

He's currently repaying his mother with a $500 payment each month; he estimates that he owes her roughly $45,000 dollars. The strain on his family, and his personal relationship with his mother, is actually *worse* than owing money: "I'm 30, living on the other side of the country from my mom, and I haven't talked to her in a couple of weeks, and she can't tell me what to do—but I owe her all this money. And that has an impact on our relationship, and it's that hold when I go home. It's in every conversation, that I owe her money. And that sucks."

Clay's story is particularly terrifying because of the nature of his purchases: clothes, restaurants, bars, and travel. He didn't purchase a home he couldn't afford, or an exotic pet; his everyday purchases eventually became a landslide, and then an avalanche, of debt. His debt, and his understanding of what it meant to buy something on credit, didn't catch up with him until the last few years.

"How could that happen?" you might think. Well, we cover this more in-depth in Chapter 4, but money—and the debts we owe when we spend money we don't have—is easy to hide from ourselves. We push it into the furthest recesses of our minds; unlike other problems, like alcoholism or drug addiction, credit-card debt is invisible. Other people can't see it, and it's generally considered impolite and embarrassing to talk about. The only person who can really wake you up to your debt is you—and a collection agency.

Clay is a soft-spoken person who speaks generously of his family, and takes absolute and total responsibility for his debt. His willingness to talk to us, and to open up his heart to us and to you, the reader, demonstrates his deep understanding of the situation he's found himself in—but it may be too little, too late.

Parents, be aware: Stories like Clay's are not created in a vacuum. Often, credit habits are modeled after our parents' spending patterns. He says of his upbringing:

> *When I was that young, I was way too strong-willed. The world was my oyster, and I just wanted to go explore, and I wasn't smart at all. I wasn't taught [about finances]. When you're getting $2,000 worth of presents at Christmas parties every year, and then next year, your parents say something like "It's kind of been a rough year—so here's only $1,500 worth of stuff." It's kind of like, "What the [heck]? Now you're going to send me off into the world, and I need to figure out [money] for myself?" It doesn't work. I would never blame my mom, but there's no reason I should be in this situation. I never had my mom sit down and do a basic budget with me—as far as how much are you making, what's your intake, what's your outtake. Nobody ever did that with me. I had to do it on my own. And I'm still learning.*

UNDERSTANDING BORROWING CAPACITY

Believe it or not, someday you'll want to borrow even more money. We have many friends who went to graduate school, including Ruth herself, and Carol's husband. Graduate school is wonderful; we've heard it described as being "back in an intellectual comfort zone rivaled only by the womb." You can hone your professional skills or spend a decade immersed in research on a specific thing; it's how you become a doctor, a lawyer, or a scientific expert. There are very few experiences that can rival the feeling of being in a room full of brilliant people, whose minds merge as they explore new boundaries of thought and interpretation. It's infectious; it's exhilarating. Unlike college or high school, you're not still "learning" in the same arduous way; your mind moves into fifth gear, along with a group of your peers. Graduate school is not only a wonderful way to grow your mind and advance your career, but it's also a place where you can make lifelong friends.

Graduate school is often used to increase your standard of living—to get you that promotion you've been eyeing, to change careers, or otherwise push your life forward: become a doctor or a nurse, or a full professor instead of an adjunct instructor. That's all well and good. We clearly like and value education, but the price of many graduate programs is significantly higher than undergraduate, with places like Harvard Business School (HBS) estimating a whopping $79,600 in cost of attendance for the 2010–11 year. If you're married and have two children, HBS estimates you'll need over $111,000 dollars each year just to make it through school. Although that may be the highest graduate cost of attendance we've ever come across, graduate school is still generally more expensive than undergraduate—about $10,000 or more, per year. On average, the annual net price of tuition for a four-year public undergraduate education is $15,500; for a master's degree at a public, it's $25,700. At private colleges, where an undergraduate education has an average annual net price of $26,300, a master's degree will cost, on average, $37,800 for tuition each year.[5]

Why so high? Well, employers often subsidize, or help pay for, graduate degrees for their employees, which drives up the price for people who are looking to change careers. In the case of professional degrees such as medicine or law, the de facto assumption that graduates will make enough money to repay their degrees (and indeed, often view either profession as a guaranteed gravy train) means that the market value of the degree—in other words, what they can get away with charging—is very high.

Some graduate programs will fund you (give you tuition and living expenses) while you study. The rest will be primarily on your own dime. Let's look at the total costs of two popular, usually unfunded, pay-out-of-pocket graduate degrees.

MEDICINE

Ouch! Excuse the pun, but it's painfully *expensive* to become a doctor. The Association of American Medical Colleges says that in 2009, the average student loan debt of med school graduates was $156,456. Depending on the repayment method you choose (and assuming it's all in federal loans, you can take out larger loans when you're a grad student), that's a monthly loan payment from anywhere of $800 to $1,800 *per month*. An $1,800 monthly student loan bill will have an enormous influence over what kind of medicine you practice, where you live, and when you can buy a home of your own, and save for your children's college and even your own retirement. So if you're thinking about med school down the line, it might be a good idea to go right out of college. Though the possibility of burnout exists, at least you could be done with your student loan payments by the time you're ready to buy a house.

LAW

If you'd like to become a passionate defender of the underprivileged, make sure you choose a law school that discounts for public-interest law. Otherwise, your student loan debt from law school will average $71,436 if you go to a public, and $91,506 if you go to a private. So following the one-to-one ratio, our debt rule of thumb, you'll need to make at least $71,000 your first year out of law school. Luckily, the average salary for law graduates is $68,500—nine months after graduation. That's around $800 per month in student loans—a big chunk out of a monthly salary of $5,700.

If you're already carrying debt from undergrad, adding the cost of graduate school to your total debt will be onerous, to say the least. It might be worth it, but you should keep further borrowing (also known as your borrowing capacity) in mind when you're looking at colleges. The more you borrow now, the less you may be able to borrow later—and the higher your debt goes, the more significantly it affects your life.

You could even be denied the job you're educated to do. On July 1, 2009, the *New York Times* reported the story of Robert Bowman, a remarkably persistent 47-year-old man who conquered numerous hurdles in order put himself through community college, graduate school, and law school. He passed the bar (the exam required to become an attorney) after three attempts. Unfortunately, he also took on so much debt that he was denied admission to the bar (the license to practice) by the State of New York. His debt had ballooned (thanks to 25 percent fees charged by Sallie Mae and a collection agency) from $270,000 to $400,000 in four years. Bowman's physical problems (a roadside accident nearly cost him a leg; a recent Jet Ski collision broke his leg in four places) and other troubles prevented him from making a single payment on his loans through the 26 years he was taking out student loans. Will he become an attorney? It's tough to say. He's asked the court to reverse its decision and at the time the article was written, he intended to sue Sallie Mae—certainly an expensive and multi-year lawsuit. Either way, he's gone through more pain, heartbreak, and disappointment than anyone would ever want—all because he took on too many student debts and didn't repay them.

THE FINAL WORD ON BORROWING

This is our rule: Don't take out a dime more than $32,000 total, or $8,000 per year. That's already a lot of money; we sincerely hope that you'll think twice about borrowing even *half* of that. So for the risk-averse among you, we'll be more strict: Don't take out a dime more than $16,000 total, or $4,000 per year. Any more than that and you'll be worried about it until you're 30.

Student loans are not free and not something to discard. They are a real and serious obligation that, if unmet, could ruin a decade of your life or more. Don't be disabled by the cost of your education; borrowing is supposed to help you, not hurt you.

A life indentured to enormous student loan payments means that at *best*, you'll spend your 20s bored out of your mind at a bill-paying snooze-fest. At worst, you'll be living under an assumed name, working cash-only jobs, and running from bill collectors. Become instead the educated person who seizes *all* the joy, adventure, and success—however you might define it—he or she can out of life. Don't borrow a dime more than $32,000 to go to college.

4

You, Your Parents, and Their Money

Welcome to the most uncomfortable part of the book! It's super serious, too. So put on your serious face. We're about to get real. Well, as real as we can through the pages of a book.

As far as conversational topics go, money is *awful*.It's unpleasant and kind of distasteful, right up there with sex and politics. Chances are, you, or your parents, or both of you together, have been putting off this discussion. You probably don't know very much about your parents' financial situation, other than that you need financial aid to go to college. Most people don't share their finances with their children, so you're not alone.

The goal of this chapter is for you to have a productive and helpful conversation about your parents' finances, and figure out how your family is going to make your EFC, or expected family contribution. If you're not familiar with the EFC, please turn to Chapter 2. In order to do that, it's helpful to have an understanding of what "making money" might mean to your parents, why it's hard for them to talk about, and why they might not have enough to give you.

Talking about money is weird and awkward for literally everyone, even for us—and we write about and think about money all the time. It's a strange thing. You'd think that because we live in a capitalist economy—one that is so nakedly obsessed with dollars, greenbacks, dough, bucks, and bread—we would have a better relational vocabulary for talking about cash. But we don't. Money is a heavily loaded topic. Conversations about money, particularly with your children, skirt the edges of ego, of fear, of satisfaction, of success, of identity.

With a little bit of empathy and understanding, you can navigate this conversation with ease. It's best to start off with FAFSA4caster and estimate your EFC, before you talk about whether or not your parents can meet it. You can do this your freshman, sophomore, or junior year of high school. You can even do it in middle school! It's *never* too early to start talking about money (but it will always be a little awkward).

Before you have "the money talk" with your parents, please ask them to read Chapter 2 as well as Chapter 5, which is written specifically for parents. It won't take them more than an hour, and it'll give everyone a good understanding of all the terms and phrases you'll need in the coming months and years. It's an easy thing to ask; just put a sticky note on top of the book with the words "Please Read Chapters 2 and 5."

STEP 1: PREDICT YOUR EFC WITH FAFSA4CASTER

Ask your parents to sit down and talk with you about paying for college—the first of what will probably be several conversations. You'll need a computer with a working Internet connection to use FAFSA4caster, and a blank sheet of paper with a pen.

When is a good time to get your parents' attention? Certainly not over the breakfast table, or at the end of a long workday. We suggest asking your parents two to three days in advance if they can set aside some time to talk to you about paying for college; you'll need an hour or so. Literally say the following words:

"Mom and Dad (or "Mom and Mom" or "Dad and Dad" or "Betty and Dad" or "Mom and Charlie" or just "Mom" or "Dad"), would it be possible for you to set aside some time to talk to me on (insert day here) about how we're going to pay college? I've been reading about financial aid, and I think we should talk about it. I need your help. What's a good time for you?"

The most important thing is to *be polite*. As German philosopher Arthur Schopenhauer so famously expressed, "Politeness is to human nature what warmth is to wax." (Schopenhauer's misogyny aside, we think it's always good advice to be polite.) Speak evenly and reasonably; if your parents won't respond favorably, just repeat, over and over, that you *need their help*. Keep asking until they relent! Persistence is one of the great traits of successful people. You don't get what you want unless you *ask for it*. And sometimes, with people, you have to ask several times. That's just the way it goes. Don't get mad. Just get what you want. You'll wear them down eventually.

It might sound smarmy, but if you did have to ask your parents several times to have this conversation with you, start by saying *thank you*. Be genuine! Thank them for their willingness to talk with you about college, for the things and opportunities they've provided for you, and for their willingness to help you invest in your future. Although it's always a choice to have children, parents sincerely appreciate being thanked for all that they've done. Expressing your gratitude (as soon as you start saying thank you, you'll find that you really do mean it) is a wonderful way to warm up the conversation and get everyone on the same page. If you need to, make a list of all the things you're thankful for.

If your parents are married to each other, talk to them together; if they're divorced, talk to them separately unless they have they have the kind of relationship that allows you to sit down together. If they are divorced, it's a good idea to speak with the parent who claims you as a dependent first; that's the parent whose financial information will be on the FAFSA. *Helpful hint*: If your parents are divorced, always file with the parent that has a smaller annual household income—household, not individual. This is assuming they live in the same city and state, and that you could reside with either parent. For some students, that's not the case; one of your parents has moved out of state, gone to Bali to eat/pray/love, or doesn't have a stable environment for you. In that case, don't worry about it. But if you can file as a dependent of a parent that makes less money, do so. That will give you a lower EFC than if you file with the wealthier parent, and you can use the FAFSA4caster to figure out what the difference would be.

Anyway, you'll ask your parents a few days in advance for their time, and then hopefully you'll sit down together at the kitchen table with a computer, a blank sheet of paper, and a pen or pencil. Turn off your cell phone (and theirs!). Your parents might ask you what kind of college you plan on going to, and how much you think it's going to cost. Frankly, it doesn't matter. Wherever you go to college, your EFC will be the same, so you should find out what it is as soon as you can. Whether you go to a public or a private, you're planning on making up the remainder of the costs through loans and aid. Show your parents the following formula:

direct costs (tuition, room and board, and fees) – EFC (what you'll figure out today) = the amount you need in aid, including scholarships and loans

Your parents *don't* have to be responsible for this amount. If they can contribute to it, great; if not, you're going to try and get enough in financial aid to make it work. *If you're in the top 25 percent of applicants at most colleges, you've got a very good chance of getting the best need- and merit-based aid award available.*

That means, if your parents ask you what kind of college you plan on going to, the answer is: "A college where I'm in the top 25 percent of applicants, and I can get funded."

Say it with pride! This is *your* education. You're taking charge. But what does that mean for your parents? It simply means they have to figure out how to meet your EFC; you'll take care of the rest. *Your EFC will be the same, no matter where you go to school.*

And although FAFSA isn't perfect, your expected family contribution is generally a pretty good indication of how much money your family *could* spend on college, and colleges take it into account when they award your aid. The federal government absolutely assumes that the first responsibility for paying for your college education rests with your parents. There's no two ways around that, and please see page 99 if your parents refuse to pay at all. And if your parents are willing to commit more than their calculated EFC, fantastic; if not, you're willing to do enough research to find a college that will fund you.

Filling out the FAFSA4caster takes about 30 minutes. You'll go online to *fafsa4caster.ed.gov*, and your parents will input their financial information. The FAFSA4caster doesn't save your information, or share it with anyone. Your parents may tell you exactly what their financial situation is; they may not. The beauty of FAFSA4caster is that they can fill it out with you, and you don't have to look at their income and assets if they don't want you to. But you *will* learn what your family's expected family contribution, or EFC, is. It's important for you to understand how much your family is expected to be able to pay for college, because you may have to make some changes as a family in order to afford it.

At the end of FAFSA4caster, you can choose to compare the average cost of a private education to the average cost of a public education, in or out of state. When you submit the FAFSA4caster it will give you a summary page; your EFC will be at the top of the page. It'll be anywhere from 0 to 99999; this is the whole dollar amount that your family should be able to pay out of pocket. Ask your parents to write it down on a separate sheet of paper. This is the most useful part of the FAFSA, and the one most germane to this chapter.

Below the EFC is a chart that estimates the amount you could theoretically get in federal aid. It includes loans, and Pell if you're eligible. We're not thrilled with this part of the FAFSA4caster; it tends to allow families to make an assumption, based on the FAFSA4caster estimate, of what the aid and loans will be—and it never looks like enough. Remember: The FAFSA4caster aid estimate is *only federal*. It does not estimate what you might get in need or merit-based aid from a specific college or university, or grants from your home state.

As you can see from your summary, FAFSA will subtract the grants and loans that you're likely eligible for from the average cost of tuition, and show you an estimated gap at the bottom of the page. Please bear in mind that the cost of tuition used by FAFSA is an average sticker price; it doesn't use data based on what families actually pay—just what colleges and universities report that they *charge*. For more information about sticker price and net price, please see Chapter 7.

The FAFSA4caster may have awarded you up to $9,000 or more in loans (two Direct Staffords and a Perkins, if you're eligible). You do *not* have to take out these loans, and *you should not use them to meet your EFC*. The EFC is a family responsibility; student loans will be yours, and you'll use them to meet your need (direct costs – EFC = your need). We're not against loans; a reasonable amount of student loans can help build credit and responsible financial behaviors, and ultimately, you, the person who is receiving the education, should be responsible for paying for as much of it as you can. But as we discussed in Chapter 3, student loans can easily become unreasonable—and unmanageable. Take out your sheet of paper, where you've already written down your EFC. Next to that, write down the amount in loans that FAFSA4caster predicts you'll be eligible for.

STEP 2: UNDERSTANDING LOAN REPAYMENT WITH FINAID. ORG

Before you start talking with your parents about how your family can meet your EFC, it's important to cover the loan question that your FAFSA summary raised. *Remember: You won't be using your loans to meet the EFC. Meeting the EFC is your parents' responsibility.* FAFSA4caster gave you an estimate of how much you'll be eligible for in loans; your parents may assume that you will take out the maximum. So while you're sitting together in front of a computer, log on to *finaid.org/calculators/loanpayments.phtml*. Multiply the loan amount you wrote down on your sheet of paper by four (for four years of college), and then enter it into the loan calculator. The calculator will give you the standard federal interest rate of 6.8 percent. Leave it there. Select a 10-year term with a minimum payment of $50. Hit enter.

On the next page, you'll see a summary of what your monthly student loan payment could be. Ask your parents if they think it's manageable. We don't think that anything beyond $32K total in loans, or roughly $368 per month in repayment, is manageable for most college graduates; your parents may think differently. So it's time to ask a few questions. Do your parents want you to take on loans to meet your remaining need? If you take on loans and can't repay them, would your parents be willing to help you? Would they give you half, or make your monthly payments until you find a job? Do they think you should take out less money in loans? What's a reasonable amount? Discuss, and try to come to a conclusion about a reasonable total loan burden for your college education. You haven't taken out the loans yet; this is just a discussion about budgeting and student loans that every family should have. Often, parents are more willing to assist their children with additional college costs (if they have the funds available) once they realize what kind of debt their child could eventually be assuming.

Remember that taking out loans doesn't change your EFC. You can apply a portion of them to your EFC, if you absolutely need to, but they'll likely be part of your aid package.

STEP 3: MEETING YOUR EFC

The FAFSA is great at divining two things: families that absolutely cannot pay, and families that have boatloads of money. But the middle class often falls into a grey area, where the EFC can look like an astronomical amount of money.

It's not as bad as you think, and you don't have to pay it all in one lump sum. Your family probably has the money somewhere—but you're going to have to change your spending habits. Most colleges allow parents to pay their EFC with a 10-payment plan that extends from June to April, or July to May. Divide the EFC by 10. Your parents will need to meet that amount each month for 10 months of the school year, each year that you are in college.

If the EFC doesn't shock your parent(s), and they think it's reasonable, ask them to multiply the EFC by 1.5. This means that an EFC of $15,000 would become $22,500; an EFC of $20,000 would become $30,000; an EFC of $35,000 would become $52,500, and so on. That extra $7,000, $10,000, or even $17,000 dollars could mean the difference between attending a school that will fund you, and a school that won't. If you've got your heart set on some highly competitive places (where you may not be in the top 25 percent of the class), you might need the extra funds to make up for the lack of a scholarship. Remember: The bottom half of the class pays for the top half of the class. If you can't demonstrate serious financial need for an elite college, and you'd be in the bottom of their academic class, you won't get much of a discount.

However, your family is probably not looking at the EFC and thinking, "That's all?" So this is where you're going to get creative. In order to meet your EFC, you and your parents are going to need to discuss the following things (this conversation is the same for both intact families and the custodial and non-custodial parent):

√ *Have they put aside any funds, perhaps in a 529 savings plan, for your education? If so, these funds should be applied to your EFC. If not, better late than never! Ask your parents how much they can start putting aside—starting tomorrow. At the end of the year, $200 per week will be $10,400; even $100 per week will make a big difference.*

√ Do they have any large purchases planned for the next few years, like cars, vacations, home repair, or care for a relative? If so, ask your parents if you can help them in some way. Instead of replacing the entire roof, would it be possible for you to help one of your parents replace the leakiest section during the summer? Could you provide childcare for your siblings more often, or commit to ferrying an older relative to necessary appointments every Saturday for the next year? Ask your parents if they're willing to put some of their savings toward your education instead, and negotiate. Ask them about any large purchases they plan on making in the next few years, and run down the list, item by item, suggesting ways in which you could help or somehow allay the financial burden. If you have a car, volunteer to sell it or give it to another sibling, and take yourself off your parents' car insurance.

√ Do you have any grandparents or great-aunts and uncles? If so, you're in luck. There's only so many bridge tallies and Cadillacs that they can buy; older relatives often love to do something real for their grandchildren, other than send new socks and checks for $27, and sometimes they have the portfolio to do so. Do your parents think they would be willing to contribute to your college education? If so, how much? Let your parents know that you don't need birthday or holiday gifts from your older relatives, and ask them what they'd prefer. Should they broach the subject with Grandma? Should you?

√ If your grandparents are willing to help, the best way to go about it is for them to open a 529 savings plan on your behalf, or use a Coverdell account or savings bonds. For more information on the 529 plans available in your state, go to our website at thefinancialaidhandbook.com.

√ Another approach, if your grandparents went to college, is to look into legacy scholarships. Are you interested in going to the same school they did? If so, there may be a legacy scholarship available for you. To find out more, look on the college's website, or call the admission office directly (you can always find the phone number on the site, under "Contact Us") and ask if there are legacy scholarships available. If your grandparents (or parents) served in the military, you might also be eligible for veteran's scholarships. Go to the American Legion website at legion.org and look through the online "Need A Lift?" booklet, which lists scholarships, tuition costs, and federal and state grants that could benefit direct descendants of veterans.

√ Grandparents also often belong to some kind of fraternal organization, like the Elks, Moose, or an ethnic-based organization (for example, the Polish Ladies' Auxiliary), the AARP, or a union. Often, those organizations have college scholarships for relatives or descendents of members. Ask your grandparents what organizations they belong to, and then contact their local chapter (or look on the website, if they have one) for scholarship information. It's not the most reliable route, but it's always a possibility, and it's worth looking into.

Be prepared to list what you're able and willing to do, aside from taking out loans, to pay for your college education. Will you be working during the summer? If, so, how many summers? Would you be willing to put a portion of your income from an after-school job toward your college education? Are you willing to babysit younger siblings, or take over chores that might be hired out (like cleaning, raking, mowing the lawn, dog walking, car washing) from now until you start college? Make a list of everything you could do, during your remaining years in high school and your summers home from college (discount the summer between your junior and senior year from college; you will likely need to take an unpaid internship during that summer) to help contribute to the EFC, if your parents need you to. Remember: It's always cheaper to save than it is to borrow. In other words, it will ultimately cost you less to *earn* the money than it will to take it out in loans.

Remember that no matter where you go to college, your EFC will be the same. So before you even *visit* colleges, your family needs to make sure that you can find a way to meet your EFC.

DIVORCED AND/OR BLENDED FAMILIES

Divorce can shatter the best-laid schemes of mice, men, and college tuition. Unless parents have carefully spelled out who pays for what, college tuition can be the last thing on their minds. (Many custody agreements expire when the child turns 18.) If your parents *do* have a written agreement, you'll have to ask them what it is, and then stick to it. If your parents need to re-negotiate the terms of their agreement (due to job loss or any other change in their financial circumstances), ask them to do that as soon as possible. But for the rest of you—those whose parents *don't* have written agreements about college tuition—you will have to have the same conversation twice. As a student, this sucks for you. We're sorry, but that's just the way it is: It's twice the amount of work. Fortunately, divorce—and everything that goes with it—is common enough that even the craziest-sounding situation will be old hat to your college's financial aid office, so for now don't worry about explaining it down the line.

In terms of the EFC, you'll have to have the same conversation that you had with your custodial parent *again* with your non-custodial parent. Although the non-custodial parent's information may not be on the FAFSA, it takes two to tango. No one impregnates themselves: Both of your parents had a hand in creating you, and so they are equally responsible for your college education, to the degree they are able. It's that simple.

The rule of thumb we like to go by for divorced parents is called *half-sies*. That's right: No matter whose financial information results in the EFC, your divorced parents should split it right down the middle. *If your divorced parents still live in the same city or town, and if you are able to live with the parent that makes the least amount of money for more than half the year, then that's the best financial decision you can make in terms of lowering your EFC.* In that best-case scenario, regardless of whose income is responsible for determining your EFC, your parents should split the cost of the EFC in half. In terms of the FAFSA, the parent who is your legal custodian may not be your "custodial" parent; for the FAFSA, your custodial parent is simply the person you lived with the most (that is, more than half the year) during the last 12 months. How do you choose whose EFC to use? It's simple. The smartest thing to do would be to calculate the EFC *of each parent* separately, then bring both numbers to both sets of parents and ask them which EFC they would rather split: the higher EFC, or the lower EFC? If they're thinking straight, they'll want to split the lower EFC. Again, whichever parent has the lower EFC is the parent who you should consider your custodial parent, and the one you should live with for more than half of your senior year of high school (if you are able to). Splitting the lower EFC makes it reasonable for both parties.

Now, there might be some griping about who makes more money, or how they spend it, or whose new wife or husband does what, or whatever ridiculous thing they can think of. But the EFC is the responsibility of both parents; if they were still married, they would share it. Just because they got divorced and decided to stop taking care of each other, that does not absolve them from taking care of *you*. We've had countless phone calls from whiny, embittered divorced parents, claiming that the other parent is responsible for more. Look: Two people make a baby. Not one person. Maybe if your parents were young enough to be born into the age of financially accessible reproductive technology, three people (your dad's sperm, your mom's egg, and a scientist), even four people (sperm donor, egg donor, surrogate, and scientist), or an entire laboratory made their baby. There are always two names on a birth certificate: the names of your legal parents. They are equally responsible for the cost of your college education; they should split the EFC right down the middle. If a wealthier parent is willing and able to contribute additional funds, great—but the other parent is not obligated to match that additional amount, if he or she is not able to.

Now, we know that halfsies might not always be possible. Sometimes parents make wildly different incomes from one another. Sometimes, you simply cannot live with one of your parents, due to location, financial circumstance, illness, or even prison. If one of your parents is insanely wealthy, he or she should probably be the one to pay for your college education. What's insanely wealthy? Let's call it more than $250,000 per year. That's a high enough income to put your EFC through the roof, and possibly make it difficult for the other parent to split the EFC down the middle. That's also an income bracket where you'll get very little need-based financial aid, and you probably don't need to be reading this book. Those parents know who they are. And if one of your parents is making so little money that he or she cannot afford to house you for more than half the year, and really cannot afford in any way to help you with college, then the burden will likely be on the shoulders of the parent who makes the most. It's an unfortunate reality, and you'll need to discuss all of this with the financially responsible parent.

WHAT ABOUT MY STEP-PARENT(S)?

If one or both of your parents have remarried, the income of their spouse(s)—your step-parent(s)—will be considered in the FAFSA (the custodial parent's spouse) and/or the PROFILE (both households, custodial and non-custodial). Step-parents, however, often have their own financial responsibilities, like their own children (your step-siblings) or their own elderly relatives (step-grandparents and step-great-grandparents). If, when one or both of your parents remarried, they signed a pre-nuptial agreement that precludes the step-parent from paying for any of your college education, that agreement is void; the reason is that two parties cannot make an agreement that binds a third party. (In this case, the third party is the federal government.) Your custodial parent's spouse is required by law to include his or her assets in the FAFSA. If, however, the financial obligations of that step-parent includes other college tuitions, that obligation will be included in the FAFSA the same way that any legal siblings (blood relatives or adopted siblings) would be. If those step-siblings consider your custodial step-parent to be *their* non-custodial parent, their information won't be included (but all alimony and paid child support will be).

Step-parents, both custodial and non-custodial, are tricky. They're not your actual parent, but they did marry into your family and, by law, took on all of your parents' family and financial obligations. They may not feel as though they should be responsible for your college tuition, but by law their information is included in the FAFSA. We recommend that you include the custodial step-parent in all conversations about college tuition; the non-custodial step-parent *does not* have to be included other than for good will among family members.

You should also know that different schools have different expectations. If you've already got a list of your top schools, go online, and look up the phone number for the school's financial aid or admission office (either under "Prospective Students," "Admissions," or "Contact Us"). We recommend that you call them, identify yourself as a prospective student, ask politely if the person on the end of the line has a moment to answer your questions, and then explain your situation as quickly and as thoroughly as you can. We do recommend that you call, because this kind of information is not usually communicated in financial aid brochures or on the colleges' website. So if you've got a list of schools going already, and you have a tricky divorce or blended family situation, we encourage you to contact your top choice schools early and learn their expectations.

If one or both of your parents are engaged, we recommend that they understand and discuss the financial ramifications of getting married while you're in college. For the soon-to-be step-parent, there are very few benefits to absorbing your family's financial responsibilities—but quite a few negatives, the largest being a legal responsibility for meeting your EFC each year until you graduate college. It's fairly simple to broach this topic with them: Just ask your soon-to-be step-parent how he or she feels about paying for your college education. If the answer is "That's not my responsibility," let him or her know that FAFSA disagrees, and that his or her additional income will change your financial aid award for the worse. Then let them know that you love having them around—but that living together until you graduate might be the best possible financial decision for everyone.

WHAT IF MY DIVORCED PARENTS DON'T SPEAK TO EACH OTHER?

If your parents don't speak to each other, then you will need to assume a role that you're probably already quite familiar with: the role of the adult. Sometimes divorced people can be so childish that we cannot believe they manage to function in other areas of life. You're going to need to ask your parents a simple question: Which EFC would they rather pay half of: the higher EFC, or the lower EFC? Calculate the EFC *of each parent* with the FAFSA4caster, and then bring both numbers to your parents. They're going to have to split one; make them choose. If they have an ounce of sense, they'll choose the lower EFC. The parent with the lower EFC is the parent that should claim you as dependent, and the one you should consider the custodial parent.

WHAT IF MY DIVORCED PARENTS ARE BEST FRIENDS?

Oh, you lucky duck. If your divorced parents are the best of pals, they can work this out between themselves. Have them each read the second half of this chapter, and ask them to make a plan! Have the three-step conversation we outlined earlier in this chapter with both of them at the same time.

DEADBEAT DAD AND MOMS

Some students, and it might be you, have one parent that is a *total jerk*. These are known as Deadbeat Dads and Moms (aka DBDs and DBMs). DBDs or DBMs mostly come into the equation when you're applying to a college that requires the CSS PROFILE, which requests documentation from both the custodial and non-custodial parent. The CSS PROFILE is administered by the College Board, a nonprofit organization that also administers AP testing and coursework. (A list of schools that require the PROFILE can be found at *collegeboard*.org.) If you're applying early decision, most colleges will require the CSS PROFILE along with the FAFSA.

Deadbeat Dads and Moms like to punish their ex-spouses by denying *you*, their child, financial support. How this punishes the other parent, we're not quite sure. Mostly, it just punishes *you*, and often irreparably damages your relationship. Deadbeat Dads and Moms are people who operate with a limited set of logic and morals. They cannot see the forest for the trees; they cannot let their love of you, their child, dissolve their hatred for their former spouse. These parents know who they are. And we, as former admission and financial aid directors, know who they are, too. That's the good news.

Every college and university that you will apply to has a protocol for Deadbeat Dads and Moms (also known as a "non-custodial parent that refuses responsibility for payment"). In order for you to be able to work within this system, you've got to start documenting your DBD or DBM today. You will need to dry your tears, find your strength, and get a pen! Write down the time and date of each conversation you have with him or her about college payment, and write down what he or she says to the best of your recollection. You must document the refusal to support you or to fill out the PROFILE in order to get a waiver of non-custodial information. That will happen down the line, after you've already applied to colleges, but it helps to document his or her behavior as soon as you can. Just write it down in a notebook or in a Word document on your computer with times and dates; if you can get other documentation, such as unpaid child support, that's helpful, too. Photocopy all official documents and keep them in a folder marked DBD or DBM. Note: DBD/DBM is not an official financial aid term. But sometimes it helps to call a call a deadbeat a deadbeat. Hopefully, you've got at least one decent parent, aunt, uncle, grandparent, or foster parent to take care of you, and you don't need a crazy Deadbeat Dad or Mom interfering in your life. So let him or her be crazy; just *document* his or her crazy. It will help you in the long run, and you don't *really* need that person to move on with your life and go to college.

WHAT TO DO IF BOTH OF YOUR PARENTS ABSOLUTELY REFUSE TO PAY OR FILL OUT THE FAFSA

Your parents MUST fill out the FAFSA if you want to get any financial aid. They may be laboring under the assumption that if they *don't* pay or fill out the FAFSA, you'll get *more* aid. That is absolutely *not true.* The federal government, which gives billions of dollars to colleges not only in federal student aid but in actual dollars, assumes that the responsibility to pay for college lies first with the family of the student. Turning 18 and moving out of the house doesn't change that; until you are 24 years of age or older, you're considered a dependent by the FAFSA. If your parents are the kind that think "good children pay for their own education," they should be aware that they will raise your college costs significantly, likely to the sticker price, if they do not fill out the FAFSA. *You won't be able to take out federal loans or qualify for any federal grants unless your parents fill out the FAFSA.*

Chapter 5 is written specifically for your parents; we recommend that they take a look at it before you sit down to discuss your EFC. And after you've taken these three steps (predicted your EFC, calculated your possible loan burden, and discussed ways you can help your parents meet the EFC), it's a great time to start looking at colleges. Go on to Chapter 6, and use our MAP (Merit Aid Profile) to begin your strategic search for colleges where you'll be in the top 25 percent of applicants. You can also page through *The Financial Aid Handbook*'s Best Bets List, our non-hierarchical profiles of some of our favorite colleges (whose financial aid budgets and practices are strong, of course!), beginning on page 221.

5

FOR PARENTS: YOU, YOUR CHILDREN, AND YOUR MONEY

The goal of this chapter is to help you and your spouse (if you have one) figure out how to predict and meet your EFC, or expected family contribution. The expected family contribution is a number, in actual dollars, that is calculated by the FAFSA, or Free Application for Federal Student Aid. The FAFSA is used by all colleges and universities to determine your child's financial aid award. You and your child will need to fill out the FAFSA if you want to receive any need-based financial aid from your child's college of choice. The FAFSA can be submitted as early as January 1st of the enrollment year. For example, if your child is planning on attending college in the fall of 2014, you may submit the FAFSA on or after January 1, 2014. It's a good idea to file your taxes *before* you submit the FAFSA, so prepare and file them as soon as you can; don't wait until the April deadline.

Luckily, you can predict your EFC at any time by using the FAFSA4caster, an online calculator at *fafsa4caster.ed.gov*. It takes about 30 minutes to complete, and anything you input will not be forwarded to the federal government or individual colleges without your express permission. We love FAFSA4caster! It's a wonderful and extremely helpful tool, and it helps you determine what your EFC might be long before your child actually applies to and enrolls in college.

No matter where your child is planning on going to college—a community college, a large public, or a small private—your EFC will be the same. You will submit your basic financial information in the FAFSA, and the Department of Education will calculate, using a federal methodology, how much you could reasonably afford to spend on your child's college education. For more information about the FAFSA and how your EFC is calculated, please turn to Chapter 2. We do recommend that you read all of Chapter 2 before reading any further into this chapter; it will give you a good understanding of all the terms and definitions you'll need to know.

After your child actually *applies* to colleges, the information from your FAFSA will be forwarded to the college itself. You'll stipulate which colleges when you turn in your FAFSA, which you can do online. Each college will then calculate your child's remaining need (that is, scholarship dollars or tuition discounts they can receive) by using the following calculation:

direct costs (tuition, room and board, and fees) – EFC (expected family contribution, which you will figure out today) = amount your child is eligible for in need-based aid, from both the federal government and the college itself

If your child is in the top 25 percent of applicants (which you can determine by following our MAP process outlined in Chapter 6), he or she will have the best possible chance of getting the highest amount of need- and merit-based aid available. We recommend that students *only* apply to colleges where they are in the top 25 percent of applicants; there are currently more than 4,400 colleges and universities in the United States, with varying degrees of competitiveness.

If you want your child to receive any *need-based financial aid, you must fill out the FAFSA.* All colleges and universities that accept federal financial aid dollars agree to the basic assumption that the primary responsibility for paying for a student's education rests with the family—not with the federal government; not with the college; not with the state government, but with the student and their family. You can't get around this. Simply declaring that you won't pay, or refusing to fill out the FAFSA or PROFILE (another form that you may have to submit; for a list of colleges that require the PROFILE, go to *collegeboard.com*) will not change that obligation.

We understand that talking with your children about your finances is a thorny road. Most people don't do it; a pretty standard reason is that children cannot keep their mouths shut. If you tell them how much money you make, they'll tell the teller at the bank, the checkout girl at the grocery store, or their friends and teachers. Children, and especially teenagers, have absolutely no understanding of what it takes to make a living, and it's difficult to explain how much money you make. Children don't understand after-tax income, debt, assets, or financial obligations in the same way adults do. No matter what you say, your child may take one look at your new car or any new gadgets, and they may automatically assume that you have more discretionary or disposable income than you actually *do*. So we don't necessarily recommend telling your children exactly what your income is, and thankfully, with FAFSA and the FAFSA4caster, you don't have to; all you have to (and should) tell your child is what the FAFSA results in: your EFC.

In the previous chapter, we've done our best to explain to your child how he or she should approach this conversation with you, and why talking about money can be difficult for families. We've encouraged your child to initiate this conversation and to fully take responsibility for the pursuit of his or her college education. You might not be able to answer every question we've encouraged your child to ask you, but we think it's important that your child have a general (*not* explicit) understanding of your household finances and obligations, and recognize his or her responsibility for the changes in household spending that you may have to make to meet your EFC.

We'll talk about the multiple ways you can meet your full EFC (and why you should) later in the chapter. For now, the most important thing is to actually calculate it with FAFSA4caster, and get an idea of exactly how much money we're talking about.

STEP 1: PREDICTING YOUR EFC WITH FAFSA4CASTER

For intact families, this process is fairly simple: You and your spouse will sit down and calculate the EFC together. But for divorced or blended families, the EFC can be confusing. Whether you're the custodial or non-custodial parent, you should calculate an EFC. Regardless of who is the legal custodian in a divorce, FAFSA considers the custodial parent to be the parent that the child has lived with the most (that is, more than half the year) in the last 12 months. We recommend that both parties fill out the FAFSA4caster and calculate an EFC because divorced parents who share custody often have trouble, unless there is a written agreement, deciding who pays for what. We think that (if you share custody and it is possible to have your child live with either parent for more than half the year) calculating both of your EFCs, then splitting the cost of the lower EFC, is the fairest way to settle this issue. And if your child is going to a school that requires the PROFILE, you'll *both* have to go through the process of submitting your financial information anyway. The PROFILE may ask both parties to contribute *more* than the FAFSA, but the difference should not be significant. FAFSA4caster is the quickest and easiest way to get an approximation of what the financial burden will be, regardless of where your child goes to college.

Filling out the FAFSA4caster takes about 30 minutes. You'll go online to *fafsa4caster.ed.gov*, and you and your spouse, if you have one, will input your financial information. You'll also input your child's financial information, if he or she has any income or assets. The FAFSA4caster doesn't save your information, or share it with anyone; you may create a profile with your e-mail, but your actual names will not be on the form. As you fill it out, you may tell your child exactly what your financial situation is; you may not. The beauty of FAFSA4caster is that you can fill it out with your child, and you don't have to share your income and assets, if you don't want you to. But you *will* learn what your expected family contribution, or EFC, is. It's important for your child to understand how much your and your spouse are expected to be able to pay for college, because you may have to make some changes as a family in order to afford it.

At the end of FAFSA4caster, you can choose to compare the average cost of a private education to the average cost of a public education, in or out of state. When you submit the FAFSA4caster, it'll give you a summary page; your EFC will be at the top of the page. It'll be anywhere from 0 to 99999; this is the dollar amount that you and your spouse should be able to pay out of pocket (from savings, income from assets, or discretionary income). Write this number down on a separate sheet of paper. This is the most useful part of the FAFSA, and the one most germane to this chapter.

Below the EFC is a chart that estimates the amount your child could theoretically get in federal aid. It includes loans, and Pell if you're eligible.

We're not thrilled with this part of the FAFSA4caster; it tends to allow families to make an assumption, based on the FAFSA4caster estimate, of what the aid and loans will be—and it never looks like enough. Remember that the FAFSA4caster aid estimate is *only federal*. It does not estimate what your child might get in need or merit-based aid from a specific college or university or grants from your home state.

As you can see from your summary, FAFSA will subtract the grants and loans that your child is likely eligible for from the average cost of tuition, and show you an estimated gap at the bottom of the page. Please bear in mind that the cost of tuition used by FAFSA is an average *sticker* price. It doesn't use data based on what families actually pay—just what colleges and universities report that they *charge*. For more information about sticker price and net price, see Chapter 7.

The FAFSA4caster may have awarded your child up to $9,000 or more in loans (two Staffords and a Perkins, if you're eligible). Your child does not have to take out these loans, and *you should not use them to meet your EFC*. The EFC is a family responsibility; student loans will be your child's (for federal loans, you will not sign on as a cosigner; the responsibility will be entirely your child's), and your child will use them to meet his or her need (direct costs – EFC = your child's need). We're not against loans; a reasonable amount of student loans can help build credit and responsible financial behaviors, and ultimately, your child, the person who is receiving the education, should be responsible for paying for as much of it as they can. As we discussed in Chapter 3, though, student loans can easily become unreasonable—and unmanageable. Take out your sheet of paper, where you've already written down your EFC. Next to that, write down the amount in loans that FAFSA4caster predicts your child will be eligible for.

STEP 2: UNDERSTANDING STUDENT LOAN BURDENS

When we outlined this step for your child, we encouraged him or her to go online to *finaid.org*, and use the Finaid student loan calculator to calculate what the monthly payments might be, and then discuss those with you. Although it may seem premature, the one drawback of FAFSA4caster is that it automatically calculates an estimate of your federal loan eligibility, and in that sense, it's front-loading the conversation. So before you start making assumptions about how much is okay to take out in loans, you should have a basic conversation about them with your child and calculate the repayment. The college, and the federal government, will do this as well—*after* your child has applied and been accepted. At that point, it's too late to change your mind. What's your child going to do: withdraw his or her application 10 days before class starts and spend another year at home? Of course not. So it's good that have this conversation now, and it will allow you to understand the various aid awards you will receive from colleges much more efficiently. So ask yourself and your spouse the following question: "How much do we think our child should take out in loans?" Although tuition costs have risen enormously—faster than healthcare and any other section of the economy—that doesn't necessarily mean that the *value* of a degree has risen enormously. Before you commit to a final answer, if you're encouraging your child to take on more loans (we consider anything more than $32,000 in total debt for four years, or roughly $368 per month on a 10-year repayment plan, to be truly unreasonable for any college graduate) and perhaps to attend a college where they are *not* in the top 25 percent of applicants (i.e., a more competitive school, where he or she may receive significantly less aid), please think about the following.

An undergraduate degree is not the same as medical school or law school degree. What we mean by this is that there is no guarantee that upon graduation your child will have a high-paying job. To put it bluntly, undergraduate degrees are no longer a money-making enterprise; they have become as requisite as a high school diploma (and in some fields, about as valuable). And if your child is interested in a career in business, law, medicine, science, mathematics, or any other traditionally high-paying field, she will likely need to go to graduate school for an MBA, a JD, an MD, or a PhD. That means your child will need to have some borrowing capacity when she graduates from college; if she takes on too much in debt for undergrad, she won't be able to afford graduate school.

We've each been in the business of college admission and financial aid for more than 35 years. We've worked with literally dozens of colleges and universities, and personally hired at least a hundred employees between us. The statement we made about the value of a college degree is our opinion, and we've formed it from our experiences in both the industry of higher education *and* as employers. It's certainly possible to find statistics on the web that claim college graduates make more than a million dollars in extra income throughout the course of their lifetimes, or that graduates of Rice University, for example, see a lifetime ROI of 11.8 percent (according to payscale.com). Here's what we have to say about those statistics: They're generally true—*for engineers*. Engineers of any stripe skew compensation data greatly. So if your child is incredible at math or science—and plans to attend an engineering school such as MIT, RPI, Harvey Mudd, or Union—he or she can usually count on making lots of money. But if your child is at all interested in the humanities, the nonprofit sector, teaching, development, politics, or essentially any other career that does not involve being a wizard with numbers, the smartest financial decision he can make is to keep his college debt as low as possible, so that he can take any kind of job he'd like to, no matter how low-paying an entry-level position in his chosen field might be. If you're not thinking about the state of the economy, or if you assume it will rebound by the time your child graduates, we've got news for you: The current recession has pushed millions of recent graduates back into the entry-level job market. They might still be there, competing for the same jobs, when your child graduates from college.

There's also the issue of where, and how, your child will live after college. We discuss this extensively in Chapter 3; if you haven't read it, we can sum it up quickly. From your perspective, it's fairly simple: Your child is about to move out of the house. You do not want her to move back home after she graduates. She will leave her stuff everywhere, drink all your wine, drive your cars, drain your wallets, and most importantly, not be leading her own life. We've both become empty-nesters (Carol for nearly a decade; Ruth for just a year) and it is *wonderful*. Don't get us wrong; we love our children, and we love having them around. We really love it when they visit. But as empty-nesters, we run around naked, we eat whatever we want, we don't watch our language, and we spend our money on ourselves. If we want to spend three days doing nothing but going to the gym, doing work, hanging out with each other, and eating takeout, we can. It's a return to the life we had before we had children, when we had zero responsibilities. Remember that time? Wasn't it amazing? You can be back there! Just don't let your children take on so much student loan debt that they have to move back home with you. As an added benefit, watching our children become smart, successful adults who we consider our friends and peers has been exceptional.

STEP 3: MEETING THE EFC

It's entirely possible that you looked at your EFC, as calculated by FAFSA4caster, and thought, "That's all?" If that happened to you, then multiply your EFC by 1.5; having that extra money budgeted may mean the difference between your child attending a school where he or she is funded (and is in the top 25 percent of the academic class), and one that's more competitive, where he or she is *not* in the top 25 percent of the class. If your child is not in the top quartile, you'll likely have to shell out more money in order to make up the difference. If your child is in the middle 50 percent of applicants at a more competitive college, he or she will probably get *some* aid, but not a lot. Having that extra .5 of your EFC may be the key to sending him or her to that kind of school.

We're going to guess, however, that you did not look at the EFC and think "No big deal!" It's much more likely that you looked at it and thought, "What on earth? Where am I supposed to find that kind of money?" As we said in Chapter 2, the EFC can appear to be an astronomical amount of money. There's one easy way to break it down, however; most colleges will allow you to pay your EFC in a 10-month payment plan. So start off by dividing the EFC by 10. You'll need to meet that monthly payment for 10 months out of the year, each year your child is in school.

If you've put aside any funds in a 529 savings plan, a Coverdell ESA (also known as an Educational IRA), mutual funds, or savings bonds, use those funds to meet your EFC. We recommend dividing the total by four, and using part of those savings each year, instead of spending it all on their first year or two.

If you've still got a few years before your child enrolls in college, and you haven't begun saving, you should *start saving tomorrow*. It's *always* cheaper to save than it is to borrow, and the sooner you become used to taking a cut from your paycheck before you calculate your discretionary income, the easier it will be to meet your EFC. Here's a quick breakdown on the most common types of college savings plans. (They should be available through your bank or any financial services you use, like Charles Schwab or Ameriprise.)

√ **529 Savings Plans:** *Also known as a qualified tuition plan, a 529 is a tax-advantaged plan designed expressly to save for college costs, and is authorized by Section 529* of the IRS tax code. If you know, without a doubt, where your child will be attending college, it's possible to use a 529 as a prepaid tuition plan; this will lock in tuition prices at eligible public and private universities. Credits purchased in a prepaid plan will always keep their value. For example, a half-year's tuition will always be a half-year's tuition, no matter how much the actual dollar cost increases. For public universities, every state, including Washington, DC, has one; private colleges use the Private College 529 program, which currently has more than 270 colleges (and you can use the credits at any of the 270 schools). For participating schools and more information, go to privatecollege529.com. Because it's often difficult to predict where your child would like to go to school, another option is to open a 529 as a college savings plan, instead of a prepaid tuition plan. You can use a 529 savings plan at any college, for any education-related expense (including books, room and board, fees, and computers). Earnings in 529 savings plans are tax-exempt; total contributions in many states cannot exceed $200,000. For more information about your home state's 529 plans, please see our website at thefinancialaidhandbook. com.

√ **Coverdell ESA:** *A Coverdell ESA, also known as an Educational IRA, is like a small IRA (independent retirement account), without some of the tax benefits. Annual contributions cannot exceed $2,000, and are not tax-deductible, but earnings and distributions are tax-free.*

√ **Roth IRA:** *A Roth IRA isn't the best way to save for college, but the laws allowing tax-free withdrawals of contributions can benefit you if an emergency arises, and you need to put some of the funds toward something else. A Roth is commonly invested in mutual funds.*

If you withdraw funds from a 529 or Coverdell account for any purpose other than education, you'll be subject to a 10 percent tax penalty.

The Final Word on Saving for College

We recommend investing in a 60/20/20 mix of 529 savings/Coverdell/ Roth IRA. This allows you to retain a small portion of penalty-free assets in a Roth should an emergency arise, and to create, if the funds go unused, a starter retirement account for your child. Because of the recent economic trend in transitions from employer-paid and vested traditional, benefit-defined retirement funds to 401(K)s and IRAs, and the emergence of a truly global free market that relies heavily on freelancers and independent contractors, a small starter Roth can make an enormous difference in the long-term economic well-being of your child and provide a small safety net of assets for you if your financial circumstances change.

If You Haven't Saved Enough or at All

If you haven't set aside savings for your child's education, the easiest way to begin meeting your EFC is to adjust your spending. That may mean some serious shifts in the way you live, and we understand exactly how difficult that is. We recommend, however, that you adjust your spending first, and think about borrowing as a last resort.

Why You Need to Meet Your EFC Using Your Current Income

For all that's been written about the adjustments that baby boomers like us will have to make in our retirement plans, the implications of the current U.S. economy are just as severe, if not more so, for those of you who are still raising and educating your families. Adjusting your mindset from the economy you grew up in, and the one you find yourself in now, is difficult, but it's incredibly important to do. We need you to re-shape the way you think about money. Why?

1. Because Your Assets May Not Have Any Value

Let's start with home equity. It's likely that your adulthood has been a time of easy credit, during which you saw your investment in your home move from something you considered *a place to live* into an erstwhile ATM, whose equity loans allowed you to pull the credit lever at will. You may have used home equity to upgrade your home, for travel, for the purchase of a second home, or for a boat, new cars, or consumer goods. It's also likely that you can't do that anymore; home equity is dead in the water. The market won't bear it and, indeed, it's an economic oddity as to *why* the market became that way. If you're assuming that the value of your home will return to pre-crash levels, think again. As economist Edward Glaser remarked in the *New York Times*'s Ecomonix blog on April 6, 2010, there are only two hard-and-fast rules that create booming prices for real estate: restricted supply (in places like Manhattan, where there is an actual limit to land), and a durable anchor for robust demand. The housing market in the early 2000s mimicked the patterns of cities with *both* of these preconditions in places that *lacked* one or both, and it's unlikely that your home (unless you live in a truly stable real estate environment, such as Manhattan or San Francisco) will ever return to it's inflatcd pre-crash value.

2. IF YOUR ASSETS DO HAVE VALUE, IT HAS DECLINED

Even outside the housing market, the pre-crash market contained other economic oddities that have probably influenced your long-term spending habits. As we said earlier, retirement funds, which morphed from employer-paid and vested traditional, benefit-defined pension funds, became 401(K)s and IRAs, which all boomed in value during the past 20 years—until, of course, they nose-dived. Too many of us (and yes, that includes us, although we may be 20 or 30 years your senior) became accustomed to looking at our quarterly 401(K) statements and assuming we *actually had that amount of money in hand*. Now, many of us don't have it and need to devote our resources to building our retirement funds back up.

3. YOU ALREADY MAKE ENOUGH MONEY— YOU'RE JUST SPENDING IT ON GARBAGE

We've come to the crux of most spending habits: the issue of *stuff*. Thanks to a globalized free market that brought both durable consumer goods and our endless appetite for acquisition to our doorsteps and laptop screens, we began purchasing things we didn't need by the bucket (or by the cardboard box from Amazon). Think about all the crap in your house. How many iPods do you have? Cell phones? Laptops? Clothing? Cable? Televisions? DVD and Blu-Ray players? It really is just *crap* that you don't need, but you're probably used to the drain on your bank account, and can't imagine living without at least a little bit of retail therapy. It used to be easy: Getting credit was a piece of cake, and your investments looked sound. That's probably not true for you anymore. So you know what? Get rid of all your crap! Sell it on eBay. Use that digital camera you bought and only take out once a year, put your stuff against a white background, and get rid of as much of it as you can handle. It might not bring you a huge windfall, but it *will* get it out of your house. Getting it out of the house is important; crap is kind of like animals. You have to keep feeding them. You need new DVDs for the DVD player. New songs on iTunes for the iPod. New expensive parts for the expensive car, new everything for the boat, new hair cream to offset the damage you did with a new hairdryer, and so on. Buying and maintaining your stuff is an enormous waste of time and money.

You, at this point, are either thinking "Yes! I am ready for a moratorium on stuff and spending! Let's clean house! I've been waiting for an excuse to free myself of my earthly possessions!" or "Why should I get rid of the things I work so hard for so that my entitled teenager can go learn about Marx, bongs, hookup culture, oversized glasses, stupid haircuts, Benjamin, patchouli, and tight pants for four years? If she wants to do that, she can pay for it herself."

We're guessing that it's the latter. We have one answer for you: *It's the economy*.

The difference in the economy from the time that you entered the workforce and when your child will be graduating from college could be measured in light years. This is not just about the recession: *The last 10 to 20 years have altered the way we do business, in America, and in the world. Forever.* Advances in technology meant the development of a truly global business environment. In simple English, that means the Internet. The Internet is not just a revolution for consumers and communicators; it has absolutely revolutionized *business*. Every single kind of business. The dot-com bubble in the early 2000s was almost a joke compared to the amount of money that the Internet has enabled the *entire* economy to make. Since the commercialization of the Internet in the mid-1990s, our GDP (gross domestic product) has increased by nearly 8 trillion dollars—more than *doubling* in size. That means that in the last 15 years, we've doubled the wealth in the United States—and it could not, would not, have happened without the Internet. When it comes to understanding the importance of the Internet's impact on every part of the workforce, we're not talking about Twitter or Facebook. We're talking about real tools, everything from Skype to GoogleDocs, which allow people to do business efficiently and meaningfully, from anywhere. Those tools simply did not exist when you graduated from high school; today's economy is completely different. It's one where the best, the brightest, and—most importantly—the *most agile* will be the ones to succeed.

The hemorrhage of jobs we experienced in the last few years also pushed millions of people into an economy where they would take whatever work they could get, further cementing a pattern of globalized freelancers. Business that survived the last few years have come to rely on, and profit from, a contractor-based business model that simply would not have been possible 15 or even 10 years ago. What does that mean? It means, quite simply, that job security as we knew it is no longer a safe bet. The new economy that we're facing means that many of the assumptions we've had as adults about the workplace will have to go right out the window. High-paying jobs with benefits, pensions, and job security for decades are becoming extinct.

Your children will be graduating from college into a world without defined benefit pension funds or high-paying starting salaries. The sheer size of their generation means that the competition, too, will be enormous; there are roughly 20 percent more graduates of the high school class of 2010 than there were in 1994. They will likely have to take unpaid internships and low-paying jobs to get their feet in the door, and later, possibly get an advanced degree. This means that asking your child to take on an unreasonable amount of debt will only handicap him or her. Taking on debt for an education he or she cannot afford, in an economy that requires so many new graduates to work for pennies (or even for free), could make your child's education a moot point—or even a negative-sum game.

Whether your own experiences have you nodding your head in agreement or shaking it in disbelief, we want you to take away one thing that we think everyone can agree on: *It's always important to be conservative about borrowing.* Asking your child to take on too much student debt, either because you don't want to pay your EFC, or because you think he should go to a "better" school, where he receives no funding, is a bad idea. The most important skills your child can have in this economy—one where big companies and big names are often the *least* effective—are not about the brand name of his or her college or university. Brand is not a skill; it might be an asset, but it won't outweigh the burden of too many student loans. What your child will need is the ability to learn quickly, communicate beautifully, collaborate with ease, and understand and master changes in technology, no matter what his field. It's that simple. Although we've said it before, we'll say it again. *No one really cares about undergraduate*; it is not law school or med school. It does not necessarily "pay you back," but it *is* something that your child absolutely has to do, just like high school was for you.

In 2018, when your child will enter the workforce, there will be more jobs for college-educated workers than for those without a college degree—even with, or perhaps especially because of, the 2007 crash. According to a 2010 study from the Georgetown University Center on Education and the Workforce, 63 percent of the 30 million new and replacement jobs in 2018 will require some college or better; of that subset, 72 percent will require a bachelor's degree or higher.

Your child *must* go to college. He should go to a school that's a great fit for him—one that challenges him intellectually, and offers him a scholarship. It's that simple. But even if your child gets the best scholarship his dream school has to offer, the college may still expect you to meet your EFC. If you pass the burden of the EFC down to your child, you will absolutely be disadvantaging him in the job market after he graduates. You will be *paralyzing* your child. Don't do it. Find a way to meet the EFC.

We genuinely believe that investing in your child's education is a worthy endeavor; it's far more valuable to you, as a parent, than dinners out, club memberships, or the latest model automobile. And we personally believe that there is, other than our own retirement funds, no better place we can spend our money than on our children's education. This doesn't mean that you should mortgage your house and your future to send Susie to her dream school, nor does it mean that you should borrow or sacrifice in order to maintain a certain lifestyle for your child. Susie doesn't need a daily on-campus latte, a shopping trip, or spring break in Cancun, no matter how much she might want those things, and if she can't get a scholarship, she doesn't need a big-brand school. But she will need you to meet your EFC.

WHERE DO I START?

You and your spouse should go through the following itemizations of how you spend your combined after-tax income:

√ *Monthly mortgage payments or rent.*

√ *Utilities.*

√ *Food.*

√ *Household insurance.*

√ *Property or school tax.*

√ *Health insurance.*

√ *Retirement contributions and savings.*

√ *Consumer debt.*

√ *Transportation (including car payments, insurance, and gas).*

√ *Care for your other children, if you have them.*

√ *Any other necessary costs, such as caring for an aging parent or disabled child.*

Those are your financial priorities; anything else, including vacations or large consumer purchases, is unnecessary. Although you've probably talked about it in the past, you and your spouse will want to discuss any assumptions your might be making about your own jobs or incomes, and any concerns you might have about your individual situations. That means potential layoffs at your place of work, mandatory furloughs, financial support for either of your own parents, commitments either one of you may have made to members of your blended family (including alimony and child support), and how long you have until your next child, if you have one, enters college.

If you're planning for multiple college tuitions, don't forget to tell FAFSA4caster (and re-calculate your EFC, if needed). Your portion of the EFC will change when you have two kids in college simultaneously—it gets divided in half, then for three children in thirds, and so on. Your children's assets and income will count only toward their own EFC. To plan, try using a laddergram such as the one shown here:

EFC with one child in college: $10,000

EFC with two children in college: $5,000

EFC with three children in college: $3,333

	2012	2013	2014	2015	2016	2017	2018	2019
William	$10,000	$10,000	$5,000	$5,000				
Barbara			$5,000	$5,000	$3,333	$3,333		
Susie					$3,333	$3,333	$5,000	$5,000
Krista					$3,333	$3,333	$5,000	$5,000

After subtracting your financial priorities from your monthly take-home incomes, you might discover that you have a few hundred, or even thousand, extra dollars. Where does it all go? We're willing to bet it goes to small things, such as $5 lattes, $6 half-gallons of fresh-squeezed juice, new clothes, movie tickets, vacations, and so on. If your bank allows on-line banking—and most of us use it—log on *right now* and set up an automatic transfer for payday, and put at least half of the extra in a savings or money market account. If you can put aside $500 with each biweekly paycheck, that's $12,500 per year (or $13,500 per year if you work all 52 weeks), and $1,000 per biweekly paycheck is a cool $25,000.

Another way to calculate is to take your EFC and divide it by 25 (half the working weeks in the year, and the number of paychecks you'll receive). That will give you exactly the number you need to auto-save from each paycheck.

But it's more likely that you've subtracted your financial priorities from your take-home pay, and come up with bupkis—or worse, a negative number. If you've got assets or savings that you've earmarked for your retirement, don't even consider touching them. We do not recommend that you cash in on, or borrow against, your own future. If you can't support yourself in retirement, the burden will fall to your child. What you'll need to do now is look at your list of financial priorities, and see where you can make changes. Go down the list, item by item, and discuss ways to cut back. We've got two important bills that we'd like you to consider first.

THE #1 DRAIN ON FAMILY FINANCES: CARS!

How many cars do you have? How much do they cost you?

Oh, we could rail against cars all day. It has nothing to do with their environmental impact, either. It's simple: Cars only depreciate in value. From the perspective of any financial planner, cars are infuriating. They are worth significantly less from the moment you drive them off the lot.

Think about it this way: if you were dealing with the stock market, you would never, ever want to invest in something that only loses value. It's not like you think that someday, your brand-new Suburban is going to skyrocket in value. You *know* it will decline in value, and yet, people continue to buy new cars. Why? It's such a waste of money! When you buy a brand-new car, you're a sucker. You've been tricked. Your car is a living, breathing, four-wheeled money pit. Gas, insurance, and monthly car payments can run you several thousand dollars a month—or they can run you a couple of hundred dollars a month. It's up to you.

So what can you do? Honestly, sell your cars to pay off your auto loans, and buy a used car that has lots of airbags. Or get a bicycle and use public transit (we know this isn't an option for most people, but hey, think about it anyway). Don't spend more than $10,000 on your "new" used car, and try to get a certified one. (Most car manufacturers will inspect their used cars, so that you know they're not lemons.)

You might be reluctant to do this. Don't be! You car is an expensive ball and chain! Free yourself of it today!

If you're still unwilling to get rid of your car, try this: Take the amount of discretionary income you calculated earlier, and add the dollar cost of your car(s) to it. Look! You could have so much more money each month! It's possible that you wouldn't need to change a single thing about your finances, if you just could *keep* the money you normally spend on cars.

YOUR HOME EXPENSES

Other than your basic utilities—heating, cooling, gas, water, electric, and maintenance costs—how much do you spend on cable television and phone bills? Add up the total costs, then get ready to start subtracting. Begin by getting rid of your cable TV; you can watch everything you need to on hulu.com for free, or get Netflix for $10 per month. Does everyone need a cell phone with lots of minutes? Or even at all? Can you charge any of the bills to your employer? If you're willing to get rid of or greatly reduce these costs, you could have an extra $250 (or more) per month.

For more detailed and creative ways to reduce your spending, check out one or more of the following:

√ *Suze Orman's* Action Plan: New Rules for New Times, *or suzeorman.com.*

√ *Chris Farrell's* The New Frugality.

√ *Mary Hunt's* "The Everyday Cheapskate" *newsletter; sign up atdebtproofliving.com.*

BORROWING TO MEET YOUR EFC

Although we strongly recommend that you significantly reduce your spending in order to meet your EFC, sometimes it's not possible. You may also need some additional funds to help your child if he or she doesn't get the highest possible aid award. *You can take out a federally backed student loan for yourself.* Parent PLUS loans are like Direct Staffords for adults; they're federally guaranteed loans with a fixed interest rate of 7.9 percent. They can only be used for educational expenses, and interest is charged from the day you take out the loan. The actual dollars will be given directly to the college, which will then disburse the funds, typically twice a year. Colleges use the funds for tuition, room and board, and any other direct fees, then give the remainder to you in a check. You can authorize any part or all of the remainder into your child's account at the school, if you so desire and expressly authorize it. The amount you can take out is directly tied to your student's aid award and the college's cost of attendance:

college's cost of attendance – your child's financial aid award = the amount you're eligible to take out in PLUS Loans each year

If you're not eligible for PLUS Loans, your child may take out more than the standard limits for a Direct Stafford—up to $12,500 per year. We do not recommend exceeding the standard Direct Stafford loan limit of $7,500 per year under any circumstance.

How Much Should I Take out in PLUS Loans?

Log on to finaid.org and use the student loan calculator (enter the interest at 7.9 percent) to calculate what your payments will be. Do the math; how much can you afford? When can you start paying it down? Will it interfere with any other debt you currently have? Don't take on a PLUS Loan until you've done the math.

What if My Child Has His Heart Set on a Particular School?

We do understand the impulse to give your child anything that he or she wants. But in this economy, it's probably not possible for you to do it, no matter how much you might want to. The old adage that would have your child going to the best college he or she can get into doesn't apply anymore. Unless your child has a very, very good chance of getting accepted to an elite college that is need-blind, you're probably going to need a scholarship.

Several years ago, we heard a father in a focus group describe his willingness to do whatever he had to in order to pay for his daughter's "dream college." He said, "If she wants the moon, I'll find a way." That was before the economy changed—and we're not even sure it made sense then. As lovely as it was to hear someone who was so devoted to his child, we wanted to shake that father and scream, "Be sensible! Don't mortgage your own future!"

You'll have to talk to your child about the school in question and determine what his or her chances of getting aid are. If she is in the middle 50 percent of applicants, she will probably get *some* aid; we cover this more in-depth in Chapter 6. Would you be able to afford the gap without taking on unreasonable debt for yourself? If not, you'll need to tell your child not to apply. If she applies, she'll fall in love (and you might, too!). It's like taking your child to a dog breeder, letting her play with month-old puppies, and then leaving—*sans* puppy. It's a bad idea that will only end in heartbreak.

SHOULD I COSIGN FOR MY CHILD'S LOAN? DO I HAVE TO?

You do not need to cosign on a federal loan (Direct Stafford or Perkins). You can take out a private loan from a bank; there are a multitude of solutions from various lending companies. These loans can look fairly cheap, and they're easy enough to get if you've got a good credit rating. Go to *studentlendinganalytics.com* for completely independent and timely information about comparative rates. But beware of two things:

1. *The minute you put your signature down as a cosigner, you're agreeing to repay the loan in full. If your child can't make the payments at any point, it will be your responsibility.*

2. *Unlike mortgages or car payments, many private student loans can't even be discharged through illness or death. If you cosign and your child becomes disabled or dies, you'll still be fully responsible for the loan. Consider purchasing a form of credit insurance to protect you, should the worst happen.*

CAN ANYONE ELSE COSIGN MY CHILD'S LOAN?

Is there someone else in your family who would want to function as the cosigner? We advocate this only if cosigning, and perhaps having to repay the loan, wouldn't jeopardize that person's financial security. If your parents are on a fixed income, for example, they're probably not the right people to ask. But your millionaire playboy brother who doesn't have any children of his own? Ask him!

TALKING TO YOUR CHILD ABOUT YOUR ACTUAL EFC

After you've gone through your finances, it's possible that you won't be able to meet your full EFC, either each year, or for all four years. Throughout the rest of the book, we'll refer to the amount of the EFC that you can actually afford to pay as your "Actual EFC." You'll need to take note of the difference between your EFC and your Actual EFC. Ultimately, it's your responsibility to make up the difference, but if you can't you'll need to take your child about what you can afford. We understand that it's difficult to say to your children that you can't afford something. It's impossible for all of us not to have some sense of self-worth tied into our annual earnings; whether we work in the profit or non-profit sector, income is seen as a proxy for personal value. So try to think of this conversation as a variation on the traditional college talk: instead of having a "reach" and a "safety" school, you're going to ask your child to apply only to school where he or she will be *funded*.

SCRIPTED CONVERSATION STARTERS

If you need some help getting started, we've got a few ideas:

√ *"Thanks for making the time to sit down and talk with us. We know this isn't on your top 10 list of things to do, but we want to let you know how proud we are of what you've accomplished in school. We want to support you in college, but there are some limits to that. We've done a thorough review of our finances, and we know that we can provide [your Actual EFC] for you each year, so you'll need to go to a college where you can get enough in aid to make up the difference."*

√ *"Here's how much we can spend: [your Actual EFC]. Here are our reasons: We have to pay for [these other things], and, while your education is important to us, those other expenditures are non-negotiable. We'd like you to keep that in mind as you look at colleges, and only apply to schools where you'll be in the top 25 percent of applicants. Although we can't give you more money, we'd love to give you our time, and help you look for schools and work on your applications."*

√ *"We don't want you to graduate from college with a crippling loan burden. Although we can give you [your Actual*

EFC, if it's larger than the EFC] per year, a portion of that will need to replace some of the loans you would be eligible for with a financial aid package. That means you'll need to get merit aid; it's important to us that you'll be able to afford to live on your own after you graduate."

√ *"We love you and we're so excited that you're ready for college, but your siblings also need to go through school. We've gone through our finances, and we can give you each [your Actual EFC]. We'll need you to give your car to your sister, and get a summer job to help cover costs. If you'd like to go anywhere besides [a local public or community college that you could pay for out of pocket], you will need a scholarship."*

FOR DIVORCED AND/OR BLENDED FAMILIES

If you're planning on getting remarried, we recommend that you have a discussion about the financial implications of remarriage and college cost with your fiancé(e). If you remarry, your new spouse's assets and income will also be considered in the FAFSA. That means he or she will be equally responsible for your child's college education, and his or her income will raise your EFC. Is your soon-to-be-spouse willing to take on this responsibility? If not, you need to have a serious discussion about this, and consider putting off your wedding until your children have graduated from college. These are modern times!

If you've already remarried, bear in mind that your spouse's finances will be calculated in the FAFSA and PROFILE. If, when you remarried, you signed a pre-nuptial agreement that precludes the step-parent from paying for any of your college education, that agreement is void; the reason is that two parties cannot make an agreement that binds a third party. (In this case, the third party is the federal government.) If you're the custodial parent, your spouse is required by law to include his or her assets in the FAFSA. If, however, the financial obligations of that step-parent include other college tuitions, that obligation will be included in the FAFSA the same way that any legal siblings (blood relatives or adopted siblings) would be. If those step-siblings consider the custodial step-parent to be *their* non-custodial parent, their information won't be included (but all alimony and paid child support will be).

If you need to discuss this with an estranged spouse, we recommend that you move beyond any petty grievances you might have and call him or her, or otherwise arrange a time to talk. Ask him or her to split the EFC with you.

Be prepared for this discussion. Get ready to talk about the FAFSA, what you can contribute, and what your child might otherwise need from the other parent. Be willing to create a deal sheet that lists commitments for both parties, and sign off on it at the end of the conversation (full names and a date).

If prior experience with your ex leads you to believe that there's no chance for a positive or productive discussion between the two of you, consider the following:

√ *Has there been a neutral party (pastor, social worker, accountant) who has helped you in discussions of your child on previous occasions?*

√ *Can you hire a mediator? We recommend this if you know that your ex has the financial ability to help your child with college.*

√ *If all else fails, would you be willing to consult the attorney that represented you in your divorce? Remember: Your attorney is paid to be your advocate, and your child's education is a priority. If you can spend enough on an attorney to come to an agreement about the next four years, it might be worth the headache.*

WHAT IF MY FORMER SPOUSE IS A DEADBEAT OR OTHERWISE ABSENT?

You'll have to talk with each college about this individually, but don't worry: All colleges and universities have a protocol for this. Your ex is not the first—nor will he or she be the last—to "decline to participate." You'll have to get a waiver of non-custodial information; be prepared to document all conversations and other evidence of refusal, such as missed child support payments or alimony, for the college itself.

WHAT ELSE CAN I DO?

Read through our next chapter, the MAP, and learn how you can help your child look for colleges where he or she has a high chance of getting aid. Help your child with the applications, and visit two or three of the top contenders. After applications are submitted, you'll file your taxes as soon as you can, then file the FAFSA, which you can do as soon as January 1st of the year of enrollment.

MERIT AID AND
THE MAP

Merit aid is part of your financial aid award. It will be awarded to you after you've already applied to colleges. If you apply to the right schools, you'll likely get enough merit and need-based aid to make your education affordable. In this chapter, we explain how merit aid is awarded, and how you can determine whether or not you're a good candidate for it, and at what colleges, using our MAP, or Merit Aid Profile. You're going to define yourself in this chapter, not just through your grades, but through your extracurriculars and interests.

WHAT, EXACTLY, IS MERIT AID?

Merit aid, also known as gift aid, a tuition discount, a college scholarship, or an institutional grant, is what you will receive if you're in the top 25 percent (or even 50 percent) of the incoming class at most colleges. Merit aid, put simply, is free money. You don't have to repay it. It can take the form of actual cash that the college itself will disburse to you, or simply be reflected in a discounted tuition rate. Merit aid is a *real* college scholarship; it comes from the college itself, and is usually significantly larger than any outside, or private, scholarship you could receive.

Colleges and universities give out merit aid for one simple reason: to get the students they want the most. Only about 20 percent of all full-time students pay the full sticker price of tuition, room and board, and fees; the remaining 80 percent receive some discount right off the top, whether it's through federal loans, grants, work-study, or merit aid.[1] As we mentioned in Chapter 1, tuition is a mutable, changeable thing, which changes based entirely on how much the college wants the student to enroll. Many colleges use the bottom 50 percent of the incoming class to pay for the top 50 percent of the incoming class.

WHY DO COLLEGES DISCOUNT THEIR TUITION? WHAT'S THE POINT?

You might wonder, if colleges are discounting their tuition for 80 percent of students on average, why not just lower the price of tuition? Well, that's because from the remaining 20 percent, they're getting the highest possible price. It's in the colleges' best interest, however odd it may seem, to use a high sticker price overall. Colleges use a process known as "leveraging," a form of economic and statistical modeling, to determine *exactly* how much money they have to give you in order to get you to enroll—no more, no less. Leveraging is one of those open secrets; everyone who works for universities knows about it, but no one, as far as we know, has ever written about it for student and families. Sticker price also positions colleges in the market, and can make them appear to be "better," or more selective, schools. It's like a department store; the retail price determines what section your product will be in. An $8,000 dress won't be placed in the "juniors" section at Bloomingdale's along with prom dresses; it'll be on the top floor, with high-end designers (whether or not it *comes* from a high-end designer).

A great example of sticker-price placement is Boston University. BU is a large private university located in central Boston with an enrollment of more than 18,000 undergraduates, according to the College Board, and it accepts 58 percent of applicants. BU's self-reported cost of attendance for 2010–11 is $54,900. BU has a sophisticated website whose colors (maroon and white) are rather reminiscent of another local college: Harvard University.

If you had to ask a group of your friends "Which school is better: Harvard, or BU?" they would likely answer "Harvard" without a second thought. That's the *perceived value* of a Harvard degree; its brand presence is exceptional. If you calculate the lifetime return on investment, or the actual possible dollar value of the degree, like payscale.com (a website that tracks compensation data) did in 2010, you'd discover that Harvard *is* a great school. Harvard is #3 on Payscale's list, following CalTech and MIT, for the highest lifetime dollar return on investment—12.5 percent on average for the Harvard graduate, or just more than $1.6 million dollars.

On that same list, Boston University clocked in at #111, with a lifetime ROI of just 7.8 percent, or just more than $702,000 dollars. That's not much higher than the overall average for the 554 colleges in the study of $627,239. So when we think about those two indexes of value—perception and documented financial value—Harvard is, by far, the better school. That's not a surprise. But what *is* a surprise is Harvard's cost of attendance for 2010–11: $53,950. Harvard is less expensive than BU. Not by much, but less expensive. Why is BU *more* expensive? Because it wants to be perceived as being *as good as Harvard*. BU wants to be perceived as a highly selective elite college, even though its acceptance rates (58 percent of all applicants) are nowhere near as selective as Harvard's (only 7 percent).[2] No matter how you cut it, BU is not Harvard—but it would like to *appear* to be, by charging the same amount or more.

Expensive, but less selective, large private schools such as BU and NYU, which we discussed in Chapter 1, are great places to get a good education. They have wonderful faculty, great course offerings, and engaged student life. But if you can't pay outright for them, or be in the top 25 percent of applicants and receive enough in aid, they are not worth borrowing to attend. It's not a logical financial risk; no matter how much they might emulate top-tier elite colleges, they just aren't. You will not see the same financial reward—but their sticker price, higher than Harvard or even Yale, implies that you *could*. It's a pricing trick. Don't fall for it.

This isn't necessarily a bad thing. It's just the way the market works. Universities are, at the end of the day, businesses. So although it doesn't do any good to complain about unfair pricing policies, it does help you to understand that at any given college, if you're not in at least the top 50 percent of the incoming class, and you're not poor enough to have an EFC that's low enough for Pell, the university in question may have absolutely no interest in funding you.

WHERE CAN YOU GET MERIT AID?

After you apply, each college that gives you an offer of admission will also, hopefully, give you a financial aid offer. That financial aid award will be made up of both need-based (what gets calculated by the FAFSA and PROFILE) and merit-based aid. Most colleges and universities hand out their aid dollars sequentially; they start with the top 5 percent of applicants, then move onto the top 10 percent, then 15 percent, and so on. The top 5 percent is often the top-fifth *academic* percentile, but not always. Different colleges have different priorities; that's where your extracurriculars and interests come in to play. They might award their need and merit dollars to students who are affiliated with the same religious organization as the college; students who have exceptional volunteer résumés; or students who are interested in digital media. It just depends on the college. Most colleges and universities cannot afford to give need-based aid to all of their students. For more information about need, the EFC, and the COA, please turn to Chapter 2.

Colleges that *don't* give merit aid are usually need-blind and meet full need, and they don't give merit aid because they don't have to. Those colleges are generally incredibly selective, and, though many of them do meet full need if they accept you, your family may still not be able to afford it. For many middle-class families, the EFC (what the family is required to pay) is still high enough that paying it outright represents a real financial sacrifice. Although it may look to the government as though your family has the assets on hand, many families do not. There's a multitude of reasons for this; job loss, asset loss (from the devaluation of investments), home foreclosure, and other expenses, such as caring for a disabled child or elderly parent, are just a few. So if you're accepted to an incredibly selective college that will meet your full need (COA – EFC), but you still can't pay a large part of your EFC, we recommend that you also apply to other schools that disburse merit aid in addition to need-based aid.

Finding merit aid is tricky. It's not recorded on any single website or in any single book. (Although meritaid.com is making an attempt, it's not fully operational, and we doubt it ever will be.) The reasons for this have to do with data reporting. Although colleges and universities report their data to various agencies, including the federal government, *U.S. News & World Report*, the College Board, Petersen's, NACUBO, and so on, much of this reporting isn't useful to anyone other than the requestor, and no single source gathers detailed enough information on aid policies. The next time we have a million dollars and a team of statisticians, we'd love to give it a shot, but for now—and likely the next decade—that data won't be available. Admission data and freshman class profiles, however, are *always* reported, and they're widely available for free and online, from the College Board (*collegeboard.com*) and IPEDS (*nces.ed.gov/ipeds*). We can also find out from those same sources how much a single college gives away in aid, and how much on average; when we compare this to their freshman class profile, you can make an educated guess about how much any given student might receive in aid.

Because most colleges award their aid dollars by funding the best and brightest of their applicants (however they define that—it may be through grades, extracurriculars, talent, or organizational affiliation) *first*, you have the highest possible chance of receiving a scholarship if you're in the top 25 percent of the incoming freshman class. If you're in the middle 50 percent of applicants, you will likely get *some* aid, but possibly not enough, unless your financial need is significant.

We've made some assumptions about you, audience. We're willing to bet that most of you are middle-class kids with great, but not spectacular, grades; you'll qualify for financial aid, but not Pell. That means you're the average applicant. If your grades and test scores put you above and beyond the average applicant, and your EFC is incredibly low (Pell or lower; go to *studentaid.ed.gov* to find out more), it's not unreasonable for you to apply to a need-blind college that meets full need, like an Ivy or Little Ivy, where you will likely get enough in need-based aid to make college affordable for you. But for everyone else—whose families might be able to just barely meet their EFC or not at all—we recommend that you apply to less-selective (read: less selective than an Ivy, not a place with open admission) private colleges and universities, or to a local public (not out of state; the costs of out-of-state publics are comparably high to privates, and they give less aid).

Based on our own experience (and the data that we report in *The Financial Aid Handbook*'s Best Bets List, beginning on page 221), those colleges might be schools you've never, ever heard of. And that's *a lot* of colleges; out of the more than 4,400 colleges and universities in the United States, how many have you heard of? Probably a handful of schools that are local to your home state, and 20–50 highly competitive schools. There are so many more wonderful places out there. You just have to start looking.

That's not to say that more selective colleges don't offer merit aid; the medium- and smaller-sized ones often do. Gonzaga, for example, is a medium-sized, private, Jesuit-affiliated liberal arts college in Spokane, Washington. Gonzaga has a DI men's basketball team, and its name is quite well-known. In 2007–08 (the most recent year for which such data was available), the cost of attendance was $41,700; its *average* institutional grant (its own money) was about $11,000; its average need-based grant was $13,450, and its average merit-based grant was $8,900. The middle 50 percent of that freshman class (the 25th to the 75th percentile) scored between 1090 and a 1280 on the combined SAT, and 47 percent of their students have a 3.7 GPA or higher. So how do you find out where you need to fall in order to get merit aid? It's simple: You need to be in the top 25 percent. Your individual SAT or ACT score should be higher than the top score of the middle 50 percent, putting you above the 75th percentile. For Gonzaga, that would be an SAT above 1280, and a GPA of at least 3.7; you should then qualify for at the bare minimum of $11,000 in aid (its average), if not significantly more. If your scores are demonstrably higher than that—say, a 1450 SAT with a 3.95—it's likely that you'd get at least $20,000 from Gonzaga (half-tuition).[3] At a less selective school, that last set of credentials would get you full tuition, and a discounted room and board, if not a full ride.

HOW WILL YOU KNOW WHAT THE TOP 25 PERCENT OF THE CLASS IS?

To find information about the top 25 percent of the class, you have a few options. Most colleges report their information to the College Board. Go to *collegeboard.com*, type in the college's name, and, on its profile, click "How Do I Stack Up?" You'll see a set of charts; most of the information that gets reported is the middle 50 percent—between the 25th and 75th percentiles. So for a college that reports a middle 50 percent of SAT scores as 900–1250, the top 25 percent of the class has a 1250 or higher; for ACT scores, a college that reports the middle 50 percent of ACT as 25–29, the top 25 percent of the class has a 29 or higher.

GPA is a little tricker, because the division doesn't always add up. GPA is reported as a spread—and it's not always even. For Gonzaga, which we mentioned earlier, 47 percent of the class had a 3.75 GPA or higher. Although it doesn't *always* align exactly, we can guesstimate by subtracting 3.75 from 4, and dividing the remainder of .25 in half, then adding it to the reported GPA—determining that the top 25 percent had around a GPA of 3.875 (3.75 plus .125, or half of .25) or higher.

Here are a few other examples of GPA guesstimates, using the College Board's data:

√ At Drew University in New Jersey, 18 percent had a 3.75 GPA or higher, and overall, 52 percent had a GPA of 3.25 or higher. We'd guesstimate that the top 25 percent had a GPA of 3.625 or higher (3.25 plus .375, or half of .75).

√ At Agnes Scott College in Georgia, 34 percent had a GPA of 3.75 or higher. We'd wager that the top 25 percent had a GPA of 3.82 or higher; we found that by dividing .25 by 34 (to discover the remaining percentage points), then multiplying the answer—roughly .007—by 10, to get .07. We added that .07 to 3.75, and got 3.82.

√ At Pepperdine University in California, 51 percent had a GPA of 3.75 or higher. That's a pretty high number; Pepperdine is a fairly competitive school. We guesstimate that the top 25 percent of the class has at least a GPA of 3.9 or higher. That's easy math: Divide .25 in half to get .125, and add it to 3.75. You'll get 3.875; we rounded up to 3.9, for a conservative estimate, because there are so many students in the top percentile.

GET TO THE POINT! WHAT COLLEGES ARE GOING TO GIVE YOU MERIT AID?

In the next chapter, we cover how to look for colleges that will fund you. Before you can start searching, you need to know who you are and what your strengths are. Stop by to see your school's guidance counselor and get a copy of your transcript, just for your own reference (it doesn't need to be sealed), then start filling out our MAP, on the following pages. You can also print out a copy from our website, or make your own.

THE MAP (MERIT AID PROFILE)

YOUR STATS

You'll need to start by defining your own stats. That's three simple things: your SAT, ACT (or both), and your cumulative GPA, on a 4.0 scale.

SAT: _____

ACT: _____

GPA: _____

If you only have the SAT and not the ACT, or vice versa, ask your high school guidance counselor about a concordance table.

Is there room for improvement? An SAT or ACT prep class costs about $200–$500 up front, but is well worth the investment. Do you have another year (or two) to bring up your GPA? Although you might be encouraged to take as many weighted (honors or AP courses) as possible, we recommend that you only do so if you're certain that you'll excel. If you're terrible at math, don't take AP calc just to prove you can pass; take whatever regular senior math class is available, and try your best to get an A. Your high school guidance counselor is the best person you can ask to help you figure out how to improve your grades and test scores.

HOW MUCH YOU CAN AFFORD TO PAY

If you haven't already, you'll need to calculate your EFC—what it is, and how much of it your family can actually afford. For more information on this, turn to Chapter 4. Here, you'll put in your calculated EFC, and the Actual EFC, or how much you can afford to pay (if it's not the full amount).

EFC: $_____

Actual EFC: $_____

YOUR LOCAL PUBLIC

Before you start looking at any other colleges, you should find out what the tuition costs at your local public are; they're often significantly less expensive than private colleges, and you may be able to live at home (which will subtract room and board, but add commuting costs). We're big champions of public education, but they're not always great for students who aren't joiners. If you're going to go to your local public and live at home, you'll have to work twice as hard to participate in the college community; living off campus can be difficult. So if you're a real joiner—if you love clubs and organizations—a public college could be a place where you'll really excel. Community colleges are also an *amazing* way to pay very little out of pocket; if you can do two years at a local community college, get extraordinary grades, and then transfer, you might be able to afford a wider selection of schools.

My local U: $_____ per year

My local community college: $_____ per year

LOCAL COSTS

Actual EFC x 4 = $_____

Local U x 4 = $_____

Local Community College x 2 = $_____

Subtract your Local U x 4 from your Actual EFC x 4, or your Local CC x 2 from your Actual EFC x 4. You might be pleasantly surprised at how much funding you have left over!

You don't have to stay near home, but it's always worth considering. We don't necessarily recommend applying to out-of-state public colleges; they statistically give out less aid, and you'll have to pay for room and board. Many states, however, have reciprocity with neighboring states, and qualifying residents of Washington, DC, may receive in-state tuition at any public college in the country through the DCTAG initiative. (For more information on DCTAG and state-specific grants, go to our website, at *thefinancialaidhandbook.com*.)

YOUR INTERESTS AND EXTRACURRICULARS

After you've defined your stats, you'll need to go over your interests and extracurriculars. This can mean a lot of things—anything from volunteer work to videos that you've posted on YouTube for a class project. It can include community activities through your church, temple, or even atheist's organization; involvement in school plays or sports; and after-school jobs or internships.

Fill out the following chart; rate yourself on a 1–5 scale (**1** being the least involved person that you know, and **5** being the most) for each activity. Don't worry if you can't fill every category; few students can! We just like to leave a little extra room. Ignore the "Buzzwords" column for now; you'll fill that in later.

Category	Description	Buzzwords	Points
Leadership Experiences			
Activities: Sports, Clubs, Performing Arts			

Honors and Awards, Recognitions			
Community Involvement, Service, Volunteer Work			
All Others, including Paid Work			

Every activity for which you've given yourself a **3** or higher on is one that you'll want to use in your application, and you might want to seek out the faculty or adult advisor that oversaw those projects. Can that person help you with a recommendation? How does he or she feel about his or her *own* alma mater? Would you consider going to that school? If you're interested in applying to a college that an adult in your life is an alumna of, it would be fantastic to have a recommendation from that person.

If you've rated yourself a **1** or **2** for any activity, is there a way to become more involved before you send off your applications? Think about it, and try to become more involved. Whether that means spearheading a new initiative (adding vegan baked goods to bake sales) or taking a leadership role, you should try to bring those **1**s and **2**s up to **3**s, **4**s, and **5**s. If you're not interested, then forget about them—and devote yourself fully to your other activities.

Colleges prioritize extracurriculars in the same way that they prioritize anything else. The ideal merit aid candidate has extracurriculars that align with a college's values. If you've got strong leadership experiences, for example, you'll want to apply to the kind of college that values strong leadership experiences. When your academic credentials are tied to other things that the college values—whether that be diversity, community service, or the arts—you have a profile that hits on all possible cylinders. It's not a guarantee at every single school, but more often than not, matching yourself to a college's values gives you, as a prospective student, a much better chance of having your application placed in the right stack. But how can you figure that out? You'll need to talk the talk—and learn how to discuss your experiences on an application within a specific context. Get a colored pen, and circle the experiences you rated yourself the highest on.

DEFINING YOUR BUZZWORDS

Again, when colleges determine what they value in a student, it's not just about test scores. It's also about "strategic priorities," or buzzwords. After you've evaluated your extracurriculars and interests, you'll need to learn how to define them through the eyes of colleges and universities.

In our consulting business, we've been responsible for helping to build the strategic profile and priorities for numerous colleges and universities. As with anything, it's not a perfect process, but we try to define the kinds of students that the colleges want—and the colleges themselves—using a list of buzzwords.

HOW DO YOU FIND BUZZWORDS?

Buzzwords will be on the colleges' website. Different colleges put them in different places on their sites. The most common places are:

√ **Mission Statement:** *Targeted to potential faculty, alumni, and other professional parties, this is not typically written for students. This is usually kind of pedantic and dull, but it's not without value.*

√ **About Us/About Our Students:** *This is often a tab on the side of the page, or at the top, in the navigational header. It can also be located in a section called "For Prospective Students," or at the very, very bottom of the page, next to "Contact Us."*

√ **Strategic Plan:** *This is usually in a section devoted to enrollment, or to future or prospective students. If the college does post a strategic plan, skim it; it'll give you a great idea about where the college puts its resources, money, and energy.*

√ **Freshman Class Profile:** *Colleges choose what information to put in their freshman class profile, and not all schools have it on their site. They also put it in different places. Using a Google site search (type "freshman class profile site: the college you're looking at" into the Google search box) is probably the most efficient way to find it. The things a college will include, and the order in which they're placed on the profile, will tell you exactly what's important to that college. This may also contain information about aid dollars, GPA and test scores, and demographic information for the most recent freshman class.*

√ **Why This College?** *(on the* **Admissions** *page): When a college pitches itself to you, it is telling you what its community* *is, and what it values. Colleges that focus on their outdoors programs are outdoorsy; colleges that focus on their math competitions are math-oriented. Colleges that highlight the political action of their students are politically oriented. Colleges that highlight the volunteer activities of their students love service; colleges that say they are affiliated with a religious organization value that organization above all others. Although they rarely come right out and say, "Here are our buzzwords," it's not that complex to define. Don't think about it too hard; just try to define what you're looking at.*

Here are some of the buzzwords, or strategic priorities, we've commonly used when building a "strategic profile," or mission statement, for a college. They're certainly not the only buzzwords out there, but hopefully they'll give you a feel for how schools often define their students. These are in no particular order.

- √ *Academically able/scholars/intellectual.*
- √ *Service.*
- √ *Spirituality.*
- √ *Green/sustainability.*
- √ *Global.*
- √ *Racially diverse.*
- √ *Geographically diverse.*
- √ *Career-oriented.*
- √ *Entrepreneurship.*
- √ *Business experience.*
- √ *Community/family.*
- √ *Wellness/fitness.*
- √ *Technologically savvy.*
- √ *Character/ethics/morality.*
- √ *Outdoorsy (vs. indoorsy).*

√ Legacy/alumni.

√ Math/science.

√ Creative/performing arts.

√ Politically aware.

√ Socially active/oriented.

Go back to the list of your extracurriculars and interests. Can you fit any of our buzzwords in the "Buzzwords" column?

Take a look at our example of Susie Senior's profile.

Category	Description	Buzzwords	Points
Leadership Experiences	Led a canoeing trip in the Boundary Waters	Outdoorsy, Fitness	5
	President of my High School Secular Humanist's Society	Community, Spirituality	5
	Led a team of my peers in a 5K charity run	Socially Active, Service, Fitness	4
	Organized the Spring Fling	Socially Active, Creative	3
	Helped bus elderly people to a local election	Service, Socially Active, Politically Aware	3
Activities: Sports, Clubs, Performing Arts	Member of the Snowboarding Club	Fitness, Outdoorsy	2
	Member of the Golf Team	Fitness, Outdoorsy	3
	Member of "Students for a Better World" recycling program	Socially Active, Green	3
	Member of Mock Trial	Career-oriented	4

	Member of GSA or GBLT	Diverse, Socially Active	3
	Mathlete, 2 years	Math, Scholar	4
	Write a style blog that documents my high school classmates	Socially Active, Technologically Savvy	5
Honors and Awards, Recognitions	Class President	Career-Oriented, Politically Active, Socially Active	5
	2nd place, State Science Fair	Science, Scholar	5
	3rd place, Regional Track and Field Championships, Javelin	Fitness	5
	Recipient of $400 Arts Grant from my town	Creative	5
Community Involvement, Service, Volunteer Work	Volunteered at a local Children's Hospital, read to inpatients	Service	4
	Play bridge with my grandmother and her friends twice a month	Service, Socially Active	3
Paid Work	Sandwich delivery, after school, 15 hours per week	Business Experience	3
	Sell my handmade jewelry at art fairs 4 times per year	Entrepreneurship, Creative	5

As you can see, Susie Senior's got *a lot* going on—and there's a fair amount of consistency as to what she's interested in. Looking at Susie—a jewelry-making outdoorswoman who plays bridge, recycles, belongs to her school's Gay-Straight Alliance, and is a secular humanist and a member of Mock Trial—at what kind of college do you think she'd excel (and have a good chance of being funded)? Probably one that values the same things Susie does: creative, outdoorsy, socially and politically active students. Susie wouldn't be a good candidate for aid at, say, Oral Roberts, Bob Jones, or Brigham Young University, all religious colleges; she also wouldn't have a very good experience at any of those schools. Although many search engines online encourage students to define the kinds of colleges they'd like to go to by choosing basic demographic information—like size, location, and cost—we think that focusing on the activities you've most enjoyed in high school is the best way to determine what kind of school is a good fit for you.

After you've figured out your stats, your interests and extracurriculars, and your buzzwords, you're almost home free. Fill out our last chart, the MAP (Merit Aid Profile), to sum it all up.

In the "Me" row, you'll put your stats—your GPA, your SAT, and your ACT—and the buzzwords that you've pulled from your interests and extracurriculars. Put as many as you'd like.

If you don't have any colleges in mind, please move ahead to Chapter 7, and leave the remainder of the chart blank. If you've already started searching, go on and complete the chart.

In the Colleges A–O rows, you'll put the stats for the top 25 percent of the freshman class at however many colleges that you're interested in (go to page 130 to learn how to find the top 25 percent), along with buzzwords that you can find on the school's website. Ideally, you'll have at least two or three of the same buzzwords. If not, you'll want to make sure that your stats put you solidly in the top 20–25 percent.

If your stats are higher than the colleges, and you've got some similar buzzwords, put a Y (for yes) in the "Chance of Funding?" column. If your buzzwords don't match, you can still put a Y, but go back and look at the school's site. Could you really see yourself there? If your stats *and* buzzwords don't match, put an N (for no). If you mark any Ns on this chart, don't bother applying to those schools—unless your EFC qualifies you for Pell. In that case, you may be able to get enough in need-based aid to make it affordable.

The MAP, or Merit Aid Profile

	GPA	SAT	ACT	Buzzwords	Chance of Funding?
Me					
College A					
College B					
College C					
College D					
College E					
College F					
College G					
College H					
College I					
College J					
College K					
College L					
College M					
College N					
College O					

Please bear in mind as you fill this out that it's certainly still possible to apply, be accepted, and get some aid at colleges where you're not in the top 25 percent. But applying can mean falling in love, and falling in love means taking on extra debt. Our MAP is essentially the simplest and most conservative method we would use with any student who needed to find a scholarship, and if you're in the middle 50 percent at most colleges, you will still get *some* aid. It simply may not be *enough* aid. The best bet you can make on a scholarship is to be in the top quartile of applicants. It's that simple.

7

The Cost- Based College Search

To be blunt, the absolute cheapest option for a college education is to attend a local community college for two years, and then transfer to another school. That allows you to get all of your prerequisites and core requirements out of the way, at an exceptionally reasonable price. The average annual tuition cost for a community college, according to the College Board, is $2,713. It also allows you to raise your grades substantially, if you need to—making you eligible for admission and merit aid to colleges that you may not otherwise be able to consider.

However, there's a fair amount of missed opportunity cost here, and not all colleges accept transfer students or all of their credits. And the relationships that you'll develop with your peers and the faculty during the first two years of college are important. It can be difficult to transition into a new environment, when everyone around you has already had two years to make that school their own. There is, too, the compulsion to *get out of your parents' house*. You're 18 and ready to go. So why wait?

The traditional college search focuses primarily on brand ranking, as determined by ratings boards such as *U.S. News & World Report, The Princeton Review*, and *Forbes*. You take your transcript into your high school guidance office, and the college counselor on hand will find the most competitive school you could gain admission to—the lowest possible threshold that your grades could overcome. Then you apply, and wait for acceptance, without considering cost as a factor. Many students simply apply to the most competitive schools they could conceivably gain admission to and pray for a scholarship, without understanding that if they're not in the top quartile of applicants, they likely won't receive enough aid to make it affordable.

Although we've covered it multiple times, if this is the first chapter you've taken a look at, we need you to understand something: The old paradigm of a "safety" and "reach" school is ridiculous. Throw it out the window. You should consider colleges the same way that many people consider graduate school: *It's about being funded.* There's no shame in being one of the best in the class, and there's so much diversity among the more than 4,400 colleges and universities in the United States—many of which have incredibly devoted and highly educated faculty members—that you'll surely be able to find an environment in which you can excel and where you won't be overloaded with debt, whether it's a "top 50" school or not.

In Chapters 3, 4, 5, and 6, we covered how you're going to define the three most important elements of your college search: how much you can afford to pay outright, how much debt you're willing to take on, and what kind of a student you are. At the end of Chapter 6, we showed you our MAP, or Merit Aid Profile. You may have filled it out only with your stats, but as you begin searching for schools, you can add in their information and begin the process of separating the funded schools from the unfunded ones. The MAP is an incredibly useful tool for two reasons: It allows you to define how your values align with a college, and whether or not you'll be in the top 25 percent. If your family is in serious financial straits, and you can't meet anything even close to your EFC, we have a different chart for you to try later in this chapter. That means doing a college search that focuses almost exclusively on cost, using net price, your Actual EFC, and your stats.

THE COST-CONSCIOUS SEARCH

If you're ready to move on with your life and get out of the house (or the idea of a community college doesn't appeal to you in any way), the next-least-expensive option is to go to a college in your home state, or in a neighboring state. That throws travel costs out the window (easily an extra $1,500–$2,500 per year). You shouldn't have a car—that's just another waste of money—but you can bus, train, or carpool with the most ease from a college located in your home or neighboring state.

To begin the cost-conscious search, we recommend looking at colleges within a 250-mile radius of your hometown. Grab your laptop, a pen, and a piece of scratch paper, and go online.

Log on to *nces.ed.gov/collegenavigator*. You can use the search box in the left rail to get a list of all the colleges—public, private, or both—in your home and neighboring states. If you use the "map" function instead of the drop-down menu, you can select multiple states with ease. After you hit "Show Results," you'll get a hyperlinked list of colleges, where you can see sticker price, graduation rates, average student loan burden, and aid dollars awarded. It's not the sexiest or most sophisticated site, but the data is sound, and it's certainly the most reputable and reliable source of admission and financial aid information out there.

You can do the same thing at the College Board's admittedly more attractive website (*collegeboard.com*), although the College Board gives you more selection criteria—not all of which is a useful filter. Its aid filters, for example, don't appear to work very well, because not all colleges report that data to the College Board, but you can use the "Match Maker" to find colleges where you'll exceed (that is, be in the top 25 percent) admission requirements. Just enter your test scores into the "Admission" portion of the application.

Using the Admission tool on the College Board "Match Maker" is incredibly useful for one reason: You can choose to only see colleges that have actual standards for admission, by selecting schools whose classes have a high school GPA of greater than 2.0. This filters out for-profit colleges, which generally have an open admission policy and are not a segment of education that we recommend to anyone.

Using College Navigator *does not* filter out for-profit colleges, unless you select public colleges and universities only.

Why You Should Stay Away From For-Profit Colleges

For-profit colleges have come under fire in the last few years, with good reason. Although many for-profit colleges are traditional trade schools, there's been an enormous increase in for-profits run by publicly traded corporations, whose interests in education lie only in increasing share value for their stockholders. Much of the outcry against for-profits has to do with their funding; for-profit educational corporations receive the same kind of federal funding (in other words, taxpayer dollars) as any other segment of higher education, roughly 26 billion dollars annually. There are currently 14 publicly traded education companies, with a combined enrollment of 1.4 million students. The largest is the University of Phoenix, whose enrollment of 458,000, is, according to an article in the New York Times, *larger than the combined enrollment of the entire Big 10 Conference schools.[1] That means, when we talk about for-profits, we're talking about private enterprise. Giving federal financial aid dollars to for-profits and their students is the equivalent of using federal dollars to buy any other product on the market—a car, for example, or clothing.*

Many for-profits make the argument that their product—education— is more beneficial to society as a whole than consumer products such as cars or clothing—but that's assuming that the education they provide has a real, quantifiable value, one that exceeds the one provided by state and community colleges. And it doesn't. Their graduation rates (less than 50 percent) are atrocious; the value of their degrees in the job market is questionable; and their costs are unreasonably high.[2] Much of the coursework (associate's degrees and certificates) offered at for-profit colleges, at prices comparable to respectable nonprofit private institutions, can be found at community colleges for just a few hundred dollars. A 2010 study conducted by the Government Accountability Office, an independent, nonpartisan agency that works directly for Congress, exposed egregious and fraudulent admission and aid violations at for-profits. Undercover tests at 15 for-profit colleges discovered that all 15 schools misrepresented the value of the degrees on offer, and four colleges engaged in recruitment practices that were flat-out illegal.

We recommend that you *first* use College Navigator, and then follow with *collegeboard.com*. The reason is that College Navigator consistently lists net price, and *collegeboard.com* does not.

Once you're looking at a list of all the colleges in your region, we recommend that you write down each school you're familiar with or interested in learning more about. Then head to the college's own website, and *read, read, read*! The college's own site is the best source of information about majors, programs, student life, and the campus and town themselves.

As of October 2011, all colleges and universities are required to display a net price calculator. However, that calculator is only required to display your eligibility for grant aid, based on averages by EFC bands; this means you may not get an accurate reading. These calculators will estimate your federal loans and grants the exact same way that FAFSA4caster does. Some colleges and universities may provide more sophisticated tools that show eligibility for merit and need-based grants, but most will probably not. The most consistent and accurate information about net price will probably always come from College Navigator.

After you've paged through some college websites—try to look at 10 or so—head back to College Navigator, and type the colleges' names into the search box. Pull up their individual profiles, and get out a pen.

WHAT ARE YOU LOOKING FOR AT COLLEGE NAVIGATOR?

What you're looking for here are two things: the admission stats for each college, and the *net price*, which is located on each college's profile under a + Net Price tab (which allows you to expand the information available). The average net price is the average amount that full-time undergraduate students actually pay per year (after need- and merit-based aid is awarded). College Navigator divides up the averages by income for federal aid recipients, allowing you to view the specific average for the range of your family's household income. Net price is the best indication of what you would actually pay as a student in the middle 50 percent of applicants; if your stats put you higher than the middle 50 percent, then you will likely receive more in aid, and a lower net price.

Using the Cost Conscious Search chart (page 150), enter your stats and your Actual EFC (calculated in chapters 4 and 5), then add in the Net Price for your household's income range and the stats for the top 25 percent for each college.

As we discussed in Chapter 6, you'll get the highest possible amount of aid at most schools if you're in the top 25 percent of applicants or higher, because need and merit aid dollars are generally awarded sequentially (the top 5 percent, then the top 10 percent, then the top 15 percent, and so on). In that chapter, we used data taken from the College Board, because it's the most commonly used site and it consistently showcases GPA. You can also use Petersen's. For test scores, it's fairly simple: You'll want to have test scores that are above the 75th percentile (which you can easily see, on the +Admissions tab, at College Navigator). But GPA is a little trickier.

How Will You Know What the Top 25 Percent of the Class Is?

To find information about the top 25 percent of the class, you want to understand GPA as well as test scores. College Navigator does *not* report GPA, so you'll have to use the College Board. Go to *collegeboard.com*, type in the college's name, and on its profile click "How Do I Stack Up?" You'll see a set of charts; most of the information that gets reported is the middle 50 percent—between the 25th and 75th percentiles. Test scores are the simplest. So for a college that reports a middle 50 percent of SAT scores as 900–1250, the top 25 percent of the class has a 1250 or greater; for ACT scores, a college that reports the middle 50 percent of ACT as 25–29, the top 25 percent of the class has a 29 or higher.

GPA is sometimes difficult, because the division doesn't always add up. GPA is reported as a spread—and it's not always even. For Gonzaga, which we mentioned in Chapter 6, 47 percent of the class had a 3.75 GPA or higher. Although it doesn't *always* align exactly, we can guesstimate by subtracting 3.75 from 4, and dividing the remainder (.25) in half, then adding it to the reported GPA—determining that the top 25 percent had around a GPA of 3.875 (3.75 plus .125, or half of .25) or higher.

A FEW OTHER EXAMPLES OF GPA GUESSTIMATES, USING THE COLLEGE BOARD'S DATA

√ At Goucher College in Maryland, 14 percent had a 3.75 GPA or higher, and 12 percent had a GPA of 3.5 or higher. This is perfectly simple math: 14 percent + 12 percent = 26 percent. So to be in the top quartile, you'll need to have a GPA of 3.5 or higher.

√ At Wooster College in Ohio, 41 percent had a GPA of 3.75 or higher. We'd wager that the top 25 percent had a GPA of 3.89 or higher. We found that by dividing .25 by 41 (to discover the remaining percentage points), then multiplying the answer (roughly .006) by 24 (the difference between 41 and 25), to get .14. We added that .14 to 3.75, and got 3.89.

√ At Eckerd College in Florida, 14 percent had a GPA of 3.75 or higher, and 17 percent had a GPA of 3.5 or higher—meaning that the top 30 percent had a GPA of 3.5 or higher, and the 25th percentile would fall somewhere between 3.5 and 3.75. We'd guesstimate that the top 25 percent of the class has at least a GPA of 3.62 or higher. We got that number by dividing .25 (the difference between 3.5 and 3.75) by 17 (the number of percentage points in between), then multiplying the answer (roughly .014) by 5 (the number of percentage points we need to subtract from our gross to get the 25 percent).

Again, in the following chart, you'll enter your stats and your actual EFC (what you calculated in Chapters 4 and 5). You stats will only go in the first row, but your actual EFC will go in every row.

For each college, you'll add in the Net Price for your household's income range from the school's College Navigator profile, and the stats for the top 25 percent for each college, which you've calculated from the College Board's website.

After you've entered all that information, you can determine whether or not your scores are equal to or higher than stats you've entered for each college. If they are, add a **Y** (for yes) in the "Chance of Funding?" column. If not, add an **N** (for no) in the "Chance of Funding?" column.

Then, subtract your Actual EFC (the amount your family can afford to pay out of pocket) from the college's Net Price (use the Net Price for your family's income range). That will calculate the Gap, or the amount of money you might need to receive above and beyond average aid. The Gap directly correlates to your chances of funding. If you've marked an N in the "Chance of Funding?" column, and the Gap is a fairly substantial amount of money (a few thousand dollars or more), then mark **N** (for no) in the "Worth Applying?" column. If there's no Gap, or you've marked a Y in the "Chance of Funding?" column, then go ahead and mark a **Y** in the "Worth Applying?" column, and request an application!

What's the Gap? The Cost-Conscious Search

	GPA	SAT	ACT	Chance of Funding?	Net Price	Actual EFC	The Gap: Net Price- EFC	Worth Applying?
Me								
College								
College								
College								
College								
College								
College								
College								
College								
College								
College								

College								
College								
College								
College								
College								

If you're interested in schools outside of your home region, by all means, apply them to this chart—but remember that you'll need additional funding for travel costs. How should you search for colleges outside your home region? Well, if you're interested in a certain state, search College Navigator or the College Board by state; if you're interested in a certain major or program, use those criteria. We also recommend that you talk to your high school guidance counselor. Make it abundantly clear that you're in need of a scholarship and that you'd only like to apply to places where you're in the top 25 percent of applicants. Specify a program and your interests, and he or she should be able to help you make a list.

Wherever you've marked a Y in the "Worth Applying?" column, go online to that college's website, and request an application. Before you send in your app—and your nonrefundable application fee—you might want to visit the school. For more information about how you can use the campus visit to connect with the financial aid office, read on to Chapter 8.

8

Everything You Need to Know Before You Hand in Your Paperwork

Before you send in your applications, you need to know exactly what documentation each school requires, and when.

After you've used either our MAP or Cost-Conscious Search chart, or both, you should have an excellent idea of where you'd like to apply. If you can establish a relationship with the financial aid office at this point in the process, before you even submit an application, that relationship could really work to your advantage. Not only does contacting the aid office demonstrate a commitment to the school and a serious level of maturity, but it allows the Financial Aid Administrators (FAAs) to remember your name and get to know you. FAAs can't advocate as effectively for students they don't know, and although every officer tries to be fair, it's always helpful to make a personal connection. In some cases, that's not possible, but either way, you'll want to know and understand all the protocols that each school has in place for its financial aid dollars before you spend hours of your time on an application.

The first step is to thoroughly mine each college's website for any and all information. Here's what you're looking for; if you can't find it on the site, make a note of it for later. You want to know:

√ Does it require the FAFSA only, or is the CSS PROFILE required also?

√ Does it require an institutional financial aid application?

√ What, if any, specific merit aid scholarships does it offer? What are the requirements for eligibility?

√ Do merit scholarships require a special application? Is there an on-campus competition, or an application deadline for consideration?

√ Does it publish a matrix or chart defining who gets what kind of merit award?

√ Does it assign financial aid officers or counselors to prospective students?

√ If not, do all aid questions get routed through the admission office?

√ Can you discover who the appropriate person is to contact for more information?

You want to introduce yourself to the right person off the bat; you don't want to be a thorn in someone else's side. If you can't determine who the appropriate contact is, send the following e-mail to the admission office (usually *admission(s)@college.edu*; look on the "Contact Us" page for prospective students to find out).

Dear Admission Office,

I'm a prospective student for the fall of [the year you would be a freshman]. I'll be applying for financial aid, and I'd like to make sure that I have all the right information at hand. Who should I contact with my questions about this? I'm happy to communicate by phone or by e-mail.

Thanks so much for your assistance; my contact information is below.

Best,

[Your name, e-mail address, and phone number]

Once you've discovered who the appropriate contact is, send the following e-mail:

> Dear [Person],
>
> I'm a prospective student for the fall of [the year you would be a freshman]. I'm very, very interested in the possibility of attending [College X], but I will need to apply for financial aid. I've read all the information on your website about the process for applying for need and merit-based aid, but I was wondering if you would be able to answer the following questions for me:
>
> [insert questions not covered by the website here]
>
> Additionally, do you have any other advice for navigating the admission and scholarship process? I've estimated my EFC at [whatever you estimated using FAFSA4caster], but my family is only able to afford [your Actual EFC, which you discussed with your family in Chapters 4 and 5], and I would like to keep my loans to a minimum. I'm a resident of [your state]. Do you have any advice for someone in my situation—specific scholarships or grants that I may not have heard of? My combined SAT critical reading and math score is [your score]; my ACT composite score is [your score]; my GPA is [your GPA].
>
> Thank you very much for your time and assistance. If you have time for a phone conversation, my contact info is listed below.
>
> Best,
>
> [Your name, your year in high school, your high school, and your phone number]

It's possible that the person you're communicating with won't be able to tell you anything that you can't learn online. But you never know; the college in question may have scholarships that it doesn't advertise or publish online; the officer in question might have gone to your high school, or sympathize with your situation. It is always, always worth asking, and you don't lose anything at all by e-mailing.

Even if he or she is not terribly helpful, keep this person's name and contact information, and be polite and grateful. No matter how unhelpful he or she is, be sure to respond with a thank-you e-mail. When you visit, he or she should be one of the first people you check in with and say hello to.

If your finances are really, really tight, we don't recommend visiting a college until you've been accepted. Visiting can be costly, but more importantly, visiting is romance; it's the equivalent of going on a full-on date with flowers, candy, a concert, and a hayride under the moon in the dark. Colleges pull out all the stops for prospective students (known many places as "prospys"), and if you haven't been admitted or you don't receive enough aid to make it affordable, you could be tempted to take out more student loans than you ought to. However, we love college fairs! They're usually in your hometown or the nearest big city, and it's a great opportunity to connect with the admission office and get all your questions answered. Best of all, they're free. Go to *nacanet.org* for more information about locations and dates for a college fair near you. You can also make contact with individual admission counselors when they visit your school; for more information about who is visiting and when, see your high school guidance counselor.

Once you've had your questions answered for each school to which you're planning to apply, you'll need to actually send in applications. Skip ahead to the next chapter to learn how to optimize your application for scholarships and merit aid.

After you've sent your applications, you'll need to finally fill out and submit your financial aid paperwork. Here's what you need to know.

FILLING OUT THE FAFSA

You can submit the FAFSA on or after January 1st of the enrollment year, but it will be easiest to submit after your parents have filed their income taxes. You can fill it out online at *fafsa.ed.gov*. You can also submit a paper application, printable from the FAFSA website, which will take longer to process, but both electronic and paper versions are free. The custodial parent is required to fill out the FAFSA. For an understanding of terms used on the FAFSA and how it breaks down, please read Chapter 2.

REQUIRED DOCUMENTS TO HAVE ON HAND TO COMPLETE THE FAFSA

For both parents *and* students:

√ *Social Security numbers (SSNs).*

√ *Dates of birth.*

√ W2, tax return 1040 or 1040 A or 1040 EZ. This includes the step-parent married to the custodial parent.

√ Record of child support to children of another household.

√ Housing, food, and other living allowances: military, clergy and others (including cash payments and cash value of benefits).

√ Veterans' non-education benefits, including disability, death pension or dependency and indemnity compensation (DIC), or VA educational work-study allowances.

√ Any record of other untaxed income not reported such as worker's compensation or disability.

√ Current total balance as of today of cash, and savings and checking accounts.

√ Current net worth and investments, real estate, Coverdell, and 529 plans.

√ Net worth of any current business or investment farm. This does not include a small business where the parents control more than 50 percent and has 100 or fewer full-time employees, and does not include the value of a family farm that the student and/or parent lives on and operates.

√ Student records of unreported untaxed income.

√ Net worth of current business or investment farms.

√ Students that are eligible non-citizens only will need to provide their A number, which can be found on their alien registration card (also known as their green card).

If any of those don't apply to you or your parents (such as veterans' benefits), disregard them.

You may find it helpful to use the "FAFSA on the Web" worksheet, which you can download from *fafsa.ed.gov*, to organize and complete the questions on paper before entering online. The questions are listed in the same order that they appear in FAFSA on the Web.

FILLING OUT THE CSS PROFILE

The CSS PROFILE is similar to the FAFSA, although it's more detailed and it's not free. Both the custodial and non-custodial parent must fill out and submit the PROFILE, which can be found online at *profile-online.collegeboard.com*. The initial fee is $25 to submit the form to one school, and $16 for each additional school report.

WHAT YOU NEED TO HAVE ON HAND TO COMPLETE THE CSS PROFILE

For students *and* both sets of parents:

√ *Social Security numbers (SSNs).*

√ *Birthdates.*

√ *Federal income tax returns 1040s and W2s (two most recent years), and any other records of money earned in the most recent years.*

√ *Record of untaxed income and benefits for the last two years.*

√ *Current bank statements.*

√ *Current mortgage information.*

√ *Records of savings, stocks, bonds, trusts, and other investments.*

√ *Temporary Assistance for Needy Families (TANF) or supplemental security income (SSI).*

√ *If either parent is unemployed, the date that unemployment began.*

√ *Civil Service or union retirement plan.*

√ *Current value of tax deferred retirement, pension, annuity, and savings plans including IRA, SRA, Keogh, SEP, 401(K), 403B, 408, 457, 501C.*

√ *Parent earning projection for current tax year.*

√ Current market value of home, value of mortgage, year purchased, original purchase price, and the same information on any other real estate owned by parents.

√ For a business owned and operated by either parent: the original start date, total current market value, amount owed on business, number of employees, who owns and percentage of ownership, other family members with ownership and their percent of ownership, other family members who receive salary (names, relationship, yearly salary or wages).

√ For a farm owned and operated by either parent: the name of your farm, number of acres, current market value per acre, current total market value, amount owed, location with address.

√ Parent child support paid to another household.

√ Parent educational loan repayment, amount paid in current and previous tax years—on their own educational loans (does not include parent PLUS loan for child).

√ Amount of medical and dental expenses not covered by insurance or a medical or dental plan.

√ Total elementary, junior high, and high school tuition paid in prior and current year, and how many children you paid for and expect to pay for.

√ Monthly home mortgage payment.

√ For non-custodial parent for current and previous years: agreement of how much the non-custodial parent will pay for college.

√ VA benefits earned/expected to earn.

√ Student tuition benefits from parent employer or student employer.

√ Student uniform gift to minor (value of account).

√ Parents report for all other children (report of all dependent family members except this student and parents):

- Where they go to school.

- Associated fees or tuition, scholarships, or grants and dollar amounts for the next two years.

- Whether they will be enrolled in high school or college the following year.

√ Year, make, and model of motor vehicles.

√ Additional real estate: year of purchase, purchase price, current value, amount owed.

√ Schedule C businesses: name, amount invested, and percent of ownership.

√ If either parent is the beneficiary of a trust or estate: type of trust, value, terms, and other pertinent information (if parent has received).

√ If another family member is a beneficiary of a trust: type of trust, value, terms, and other pertinent information.

√ Credit card information to pay the fee for the PROFILE ($25.00 application fee, $16.00 per institution sent).

ADDITIONAL DOCUMENTS THAT MAY BE REQUESTED BY COLLEGES

Signed copies of the federal tax return for the student, the parent, or both, are frequently requested by colleges, as are copies of W2s, even if the student's FAFSA has been approved without being submitted for verification.

Verification happens when the college in question confirms the data reported on your FAFSA. Your school has the authority to contact you for documentation that supports income and other information that you reported. Colleges have the right to withhold financial aid offers until requested documentation is received. Be careful when you fill out the FAFSA: Students are selected for verification when there is mismatched information. If your SSN is incorrect or missing for either the student or the parent, names don't match, the number of people in the household doesn't look right, or any calculations are not reasonable, you will be selected for verification. Colleges are required to verify the information on all students selected as a result of the federal processing system, and any students for whom the college determines there is a conflict of information in the data provided. Colleges must also write and follow a policy for the selection of additional students for verification incompliance with current federal regulations.

SPECIAL CIRCUMSTANCES

Documentation must be provided for specific expenses not listed in the FAFSA or Profile that occurred since filing or not listed at all. As an example, supporting an elderly relative's nursing home expenses, recent parent job loss, or a disabled child all qualify as "special circumstances." Colleges may require copies of payment made to a nursing home or care center, or a letter of termination of employment. In other words, you need to prove it happened.

NON-CUSTODIAL PARENT WAIVER

For colleges that require the non-custodial PROFILE, and the non-custodial parent refuses to comply or can't be found, then the college will likely require documentation. Institutions may supply a Request for Waiver of Non-Custodial Parent Information form that outlines the acceptable documentation, or they may simply request specific documents, like evidence of non-payment of child support. A letter of support from an individual with knowledge of the family situation may be required, such as a counselor, minister, or officer of the court.

SELECTIVE SERVICE REGISTRATION

All males aged 18 who are U.S. citizens *must* register with the Selective Service. The federal government will conduct a database check when you file the FAFSA. Men may register on the FAFSA, if they complete it online. If the student is exempt from registering for the Selective Service a copy of the Status Information Letter may be required.

FURTHER UNDERSTANDING FINANCIAL AID POLICIES

SUMMER EARNINGS

If you are applying for financial aid, many colleges will expect that you, the student, will earn money in the summer to use for school. It may or may not say so on the website, but it may be listed as a resource on your financial aid award, when it's ultimately sent to you. If you can't have a job or take paid work in the summer for any reason, discuss it with your financial aid officer. Although it isn't likely that you'll be let off the hook for summer earnings, it doesn't hurt to ask.

OUTSIDE SCHOLARSHIPS

Outside scholarships, also known as *private* scholarships, can come from anywhere that *isn't* the college itself, or the state or federal government. They can come from corporations, from fellowship organizations, and from community or religious institutions. Your college may adjust your financial aid as a result of your receiving outside scholarships.

√ *If your college met your full need, meaning that the combination of your EFC and your financial aid package equals the total cost of attendance, and you have federal grants or work-study, then you generally can't have more financial aid than the cost of attendance. This is known as an "over award," and the college will likely reduce your financial aid package. But don't worry: It will begin by reducing your loans and/or work-study. If that's still not sufficient (because you have some amazing, enormous scholarship), only then will the college reduce the amount of its money (institutional dollars) that you're receiving. Not all schools do this; some schools might try to replace their money first. If this is the case, lobby to have them reduce your loan or work-study first. Begin by sending an e-mail, then call the officer in question as a last step.*

√ *If you are only receiving merit aid (in other words, not need-based aid), your college should have a published policy for outside scholarships on its website. What you want is for the college to "stack" the outside scholarship on top of your merit aid from the college itself, so that you can get the full amount of both. Not all colleges will do this, however. You can try to lobby for scholarship stacking, but you will probably not be successful if the published policy states otherwise. If any other school to which you've been admitted with an equal offer (against the cost of attendance) agrees to stack the outside scholarship, make sure you get it in writing—then use that document in an appeal to keep the full amount of your outside scholarship at your first-choice school.*

SATISFACTORY ACADEMIC PROGRESS

The federal government will expect you to make regular progress toward receiving your degree. The school's course catalog (updated each semester or annually) will inform you of those requirements.

MERIT AID RENEWAL POLICY

Many colleges have minimum GPA requirements for scholarship renewal from year to year. They're typically listed on the letter offering you the aid. Know what the requirements are, and keep up that GPA.

SCHOOL-SPECIFIC POLICIES FOR PAYMENTS, INTEREST CHARGED, WITHDRAWAL FROM COURSES, AND REFUNDS

These policies, which are different at each college, will be listed on the colleges' individual websites and in their course catalogs. If you don't follow their policies, the fees can stack up, and prevent you from enrolling in your courses, or even graduating on time. Parents: Put the required dates on a calendar each semester, and give a copy to your child.

THE FINANCIAL AID TIMELINE

We've put together a time line of every single thing you could possibly do during the college admission process, from the beginning of your junior of high school to the day you enroll in college. You don't have to do all of it, but you should do most of it. Rip it out of the book, or print it out from our website, and tape it to your refrigerator or desk. Check things off, cross them out in red pen, or even use Wite-Out so that your tasks slowly disappear from the page—whatever you need to do!

Timeline	For Parents	For Students	What Chapter?
September–October, Junior Year	*Complete FAF-SA4caster, at fafsa4caster.ed.gov.* *Have a candid discussion with your spouse or former spouse about paying for college.* *Start making a plan to modify your budget.*	*Take PSAT or ACT Plan.* *Meet with high school counselor.* *Attend a college fair.*	*1, 2, 5*
November–January, Junior Year	*Have a family discussion about your Actual EFC.*	*Have a family discussion about paying for college.* *Start saving, get a part-time job, stash money away for college expenses. Get rid of your car?*	*3, 4, 5*

January–March, Junior Year	Help your child search for schools, and help him or her fill out our MAP and Cost-Conscious Search charts.	Search for colleges. Complete our MAP and Cost-Conscious Search charts.	6, 7
April–May, Junior Year	Revisit your conversation about paying for college. Are you on track? Have you had any major changes in your financial position? Look at the net prices you calculated using our Cost-Conscious chart in Chapter 7. Can you still afford that?	Take SAT and/or ACT.	4, 5, 7
June–August, Summer before Senior Year	Do some local college visits, if possible. (We recommend that you save your money, and don't go on expensive visits until your child is admitted.)	Sign up for FASTWEB.	9
September, Senior Year	Put important dates on your calendar.	Take SAT and/or ACT again, or take an SAT/ACT prep course. Build a calendar of admission and scholarship deadlines.	6, 7, 9

October, Senior Year	Make sure your child is organizing his or her admission materials correctly.	Attend college fairs. Use the MAP and Cost-Conscious Search charts again to narrow down your choices. Request applications, and fill them out. Update your deadline calendar.	6, 7, 9
November, Senior Year	File PROFILE for Early Decision Profile schools. Read your child's essays and review applications for accuracy. Send all materials via U.S. mail, receipt requested, to prove your child has met deadlines, if you're not using electronic applications.	File CSS PROFILE for Early Decision PROFILE schools. Retake the SAT and/or ACT. Fill out applications for admission. Check your deadline calendar. Keep copies of everything you send.	2, 8
December, Senior Year	Watch for admission and scholarship offers. (Many scholarship offers are sent immediately following admission.)	Watch for admission and scholarship offers. (Many schools send them electronically as e-mail or through a portal in their website.)	10

January, Senior Year	File federal taxes. File FAFSA (available January 1st).	File federal taxes. File FAFSA. Make sure you list the codes of all schools on your list. (You may list up to 10.) Complete scholarship competitions (applications and essays and referrals if necessary). Go to scholarship events/interviews at your colleges.	2, 8
February, Senior Year	Get that FAFSA submitted. (Many colleges send financial aid packages to students online.) Use the charts in Chapter 10 to track your child's offers.	Get that FAFSA submitted. Watch your e-mail for your admission letter and financial aid package. Use the charts in Chapter 10 to track your offers.	2, 8, 10
March, Senior Year	File your FAFSA immediately. (Many state deadlines are March 1st.) Immediately meet any requests for subsequent information for financial documentation.	File your FAFSA immediately. (Many state deadlines are March 1st.) Meet any requests for subsequent information for financial aid. Use the charts in Chapter 10 to track your offers.	2, 8, 10

April, Senior Year	Go to admitted student events and/or a private campus visit. Meet with financial aid officers to discuss the financial aid award. Pay your enrollment deposit (by May 1st.)	Go to admitted student events and/or a private campus visit. Meet with financial aid officers to discuss the financial aid award. Pay your enrollment deposit by May 1.	10
May, Senior Year	Pay your enrollment deposit by May 1st. Find out the payment options for your child's school. Many first payments are due in June. Deposits are refundable until May 1st, so pay early to get priority for housing and registration, if that is offered by your child's first choice school.	Pay your enrollment deposit by May 1. Go outside. Stop thinking about college.	
June, Senior Year	Pick dates for summer orientation, if possible.	Sign up for summer orientation, if possible.	

July, Summer before College	Apply for Parent PLUS loan. Get your child's immunization records from your doctor. Read Letting Go by Karen Levin Coburn and Madge Lawrence Treeger.	Apply for Direct Stafford loan. Contact your roommate as soon as you get the name. Submit your immunization form.	2, 3
August, Summer before College	Complete promissory notes. Have your child pay the bill. Take your child to college!	Complete promissory notes and electronic entrance counseling (required). Pay your bill. Enjoy move-in day, and get started!	

9

Merit Aid and the Application

Before you can get any aid, you do have to be admitted. This chapter outlines the basic steps you need to take for an efficient and low-stress application process, and how to tailor your applications to ensure that you're an excellent candidate for any and all merit aid dollars available.

Now that you've narrowed down to a list of schools where you can get funded, either using our MAP in Chapter 6, our Cost-Conscious Search chart in Chapter 7, or both, you're ready to send off applications.

You may be thinking that you'd like to visit before you apply; we recommend that you wait to visit until after you've applied and been accepted. As we've said before, visiting can mean falling in love—and you're not ready to say "I love you, College" just yet. Hold off on the declarations of forever and always until the college has made you an offer of admission, and hopefully given you a financial aid award.

How Many Colleges Should You Apply To?

We recommend that you apply to seven schools or less; certainly no more than 10. Even if you're applying online, using the colleges' own forms or the Common Application, applying to more than 10 schools is a waste of your time and money. If you've done your research, and you're between the 50th and 75th percentiles of applicants, you'll likely be accepted; it's not a game of chance, so you don't need to apply to every college on earth. We recommend that you apply to only two or three schools where you're only in the top 50 percent of applicants; you'll still get aid, but you may not get enough to make it affordable.

If your list is small, apply to at least three, if you can. We don't want you to leave all of your eggs in just one or two baskets, even if you're in the top 25 percent at each place.

There are several reasons why you should keep your applications between three and seven. The first, and most important, is for your own peace of mind. College applications are a fair amount of work, and each requires a different essay and supporting materials (even if they use the Common or Universal College Application). Each application should take you a few hours of effort or more. They'll also all have different deadlines and due dates. Don't you have enough to keep track of in your life? And really, if you're applying to more than 10 colleges, all you're doing is postponing the final decision. After all, you can only attend one.

Cost, too, is a factor. Many schools charge a processing fee when you're submitting paper applications instead of electronic ones, usually somewhere in the range of $25–$75.

For colleges that require the CSS PROFILE, you'll pay a fee to the College Board of $25 for the first college and $16 for each subsequent school. You'll need to submit your test scores to each school, which costs $10 per score for the fifth score and up for the SAT and ACT, and your school may charge you to send out transcripts.

Most colleges will ask you what other colleges you're applying to; the more you list, the less seriously they'll take your candidacy. This is serious business: If colleges see that you're applying to a set of schools that make no sense whatsoever, they'll question your ability to think critically and self-reflect. For example, a student who lists his or her application pool as the University of Chicago, Kettering University, Hollins College, the University of Florida, and West Point—schools that have very little in common with each other, and nothing in common as a whole—will automatically draw a few raised eyebrows in the admission office of any one of those schools. They'll wonder if you know anything about yourself, or if you bothered to do even one iota of research. You will, to be blunt, look like a flake. And maybe you *are* a flake (some people just are), but colleges certainly don't need to know that.

SHOULD YOU APPLY EARLY DECISION?

Early decision is binding. That means that if a college accepts you, you've already agreed to enroll. Early decision is perfect for your number-one choice, but only if you're absolutely sure you can afford it. So if you've done all the research you can, and you know, without a doubt, that you're not only in the top 25 percent of the class, but your other credentials are aligned with the college's values, and you would go there in a heartbeat, then yes. Go ahead. But if you can't assure yourself of any or all of those things, then use an early notification deadline; that will signal to the college that you're serious about enrolling. We recommend using early notification deadlines whenever possible, as long as they're not binding.

HOW DO YOU GET STARTED?

The absolute best way to begin is to make a paper calendar and a to-do list. You can certainly use Google Calendar as well, but we like paper calendars; most people find that they internalize the information more easily once you write it down by hand. Mark down application deadlines for each college (again, using as many non-binding early notification deadlines as possible), dates to arrange sending your test scores and transcripts (spring semester, if possible), and dates to request recommendations. You can also use Google Calendar; if you have a smart phone, you can set Google Calendar to beep your phone and remind you of all of your deadlines.

You'll send your SAT and ACT scores using *collegeboard.com* and *act.org*, and for your transcripts, you'll need to set up an appointment with your high school guidance counselor. If you take either test again, make sure you send those new scores (only if they're higher), no matter when you take it. A higher score—even if it's sent in during your spring semester of senior year—may allow the admission and financial aid office to increase your financial aid award.

HOW DO COLLEGES DECIDE WHO GETS IN?

Admitting any student is essentially a five-step process, beginning with the simplest method of evaluation colleges have: your academic credentials.

At each step, your application will move from one pile (or electronic folder) to the next. We cover the specifics later in this chapter, but we'd like to give you an outline of how we've admitted students in the past.

1. ACADEMIC CREDENTIALS

Many colleges will recalculate your GPA, creating a core GPA of only academic subjects, and will give you a weighted advantage for AP and Honors courses. They'll also assess your SAT and ACT scores. This is the first hurdle, and hopefully you've already assessed whether or not you can pass it with flying colors.

2. TALENTS, LEADERSHIP, INTERESTS, AND ACTIVITIES

Do you value what the college values? This ties back to the buzzwords we defined in Chapter 6. If you're an atheist who supports a woman's right to choose, for example, Bob Jones University will have absolutely no interest in you; conversely, Oberlin is less likely to be interested in an evangelical Christian who is a member of the NRA and junior supporter of the Tea Party. Openly gay or transgender peaceniks might not find comfort at the Naval Academy or any other military school, and ROTC kids who love structure may not find a home at Hampshire College, where there are no grades. You get the idea. A college whose values oppose your own may admit you, but they certainly won't waste a single dime encouraging you to attend.

3. CHARACTER AND VALUES

What do your references say about you? Are you a "good kid," or are you "one of the most sportsmanlike and gracious intramural athletes I've ever seen"? The more specific your recommendations can be, the better. Recommendation letters are always positive; yours should highlight what's special about you, not just what's good.

4. ADVOCACY

If there are more qualified applicants than a college needs to fill its freshman class, the admission officers will have a committee meeting, and discuss your case for admission (and/or aid). This is when your admission counselor can *really* help you. She or he will be your advocate, but will only support you as much as you enable her or him to. You've got to let your admission counselor get to know you! Respond to e-mails and answer her or his phone calls; often, she or he has the discretionary power to improve your merit aid by $1,000–$2,000 or more.

5. Demonstrated Interest in Attending

Is it clear that this college is one you would absolutely attend? Admission officers can smell ambivalence a million miles away—and you make it easier when you write on your application that this school is a second, third, or even fourth choice for you. If there's a space for it, always, always tell them that [College X] is your #1 choice. If the college gives you the best financial aid offer, it will be—it's not a lie, it's a conditional truth.

As you can see from this process, although grades are the first hurdle to surpass, intent and fit play a very large role. If you haven't used our MAP in Chapter 6, please go back and try to define the values of each school you're applying to. You'll need to remember those values for your application.

What Goes on Each Application?

In order to make it past hurdles #2 and #3, you'll need to make sure that you've highlighted the right activities (and garnered the most appropriate recommendations) for each college. Use our MAP from Chapter 6 to define each school, then make a list for each college that connects its values with your specific extracurriculars. *When you list your activities, talents, interests, and extracurriculars on each application, make sure that the activities that align best with the college's values are at the top of each section.* Order is a tricky thing; it signals rank, importance, and intent, without *technically* doing so. Admission officers are human, just like anyone else; they'll see an extracurricular at the top of a page, and assume it's either something you're incredibly passionate about, something you absolutely excelled in, or both.

Example: Susie Senior's Applications

Remember Susie Senior from Chapter 6? Well, Susie, a resident of California, is applying to several different kinds of schools up and down the West Coast. She doesn't know what she'd like to major in, but she poked around, and created her MAP with the following colleges and the data she collected about their top 25 percent.

	GPA	SAT Verbal	SAT Math	ACT	Buzzwords	Chance of Funding?
Susie Senior	3.62	730	650	31		
Whittier	3.59	580	590	25	Creative, community, scholar, fitness	Y
Evergreen State College	3.6	640	590	26	Green/sustainability, outdoorsy, creative	Y
Lewis & Clark	3.9	710	680	30		N
Pomona	3.95	780	770	34		N
University of Puget Sound	3.8	680	680	32		N
UC Berkeley	3.95	710	760	NR		N
Otis College of Art and Design	3.6	560	590	24	Creative, community, socially active	Y

Now, Susie has an absolutely amazing sheet of extracurriculars, but she's not at the top of her class. We're guessing that she's a lot like you: active, engaged, and smart. Susie is someone who is better at actively *doing* than taking tests and getting perfect grades. And if she'd like to apply to either Lewis & Clark, Puget Sound, or UC Berkeley, she *may* get enough in aid because of her spectacular extracurriculars—but her grades alone won't guarantee that, which is why she marked **N**s for those colleges. Susie needs a guarantee; she absolutely needs a scholarship. And she doesn't stand a chance of getting merit aid at Pomona, although she could certainly get admitted.

Susie defined those buzzwords by looking at those colleges' websites. She's going to make sure that on each of her applications to Whittier, Evergreen, and Otis, her activities line up with what they're looking for. When Susie profiled herself, this is what she came up with:

Category	Description	Buzzwords	Points
Leadership Experiences	Led a canoeing trip in the Boundary Waters	Outdoorsy	5
	President of my High School Secular Humanist's Society	Community, Spirituality	5
	Led a team of my peers in a 5k charity run	Socially Active, Service	4
	Organized the Spring Fling	Socially Active, Creative	3
	Helped bus elderly people to a local election	Service, Socially Active, Politically Aware	3
Activities: Sports, Clubs, Performing Arts	Member of the Snowboarding Club	Fitness, Outdoorsy	2
	Member of the Golf Team	Fitness, Outdoorsy	3
	Member of "Students for a Better World" recycling program	Socially Active, Green	3
	Member of Mock Trial	Career-oriented	4

	Member of GSA or GBLT	Diverse	3
	Mathlete, 2 years	Math, Scholar	4
	Write a style blog that documents my high school classmates	Socially Active, Technologically Savvy	5
Honors and Awards, Recognitions	Class President	Career-Oriented, Politically Active, Socially Active	5
	2nd place, State Science Fair	Science, Scholar	5
	3rd place, Regional Track and Field Championships, Javelin	Fitness	5
	Recipient of $400 Arts Grant from my town	Creative	5
Community Involvement, Service, Volunteer Work	Volunteered at a local Children's Hospital, read to inpatients	Service	4
	Play bridge with my grandmother and her friends twice a month	Service, Socially Active	3
Paid Work	Sandwich delivery, after school, 15 hours per week	Business Experience	3
	Sell my handmade jewelry at art fairs 4 times per year	Entrepreneurship, Creative	5

For Whittier, a former Quaker but now secular college, which values creativity (its mascot is the Poets), community (its website stresses paired and team-taught coursework), scholars (the website emphasizes leaning and engagement), and fitness (those Poets play a lot of sports), Susie's going to make sure that she lists the following experiences at the top of each category:

- √ *President of her High School Secular Humanist's Society.*
- √ *Mathlete.*
- √ *State Science Fair.*
- √ *Regional Track and Fitness Championships.*
- √ *Arts grant recipient.*
- √ *Handmade jewelry sales.*

Even though these aren't necessarily Susie's most stand-out experiences—class president is certainly a very big deal—listing them first shows that Susie *valued and cared about those experiences the most.* Admission officers won't disregard what's listed underneath them; they will still take your entire résumé into account. But Susie is sending a message to Whittier that she cares about what they care about—even if she wasn't always the "best."

For Evergreen State College, which values the outdoors, green/sustainability, and creativity, Susie will make sure the following experiences are at the top of each category:

- √ *Canoeing trip in the Boundary Waters.*
- √ *"Students for a Better World" recycling.*
- √ *Golf team.*
- √ *Snowboarding club.*
- √ *Arts grant recipient.*
- √ *Handmade jewelry sales.*

And finally, for Otis College of Art and Design, an arts school that values creativity, community-minded, and socially active students, she'll highlight:

- √ *Arts grant recipient.*
- √ *Style blog.*

√ *Class president.*

√ *Handmade jewelry sales.*

√ *President of her High School Secular Humanist's Society.*

√ *Spring Fling.*

Just as Susie did, you'll want to highlight the experiences and activities that make you the best possible match for each school. Try using a few colored pencils on your personal profile—Green for College A, Blue for College B, and so on—and circle the experiences that work best for each school.

Don't be afraid to really redefine your paid work experiences, as well. If you've had an after-school job, think about what kind of business it was (retail? service?), what you learned about the product, and how it altered or enhanced your own character. Paid work experiences are wonderful material for your personal statement, too.

You'll also want to tailor your recommendations for each school, if you can. For the activities that align most closely with each school, find out if you can get a recommendation from the faculty advisor or adult who led your group. What would Susie do? Well, for Whittier, Susie would ask for recommendations from the faculty advisor for the Secular Humanist's society, and possibly the town official who oversaw her $400 Arts grant, or the Mathlete coach. For Evergreen, Susie would focus on her group from the Boundary Waters; she could get a group letter from them, detailing her leadership, and ask either of her coaches from the Golf team or Snowboarding club to write not just about her athletic prowess, but her behavior as a teammate. For Otis, Susie would want to get an amazing letter from the town official that oversaw her $400 Arts grant, any faculty advisor that oversaw her style blog, and the faculty advisor for the Spring Fling dance committee.

Working those two angles—highlighting the right experiences and tailoring your recommendations—are absolutely the best ways to ensure that your application gets considered for the best merit aid available. But when it comes to the application, there's always more. We'll keep it brief; there are dozens of books out there about how to write an outstanding application. But you've *got* to know the basics and what mistakes to avoid, no matter what. Read on for our application basics, and skip to the end of the chapter if you're looking for ways to supplement your application, go the extra mile, or address slip-ups in an extra essay.

THE PERFECT APPLICATION: COMMON MISTAKES AND HOW TO AVOID THEM

The biggest mistakes that students make are really, really simple ones, and they usually fall into one of two categories: misspelling the name of the school, your own name, or anything else on the application; and sending the wrong materials to the wrong school. When Ruth was an admission counselor at Gustavus, they used to get about a dozen essays for St. Olaf annually—because students put their essays in the wrong envelopes. If you can't get the basics right, your admission counselor won't be able to advocate for you very effectively. Don't do this. Make sure that everything goes to the right place. We like to use color-coded Post-its to make sure that we don't misplace anything.

For spelling, you've got to check, double-check, and check a third time. You're asking admission officers not only to admit you to a competitive academic program, but to give you money as well. Don't give them any excuse to pass you over (or an opportunity to advocate for someone else). When it comes to grammar, you *must* have someone else read your work. We've all had times when the sentence at hand seemed clear as day to us, but completely muddled to someone else—but we've become sentence-blind, so to speak, and we can't see it. Watch out for misplaced modifiers and double entendres. Carol remembers vividly a girl who wrote an essay about her volunteer work in Africa where she proudly told us she "treated wounds in the bush," which may be an acceptable colloquialism in Australia, but certainly not in the United States. Seemingly simple yes-and-no/either-or questions can also get easily confused. For example, if the application asks about sex instead of gender, the correct answer is M or F, not, as we once saw, "only once, in Duluth."

Essays and short answers on your admission materials are *not* the right moments to try to expand your vocabulary. It is especially not the time to use archaic or obsolete terms just to demonstrate that you can a) use a thesaurus, and b) spell them correctly. If you volunteer every two weeks with Habitat for Humanity, say just that—don't say that you "go on a fortnightly basis." Or if you come from a big family, say that—don't go with capacious, colossal, or commodious. We're not saying that you should be casual, but you don't need to beat the admission office over the head with your club of $10 SAT words. It looks ridiculous, and more often than not students display how *poorly* they understand language, instead of how well. You do not want to be the student whose essay or short answer is read aloud at lunch to provide some cheap laughs for the admission office (and yes, every admission officer does that now and again).

If you're sending in a paper application (which we don't recommend; there's almost always an additional fee, and most schools have free electronic apps), do not use glitter, stickers, colored markers, photo collages, or anything else that you wouldn't use when applying for a job. This will make your admission officer either throw your application in the trash, or simply refuse to advocate for you. No one likes a glitter bomb in a manila envelope, confetti, or scratch-and-sniff stickers. No smiley faces or doodling in the margins; no calligraphy or cursive. Use pencil, have someone double- and triple-check for accuracy, then rewrite in blue or black pen, and write clearly, in print.

THE PERSONAL STATEMENT AND/OR THE ESSAY

Remember that, just as you did with your extracurriculars and activities, you should tailor your personal statement to each school. Let's take a look at what Susie Senior would do:

√ *For Whittier, Susie would focus on her scholarly achievements—perhaps what it's really like to be a girl in the Mathletes, or how Secular Humanism reflects longstanding religious tenets from all cultures (just without a godhead).*

√ *For Evergreen State College, Susie would focus on her commitment to the outdoors, starting perhaps with an anecdote from her canoeing trip, or her recycling club.*

√ *For Otis, Susie would highlight her most creative pursuits, and how she's brought them to the public sphere. That could draw from her experience applying for her Arts grant, selling her jewelry, or even decorating the Spring Fling dance.*

No matter what you end up focusing on for your statement or personal essay, you'll want to capture the reader's attention, and maybe even allow him or her to feel the emotion of the moment. The most powerful essay

Ruth ever read, for example, came to Agnes Scott College from a young woman who wrote about her family's escape from Thailand. They fled in the middle of the night, and she described each detail of the journey: hurrying along the streets toward the shore, getting into a tiny boat, and floating for days until a larger boat rescued them. They had no water, no food, no restrooms—just fear and a hot sun all day, and a cold moon all night. It was the description of the cold moon that really got to Ruth; she didn't feel sorry for the girl, or pity her. She just felt as though she knew something *real* about her. Ruth could picture a tiny, dark-haired little girl staring at a big moon on the ocean. And she knew without a doubt that she wanted to admit a person who would share something so big, and so real, with a total stranger.

This doesn't mean you need to mine the depths of your worst experiences, or manufacture one. You just need to share something that really mattered to you—and try to keep a modicum of perspective when you do so. Another applicant Ruth had, for example, wrote an entire essay on how the death of her pet turtle was the most impactful moment of her life. It wasn't a metaphor; it wasn't a complex allusion to contemporary politics; it was literally just an essay about the loss of her reptile. It wasn't funny. She didn't sell it, or make it real. To Ruth, it seemed like the girl was simply saying "Here is my essay about something sad that happened.... That's what you want, right?" And it's not about the sad, although sad moments can be great material; it's about finding the moments or experiences you can really, truly describe.

The best way to become a more effective writer is to read, read, read, and read some more. Devour as many nonfiction essays as you can before you write your own statements; they'll inspire you, teach you, guide you, and entertain you. For great contemporary nonfiction essays, we recommend checking out the archives of the *New Yorker* magazine online at *newyorker.com*. As of this writing, they're free to access. We also love *Granta*, a literary journal available from your local library, and Timothy McSweeney's Internet Tendency at *mcsweeneys.net* (where you can also find information about 826 Valencia's free writing and tutoring centers, located in many major cities), and we're also very partial to *Consider the Lobster*, a collection of essays by the late David Foster Wallace.

"Why I'm Interested in University X"

You might be asked to detail exactly why it is that you'd like to attend University X. A general statement that could be applied to all the places you are applying to, such as "I want a strong liberal arts program with the opportunity for study abroad" is not nearly as persuasive as one that directly addresses the attributes of the school you are applying to. For example, "I am very interested in the possibility of double majoring in math and music, and St. Olaf's strengths in those programs, as well as the curricular structure that allows for double majoring, are a perfect fit. Added to that is the opportunity to do a year-long study abroad combining the two and to participate in the sustainability initiatives on campus" is much more convincing. Get specific, and don't worry about BS-ing a little bit; you have the right to change your mind once you get on campus, and no one is going to hold you to the statements you make on your application.

Also reference any personal interactions you might have had with the campus, admission counselors, alumni, or staff and faculty members. Again, this lets the campus know that you're truly interested—not just sending off one of three dozen applications.

SUPPLEMENTING THE APPLICATION: WHAT THEY DON'T ASK FOR, BUT WOULD LOVE TO SEE

Remember: Admission officers are human beings, just like anyone else. Cover letters are great; if you can attach an additional document, or print it out and forward it to the admission office. If you've got a portfolio to submit, do so electronically; burn it to a disc (make sure everything is converted to a PDF) and mail it in. For video of any kind, post it on YouTube or Vimeo, send a link with a description of the video, and make sure it doesn't connect to anything ridiculous or inappropriate. What constitutes the "ridiculous"? Well, for example, Carol's son and his friends built a potato gun in high school, and liked to take pictures of themselves shooting spuds into the river. Thankfully, this was in the days before Facebook and YouTube, but ridiculous things also include:

√ *Personal video diaries.*

√ *Anything where you swear or use profane language.*

√ *Images or video of you doing anything illegal.*

If you have to ask, it's not appropriate.

Make sure your profile on any social networking website is clean and appropriate, and that links don't have metatitles that include profane or inappropriate language.

For charity work, art projects, essays, or class projects that include a written description or file, attach it to the electronic application (if possible) as a Word doc or RTF file, or burn it to a CD and mail it in.

Anything that gets mailed in additionally should include a handwritten note, in blue or black ink, that states the following:

> Please consider the attached project, my [charity work, art project, video essay, class project, etc.], as a supplement to my application. Thank you for taking the time to add it to my file.
>
> Best,
>
> [Your name]
>
> [Your address]
>
> [Your high school]
>
> [Your e-mail or application #, if applicable.]

If you do get the chance to meet with an admission officer, faculty member, or alumni for an interview, always, always, always send a handwritten thank-you note, thanking the person for his or her time, and try to include a personalized comment about how much you enjoyed your conversation or interview. We're serious about this. Students rarely send them any more, and it will absolutely help you to stand out. But remember: No glitter, no smiley faces, no stickers, and no swearing.

ADDRESSING SLIP-UPS IN AN EXTRA ESSAY (TRUST US, IT'S WORTH DOING!)

If you had one of those semesters in high school during which you messed up left and right, you may be thinking about trying to sweep it under the rug. *Don't*. Just like any corporate disaster or malfeasance (BP, anyone?), the worst thing you can do is stonewall and pretend it didn't happen.

Your best option is to demonstrate your maturity, and address it head-on in a separate essay or letter. Sometimes there are good excuses, like your health, or that of a family member; sometimes, people just make bad decisions. *Everyone* makes mistakes, and admission officers have seen them all. Whatever it is, own up to it, and try to address what you've learned from it.

For family issues, lay them out. Be completely direct and honest, even—perhaps especially—with the ones that are embarrassing and painful. Mom in prison? Dad in rehab? Did your younger sister pull a Bristol Palin, and now there's a baby in the house? Think of this letter as an opportunity to demonstrate maturity; you're not looking for pity, just understanding. Believe us, everyone's got family problems, and your admission officer will likely empathize with you.

For your own personal bad choices, there's a whole range. Some of the most common slip-ups include the following:

√ *Low-impact course selection (aka slacked off). Does it look as if you're taking the senoritis train to Lazytown? If you are, own up to it. If not—if, for example, you've exhausted all the tougher courses—then explain that.*

√ *Chose extracurriculars over academics. Susie Senior loves her extracurriculars, and her grades suffered as a result. Or maybe Susie just recognized that her strengths don't always lie in a classroom. Talk about the choices you've made, and try to advocate for yourself.*

√ *Ignored your DARE class, and smoked yourself right off the golf team. If you've made some really bad choices and wound up tossed off a team or extracurricular, then be up front about it. Explain what you did, or maybe even why you thought (or didn't think at all) it was a good idea at the time, and what you've learned as a result. You don't need to spout 12-step rhetoric to prove you're off the pot or spiced rum or whatever it was; just be honest, and emphasize that you understand that drugs or illegal substances interfered with your education, and that you won't let it happen ever again.*

If colleges ask for *anything* else—like a seventh-semester transcript, letter of recommendation from a math teacher (because of that D in your junior year, for example), or an additional writing sample—comply ASAP. If you can't return anything on time, your admission counselor will not be impressed.

Before you send off your applications, make sure that you have a qualified adult—like a teacher or your high school guidance counselor—look at your application and any additional materials you might be sending in.

Once you're done with your applications, take a month (or two) off. Just relax. You don't need to take any more steps (including visiting) until you've been accepted.

10

MAKING THE CHOICE: AN APPLES-TO-APPLES COMPARISON

Congratulations! You've been accepted to more than one place, and now you've got to choose. If you've got the time and the inclination, we do recommend visiting. An on-campus visit not only allows you to make the final gut decision about your preferences, but often allows you to connect with the financial aid office, and possibly appeal for a higher aid award. But before you take that step, you've got to look at your aid offers and do the math to figure out what each school will actually cost you.

Don't just accept the first offer you receive; wait to hear from each school. You have until May 1st to decide. No need to jump the gun; collect all your aid offers together, and then use the following charts to understand what they mean.

In nearly every chapter, we've discussed the COA (cost of attendance). All colleges report their COA to College Navigator (*nces.ed.gov/collegenavigator*), and most will list their COA on their own websites as well. The COA is the absolute largest estimate that the college could make about how much each year will cost you. The COA includes direct costs (tuition, room and board, and fees) as well as books, spending money, travel costs, and other personal expenses. Although direct costs are generally outside of your control, you *do* have a fair amount of power over how you manage your other costs: books, spending money, travel costs, and personal expenses. You can choose to have a $4 on-campus latte every day, or not; you can choose to buy new or used books; or take a bus, plane, or carpool home for school holidays. A review we conducted of College Navigator shows that colleges estimate those other costs at anywhere from $700 to $4,100, and in order to *really* understand where your various aid offers stand, you've got to parse those "other" costs from the actual direct costs.

You'll also need to remember that the self-help you've been "awarded"—loans and work study—is optional. You don't have to take on the full amount of loans; you can choose to take on any amount.

The absolute simplest way to understand what each school "really" costs is to make a chart, comparing each school's direct costs and aid offers. You can find each school's direct costs at College Navigator, on its own website, or, sometimes, on your aid award itself.

Here's an example. We've included blank charts for you. Feel free to enter one college in "College E" to get the hang of it, and then fill out your own chart once you've got a handle on the math.

Direct Costs	College A	College B	College C	College D	College E
Tuition + Fees	40,004	31,760	24,300	17,616	
Room + Board	10,480	7,900	6,700	7,444	
Total Direct Costs	50,484	39,660	31,000	25,060	

Less Funded Aid (not including loans	18,000	15,000	15,000	8,000	
= Net Direct Price	32,484	24,660	16,000	17,060	—

In this case, Susie Senior and her family can expect to pay $32,484 at College A, and $17,060 at College D, with a spread in between. But that's not the whole story. This chart doesn't break down the ways your family is planning to pay, and doesn't include the student's contribution. We also haven't calculated what you'll spend on those "other" costs. Next, we'll calculate the total cost of attendance with both direct costs and other costs, and determine what you and your family can afford to pay out of pocket.

	College A	College B	College C	College D	College E
Net Direct Price	32,484	24,660	16,000	17,060	—
Books/ supplies	1,100	1,080	1,400	980	
Personal spending	700	1,200	1,200	850	
Travel/ transport	1,000	500	500	500	
Total Costs	35,284	27,440	19,100	19,390	
Parent Payment					
From income	6,000	6,000	6,000	6,000	

From savings	5,000	5,000	5,000	5,000	
Student Payment					
From savings/ summer	5,000	5,000	5,000	5,000	
Total payments	16,000	16,000	16,000	16,000	
Costs – Payments = Gap	19,284	11,440	3,100	3,390	

We've given different costs for different colleges, based on location, travel, and cost of living. When you complete this chart, do the following:

√ Estimate books and supplies using the college's own data, posted on its website.

√ Have a discussion about personal spending, and what's acceptable for the nine-month school year. You can also use the college's own estimates, although you certainly don't have to. For College A and College D, we're assuming Susie Senior's got a relative in the area, who can cook her the occasional home-cooked meal and give her rides; for B and C, where she doesn't have family, she's all on her own.

√ Estimate your own travel costs using a flight aggregator site like Kayak.com, Amtrak.com for train prices, and Greyhound.com. Use the lowest price point possible.

The gap that you've calculated here is what you'll need to cover annually with loans and work-study. Remember: Before you take on *any* loans, you'll need to do the math for all four years, and calculate your repayment. Please see Chapter 3 for more information. After you've determined how much you'd be willing to take in loans, you'll need to look at your individual aid awards, and determine what you're eligible for at each college, using the following chart:

How to Meet the Gap	College A	College B	College C	College D	College E
Gap Amount	19,284	11,440	3,100	3,390	
Student Direct Loan	5,500	5,500	3,100	3,390	
Student Work Study	2,500	3,000	0	0	
Other sources	0	0	0	0	
Total	8,000	8,500	3,100	0	
Disparity	11,284	2,940	0	0	

Remember that you don't have to enter *all* the loans you're eligible for; you may also enter the amount of loans you're *willing* to take on. You should understand the *total* amount of the loan over four years, which includes interest, and what your monthly payments should be, if you haven't already. Go to *Finaid.org* and use its loan calculator to discover the total loan amount, and calculate your monthly payments. If there's still a disparity, and the school in question is a college you'd really like to attend, consider either upping your loans, asking your parents to take out a Parent PLUS loan (see Chapter 5), or appealing, either now or when you visit. We discuss the appeal and the visit later in this chapter.

Here's a set of blank charts. If you run out of room, just re-create them on a sheet of scratch paper.

STEP 1: CALCULATE DIRECT COSTS USING COLLEGE NAVIGATOR

Direct Costs	College A	College B	College C	College D	College E
Tuition + Fees					
Room + Board					
Total Direct Costs					
Less Funded Aid (not including loans					
= Net Direct Price					

STEP 2: CALCULATE OTHER COSTS AND OUT-OF-POCKET PAYMENT AND GAP

	College A	College B	College C	College D	College E
Net Direct Price					
Books/ Supplies					
Personal Spending					

Travel/ Transport					
Total Costs					
Parent Payments					
From income					
From savings					
Student Payments					
From savings/ summer					
Total Payments					
Costs– Payments = Gap					

STEP 3: CALCULATE LOANS, WORK STUDY, AND THE FINAL DISPARITY

How to Meet the Gap	College A	College B	College C	College D	College E
Gap Amount					
Student Direct Loan					

Student Work Study					
Other sources					
Total					
Disparity					

APPEALING YOUR FINANCIAL AID AWARD

Not all colleges will accept or process an appeal, but it doesn't hurt to ask. When they *do* process an appeal, it's usually for one of two reasons: You've had a demonstrable change in your financial circumstances since the filing of the FAFSA, or you have a better offer from another school that they may be willing to match or exceed. When we say "match," we mean that you're asking for your award to be adjusted to match the final net price. In order to appeal, you'll have to contact the financial aid office directly. There may be instructions about this on your aid award paperwork, but if not, you should e-mail.

Your aid award should include the contact information for your financial aid officer, or the office itself. If it doesn't, contact the admission office, and let them know that you'd like to file an appeal of your aid award. If you have a reason (job loss since the filing of the FAFSA or any other family emergency), say so. It's also possible that you've received a better aid award from another school, and you'd like to know if the college in question can match it. The best way to do this is through e-mail; use the following templates. We've got two here. One is for a documented family financial loss, and one is for award comparison. Obviously, you should only appeal to your first-choice college.

FOR A DOCUMENTED FINANCIAL LOSS OR OTHER CIRCUMSTANCE

Dear [Admission or Financial Aid Office/r, whatever contact you have available],

I was thrilled to receive my offer of admission and aid award from [College X], and I would very much like to accept. However, I would like to file an appeal of my financial aid award. As of [insert date], our family financial circumstances have changed due to [job loss, medical emergency, or other financial issue]. I am willing and able to document this, and I am very committed to enrolling in [College X], but cannot do so without a financial aid award adjustment. Would it be possible to file an appeal, or ask for a review of my award? Again, I am fully committed to enrolling, and I would be heartbroken if I was not able to accept your offer of admission.

Thank you for your time and assistance.

Best,

[Your name and contact information]

FOR AID OFFER MATCHING

Dear [Admission or Financial Aid Office/r, whatever contact you have available],

I was thrilled to receive my offer of admission and aid award from [College X], and I would very much like to accept. However, I have received another, larger offer from [College Y], and although [College X] is still my first choice, my family cannot afford to enroll me. Would you consider increasing my aid so that my net price is the same as [College Y]? Again, I am fully committed to enrolling and [College X] is my number one choice, and I would be heartbroken if I was not able to accept your offer of admission and enroll. I've included a photocopy of [College Y]'s offer. Please let me know what you require on our end for additional documentation.

Thank you for your time and assistance.

Best,

[Your name and contact information]

NOTE: Do not forget to include a photocopy of the offer from College Y.

APPEALING AFTER YOU VISIT

If possible, you may want to consider appealing after you've visited. Visiting will serve two purposes; it will:

√ *Allow you to discover where you really, really want to go.*

√ *Allow you to connect in person with admission, the financial aid office, and faculty members.*

Don't underestimate the power of a personal connection! Although you can't force it, if you can get an admission officer or financial aid officer on your side, you may be more successful in your appeal.

Read on for more information about the visit, and how you may be able to make a personal contact.

THE CAMPUS VISIT

The visit can be the number-one deciding factor for most families, and can often influence decisions about cost and loan burdens. Because of this, we recommend that you *first* calculate where you're getting the best offer, and *then* set up a visit. This will prevent you from falling in love with a college you cannot afford.

College campuses are electric. There's something to be said for the simple effect of putting a bunch of quick-thinking minds in the same geographic space; it's exciting in a way that the working world is not. There's a real energy to a campus, and that energy is different at each one. Although it's possible (and certainly easiest) to visit on a weekend, we don't recommend it, because students won't actively be going to class. You want to see the campus as it is during the week. The best possible time to visit is on a weekday, when school is in session.

We recommend that you take at least one parent with you, and plan as far in advance as you can. One of your parents may need to take a personal day from his or her job. You'll want to prepare a list of questions for the college, or just use one of our favorite resources, "A Pocket Guide to Choosing a College," from the National Survey of Student Engagement. It's available for free, in English or in Spanish, from *nsse.iub.edu*, and all of the questions are great ones. Bring a notebook with you so you can write down the answers, and collect contact information from the people you meet with.

You'll also want to consider the costs of the visit. Can you drive? Bus? Train? Will you need to stay overnight in a hotel? Often, colleges offer an overnight for prospective students, where you can bunk with a current freshman or sophomore. We *highly* recommend an overnight. They're so fun, and they allow you to *really* connect with the student body. But if your parent is accompanying you or there's no overnight on offer, he or she is not going to want to sleep in a dorm room. Most colleges will make prospy (prospective student) deals with local hotels or motels; check the website or call the admission office to find out what those offers might be. If not, we recommend using kayak.com, a flight and hotel aggregator, or lastminutedeals.com, a hotel discounting site whose packages often include airfare and/or a rental car, or simply calling the hotel in question and inquiring about a prospective student rate. Many hotels—particularly those in large college towns—will have package deals for prospective students and their families. (Parents: If your child's going to be there for four years, they want your business!)

For each campus visit, be prepared to spend:

√ *Gas, train, or airfare to get you to and from.*

√ *A taxi to and from the airport, if necessary.*

√ *Meals. Most colleges will spot you at least one meal in the dining halls, but for the others, you've got to be prepared.*

Don't spend your money on:

√ *Merchandise! Oh, those bookstores with their overpriced Hanes sweatshirts are so enticing. But you might not have made your final decision yet—or received your final offer. Are you really ready to commit to that $55 sweatshirt?*

You've generally got two options for a campus visit: a group visit or a private visit.

THE GROUP VISIT

All schools host "group visit" or "campus visit" days that are open to everyone, and include just about everything you can think of. They're usually held on weekday holidays, such as Veterans' Day or MLK Day, which is a wonderful advantage for travel. The drawback? School's not in session, and although the group visit is almost overwhelmingly informative, there's little to no personal attention.

Here's a sample of what a group visit might entail:

9:00: Welcome speech! Often, the President of the college will greet you.

9:15: Faculty speech. Colleges love to show off their top dogs. This is usually pretty entertaining.

9:30: The Dean of Admission will probably give you a marketing speech that will differentiate the college from the competition. He or she will tell you what "makes them different," without giving specific comparisons to other schools.

9:45: The Director of Admission will give you the nitty gritty about the application process.

10:00: Students and parents will split up. Students head to a student-only discussion, which is always fun and very candid. It's often the best part of the talking heads lineup, and your parents are out of the room. Now is the time to ask about where the best parties are.

Parents will head to a separate panel. Ask the tough questions, about safety, security, and on-campus healthcare Colleges are required by a federal law, the Cleary Act, to provide actual crime statistics. You should be able to get a brochure about crime statistics in print, or online. Obviously, they don't put this brochure in your visit packet; you've got to ask for it.

11:00: Campus tour, led by trained current students.

12:00: Lunch, probably in one of the dining halls. If it's catered, that's a sign that the food may be terrible, so ask your student host about the dining halls.

1:00: Concurrent programs. Divide and conquer with your parent(s). These should include:

√ Financial aid.

√ Career service.

√ International education/Study abroad.

√ Housing.

√ Special programs (Honors Program, etc.)

2:30: Individual appointments in Admission and Financial Aid. If this isn't offered, ask for it in advance of your visit. Some schools won't take individual appointments on group visit days. If that's the case, skip the group visit, and go for a private visit, on another day. On a professional note, we consider this lousy customer service, and it may be a symptom of a pervasive attitude at the institution.

That's a typical schedule for a group visit, and it's a great plan for a school that may not be your first choice. Your parents usually won't have to take off work to attend, and you won't have to take off school. However, we really recommend, for your top two or even three choices, that you set up a private visit. All colleges offer private visits, and they're the ideal way to see the campus. They're all about you, not just a song-and-dance lineup for the masses. The only drawback is that you, and your parents, will have to take off a weekday.

THE PRIVATE VISIT

The itinerary of a private visit may look like this:

9:00: You'll arrive at the admission office, and have a general session or interview with the admission counselor assigned to you. You're interviewing them, and they're interviewing you. Ask good questions; as we mentioned earlier, we love the "Pocket Guide to Choosing a College," from the National Survey of Student Engagement. It's available for free, in English or in Spanish, from *nsse.iub. edu.* If you ask good questions, you'll impress them. Take notes, and be attentive, respectful, and polite. It's isn't more complex than that, despite what other books might tell you. We recommend that you meet alone with the admission counselor, and ask your parents to wait outside. It'll give you a chance to shine, and also give your parents an opportunity to ask their own questions.

10:00: Individual campus tour with a student.

11:00: You'll likely sit in on a class. Choose something you're interested in!

12:00: Lunch with a current student.

1:00: You'll meet with a financial aid officer.

2:00: You'll meet with other campus specialists (coaches, music faculty, etc.)

3:00: You'll have an exit interview with your admission counselor. If you need to appeal your award, we actually recommend that you don't bring this up now. Wait a few days, send a handwritten thank-you note, and then follow up with a written request for an aid appeal a week or two later. The counselor will remember you and won't feel blindsided.

If the admission dean or director comes out to greet you—just to say "Hello," or "Welcome"—that's a great sign. It means the college is really interested in *you*.

Hopefully, you'll be able to narrow down your options, by figuring out the final net price, your loans and work study, and making a visit to campus. We've helped you figure out the cost; the rest of the decision is up to you and your family. But sometimes, things don't work out the way you want them to.

If you're not able to appeal a truly unhelpful aid award, or you simply can't afford any of your options, don't panic. It's not going to be the end of the world if you don't go to college right away—and if you take an extra year, either at a community college or working and volunteering, you might be able to bring down the price at your college of choice if you re-apply as a stronger applicant. Read the next chapter to find out more.

11

An Intentional Alternative Plan

If you crunched the numbers in Chapter 10 and discovered that you'll have to take on an excess of $8,000 per year in student loans in order to go to college, it's time to think again. If you can't meet our $8K Debt Challenge, you likely cannot afford to go to college this fall. Sure, the *loans* are there; there are eager lenders on every single college website, popping up through insidious little boxes like the "SimpleTuition" ads on the Princeton Review, showing up in your in-box, and, yes, still through the U.S. mail. But unless you're planning on majoring in math or one of the hard sciences (and there's *absolutely no way* you'll change your mind or major), you're at a statistical disadvantage; your risk will likely garner no reward. By taking on more debt than you'll be able to repay, all you're doing is handicapping yourself. We *promise* you that's the truth. We can't stress it enough. If you haven't read Chapter 3, please go back and take a look.

If you're from a family background that isn't financially stable, you might think that taking on college debt will be your ticket to security. But if you exceed $8K in student debt per year, you could end up in worse shape than you've ever been. Instead of an express elevator to the top floor, your debt will be a cartoon anvil attached to your ankle. It'll pull you out the window and down 25 stories into the street. College, for now, may have to remain a dream instead of a reality.

Before you collapse at the kitchen table with an uncontrollable sob, hear us out: We've got an (intentional) alternative plan for you to consider.

There are dozens of reasons that you could be unable to meet out $8K Debt Challenge, but we're guessing they fall into one of two categories:

√ *Your academic credentials didn't make the cut. You got senioritis…or junioritis, or sophomoritis, or freshmanitis. Whatever it was, at some point, you stopped caring about your grades, or you weren't able to do very well on the SAT or ACT. And we understand: High school is boring. Sitting in an uncomfortable chair for eight hours a day, reading thoroughly dull textbooks is no way to learn (although it's not as though we have a better solution for public education), and some students are just better at sucking it up and running the gauntlet than others. That's really what getting through high school is about: endurance. Not ability; not IQ; not natural talent—straight-up endurance. And if you got lazy or slacked off, your grades probably suffered, and so did your test scores.*

√ *Or, you've applied to colleges where your credentials only qualified you for admission—but not for any merit aid. In other words, you weren't even close to being the best, or one of the best, in the class.*

Your life starts *now*. You're about to have a fresh start. Get ready to embrace it—even if it's not at your dream school just yet.

We're so sorry to tell you that you can't go to college this fall; we can almost see your face through the pages, and your parents' faces as they read this chapter—perhaps reflecting on their own debt, and wondering how they can break the news to you. But this is *not* the worst thing in the world. It will actually be wonderful for you. Just wait, and you'll see. Our intentional alternative plan is actually kind of fun.

Tomorrow morning (or whenever the next business day is), wake up and call the admission officer at your top three choices—the ones you can't afford. Tell that admission officer that you simply can't afford to start as a freshman, but you're going to go to your local community college for the next year or two, *starting this summer.* Yes, we mean this summer, as in the one after you graduate from high school. Look on the bright side: At least you won't have to work as much—and some of your classmates will be doing the same exact thing. Ask that admission officer to send you a list of exactly what community colleges it takes credit from, and for what courses. Ask if the college gives scholarships to transfer students, and find out what GPA you'll need to qualify for one. You'll need to make a plan; you will need to think about each class you enroll in. And you're going to live at home, without a car. Get rides. Take the bus. Get a bicycle (they're really good for you)! If you have a car, you're going to sell it. "Well," you might be thinking, "How am I going to get to work?"

You'll take the bus to work, just like millions of people without cars do. But you're not going to work very much; at most, you should work 10–15 hours a week at a part-time job. Why? Because you're going to be devoting most of your energy to getting an A in every single course that you take at a community college, and you're going to ask your parents to help you.

If you've slacked off in high school, they likely slacked off with you. Now is the time to change. Your parents are going to start quizzing you weekly; helping you with flashcards and essays; and giving you rides to and from class. *For this year, your number-one priority is getting an A in every single community college course you take.* But don't worry; community college is not that hard. You can absolutely do it. If 90-year-old women who didn't learn to read until they left the family farm at age 20 can do it, so can you. That's the beauty of community colleges: They are structured to teach everyone, regardless of age, ability, or background. They are first and foremost places to *learn.* Your instructors and professors are there because they really want to help you learn—and you will absolutely learn something. You might find, especially if you've been slacking off, that it feels really good to learn something, and get good grades.

It's important to start as soon as you can at a community college, preferably during the first summer session. That way, you're maximizing the number of grades you can report when you re-apply as a transfer student to your dream colleges. If you know that you still won't cut it at those schools, use our MAP to find colleges that *will* fund you. It's time to change your dreams—but that doesn't mean shattering them. There are so many wonderful ways to *be* in the world, and setting your sights on different goals doesn't mean giving up; it means being smart. Remember: When you do graduate from college, you'll get to do something *amazing.* Those amazing things could include:

√ Getting the classic Eurail pass and bumming around Paris, or Prague, or Rome for a few months.

√ Teaching English in Japan or Korea. (No, they don't pay you very much.)

√ Working for the Peace Corps and aiding impoverished communities throughout the globe. (They really don't pay you very much.)

√ Starting your own arts project out of an Airstream trailer and traveling the country. (Will you be paying yourself? Maybe not, but you'll need gas money.)

√ Touring with your band.

√ Following someone you love halfway across the world.

√ Taking an unpaid internship working for a person or publication you've worshipped. (You'll have to work part-time for pay.)

√ Living on a houseboat in Amsterdam working for Greenpeace. (You'll be making just enough to eat, but you'll be living your idealism.)

Those are real things that real students we've known did right after they graduated from college. If they'd had to worry about paying off a huge student loan payment, they wouldn't have been able to do any of those things. They'd be living at home with their parents, working in coffee shops, in restaurants, or as nannies, like other, less-fortunate students we've known—or working jobs they hate just to pay the bills.

Living at home with your parents for the next year won't be so bad, we promise. *Under no circumstances whatsoever should you move out and get your own apartment*; it's a waste of money. If your parents were counting on your absence, try to make a deal. What can you offer? Childcare for a younger sibling or assistance for an older relative? Home repair? Double the chores? Negotiate, negotiate, negotiate. Now is *not* the time to start paying rent.

If you can't meet our $8K Debt Challenge, we recommend that you try our intentional alternative plan. The end of the game is your college degree. No one ever asks what college you started *at*; they just ask where you graduated *from*. The point isn't how you get to your diploma; it's getting there at all that really counts.

What's in a Name? Understanding Ratings and Rankings

College ratings and rankings assess the "good," the "better," and the "best." They are an inevitable by-product of higher education; if we're paying for college with our money, our time, and our energy, we'd like to know what the "best" colleges are. And why shouldn't we? Our time and energy aside, college tuition has grown at a faster rate than *healthcare* costs. Measuring the lifetime value of that expense is an incredibly worthwhile enterprise for the consumer, and we encourage you to investigate the data available about your intended major or career path and ideal colleges as thoroughly as you can before you sign on the dotted line. Throughout this book, we've repeatedly quoted a 2010 study from payscale.com, a website that tracks compensation data, to indicate that bachelor's degrees from some colleges and universities *do* have an enormous dollar value—and many do not. But Payscale's study isn't *anything* like the rankings books, which is why we like it so much; it's a simple calculation of the dollar value of a bachelor's degree. Rankings and ratings lists *do not* calculate that, no matter what they imply.

For many people, particularly anyone who wants to major in the humanities or soft sciences, college isn't—and *cannot* be—just about the dollar value of the degree. We asked Carol's daughter, who majored in English at a large public university, what her college experience meant to her. She replied,

> *The best parts of my college years were the ones when I was writing and I really felt that I knew what I was talking about; when the culmination of lectures (seemingly irrelevant at the time), notes, readings, and gallery visits resulted in the ability to create at least one apt paragraph. I arrived occasionally at a state of scholarship that one of my professors described as "a place most of us get to for 15 seconds a year, if we're lucky." And I was lucky.*

> *At some point, I felt that everything I saw in the world was a part of everything I was learning. Connections and cross-references bubbled up in every conversation, at every bar, and just walking down the street. The world became an infinite echo chamber of productive thoughts and phrases. I saw my intellectual heroes lurking in a street corner argument between a young couple. I saw them standing behind a mother, telling her tiny, identical daughter to be quiet. It might sound silly, but it was true for me. The leaders of my life of the mind came to life themselves, and their theories, arguments, thoughts and expressions were illustrated in the movements of every single person that surrounded me.*

You might have noticed that she didn't talk about where her degree has *gotten* her in the world, but rather what it *gave* her, personally and intellectually, while she was in school. There's no way to quantify that kind of engagement. It's a qualitative issue, rather than a quantitative one.

Nonetheless, we want to know what our investment is going to get us—and the industry of higher education is ready to sell us an answer, even one that's only half-true. The whole truth is that it's impossible to assess the real and total value of colleges in any given study. Trust us, we've tried. There is so much more to a college education than the *numbers* we can crunch; there is engagement (short- and long-term; micro and macro), there is professional success and satisfaction (without a lot of money), there is friendship, there is love, there is participation, and above all there is intellectual satisfaction. And the biggest uncertainty of all is *who you are*; identity is nebulous. Where do you stop and your education begins? We just don't know the real answer to that. Statistically, we can say that the rich are different; students from wealthy families are better "achievers" than other kinds of students. But who is defining achievement? Is it really just about grades? Where does that leave everyone who *doesn't* come from a wealthy family? What comes out of the classroom, across the board and for every kind of student, is something that every single facet of education tries to calculate, and they can't. If they could, we'd have perfect public schools with 100 percent graduation rates. But we don't. We simply cannot do the math on an *experience*. That means that ratings and rankings are in many ways a near-perfect conflict of logic; they assess an experience that is definitively qualitative and relativistic (that is, the development of critical thinking) in a quantitative and hierarchical manner.

Or, to put it differently, ask any college professor: "Who is better: Kant or Jung? Plato or Socrates? Barthes or Foucault? Henry Field or Alan Turing?"

There's no right answer, he or she will tell you. The very premise of your question—that one kind of knowledge or thinking can be "better" than another—is impossible in a post-structuralist intellectual environment like the one we have now. Asking a question such as "who is better?" is literally the opposite of the purpose of higher education, which is to see the world in shades of complexity and nuance, in shades of *gray*, rather than in black and white. There is no "better" shade of gray; there are only *different* shades of gray.

If college were free, and required very little time or emotional investment on the part of the student, then professors everywhere could decry *U.S. News & World Report*, the *Princeton Review,* and so on as truly meaningless analyses of the relativistic experience. They could simply throw those rankings in the trash and be done with it. But college is not free. As we've said, over and over throughout this book, it's extraordinarily expensive. Rankings, too, are big business; those books and websites aren't free. You've got to pay for them, either for a hardbound copy of the books themselves or for full access to the websites and their data. You want an answer, so like anything else, someone is willing to sell you one. But that doesn't mean it's the entire answer.

Ruth was on the board for the *U.S. News & World Report* College Rankings board for seven years, beginning when she was director of admissions at Ball State University, and through her time as director of admissions at the University of Illinois Urbana/Champaign. The rankings advisory board is made up of admissions directors and deans from all over the country, who pay their own expenses to attend meetings to review the methodology for the rankings, and provide feedback. Seventy-five percent of the rankings are calculated using data collected annually by the federal government, known as IPEDS; that data is available online for free, either at *nces.ed.gov* or *nces.ed.gov/collegenavigator*. That data includes two primary components:

1. **Input data:** *This means the makeup of the most recent incoming freshman class—GPA, test scores, and so forth. This might tell us how difficult it may be to gain admission, but it doesn't tell us anything about the quality of the education after four years (or even one semester).*

2. **Asset, or resource, data:** *This includes the size of the endowment, the number of faculty, the number of books in the library, the value of the physical property, and so on. Does a $10 million parcel of land on a river really make the education better? Probably not. But, it's got a dollar value, so it's part of the formula.*

The remaining 25 percent is simply our personal opinion. We asked college presidents and admissions directors what they *thought* about other schools in an annual survey. It's that simple—and, in a way, that irresponsible. No one can know all the schools in the running, of course. What they do know, quite simply, are the most well-known schools. It's a popularity contest, plain and simple.

What we'd like you to understand about input data, in particular, is that it says absolutely nothing about the school itself. It only says something about the academic backgrounds of the students. It's a correlation—*not* a causality. It's not a guarantee of anything, other than that the schools that top the list are thought highly of by other academics. If you're not an academic, does it really matter? There's no way to know—and it's certainly not worth banking on with student loans. If it comes down to a brand-versus-price scenario—and your understanding of brand is informed by a rankings list—please check Payscale.com's ROI study for an assessment of that college's return on investment.

On the other end of the spectrum, the *Princeton Review* and *Forbes* create their own annual rankings, using different types of data that focus primarily on current, not just incoming, students. The *Princeton Review* rankings come from an 80-question survey of more than 122,000 current students conducted online at *survey.review.com*. (Current students are defined by those who have a valid university e-mail address.) The questions in the survey range from campus life and academics, to the students' thoughts on fellow students' attitudes and opinions. The catch? The *Princeton Review* only surveys students at 373 colleges, a list that is chosen by their board. At the end of the day, it's just a list they put together; it's not a calculation of every college (more than 4,400) in the country—not even close.

The *Forbes* rankings attempt to use quite a bit of alumni data, using salary, student loan burdens, default rates, graduation rates, competitive awards, and listings from "Who's Who in America" and the annual Forbes/CCAP Corporate Officers List. Their student satisfaction surveys come from RateMyProfessor.com, the website college students use to say hurtful things about classes in which they've received a bad grade. It's an academic Yelp, so to speak, and we think it's statistical garbage. Though the people in "Who's Who in America" and the Forbes/CCAP Corporate Officers List are probably important and financially successful, they're not *everyone* that's important or successful. It's a limited group, one that, perhaps rightfully, reflects the *Forbes* worldview of corporate success and entitlement. So although we applaud them for using student loan burdens and graduation rates, we think you should take their ratings with a large handful of salt.

What ratings or rankings do we recommend that you use? Ideally, none of them. But we know you're going to, so please keep their methodologies in mind, and remember that rankings are *never* the whole truth. And though we've referred to Payscale's ROI survey quite frequently, to be fair, it's got problems, too. From the tuition calculated (they use sticker price, not net price) to the inability to weight income by region of the country ($87,000 annually goes a lot farther in Montana than in Manhattan), not to mention the conclusion that the only kind of success is financial success, the Payscale ROI has problems. But it *does* calculate something: the dollar value of a degree. And we think, if you're looking at an expensive brand, you should at least think about what it can give you in dollars— because there's no way to predict what it will give you in *sense*. We can't tell you who is going to give you the best education. It's like falling in love, and only you can figure that out. You'll know it when you see it. You'll feel energized and engaged, and you will *want* to participate. Beginning on page 221 you will see we've created our own list of places with which we have fallen in love (*The Financial Aid Handbook*'s Best Bets List).

13

What Color Is Your Passport? Advice for International Students

In Chapter 2, we explained need, the Free Application for Federal Student Aid (FAFSA), the PROFILE, and all other admittedly arcane federal processes, terminology, and acronyms—all of which are important for U.S. citizens, U.S. nationals, and eligible non-citizens. Eligible non-citizens generally include the following:

√   U.S. permanent residents, with a Permanent Resident Card (formerly known as an Alien Registration Receipt Card or "Green Card").

√   Conditional permanent resident (I-551C).

√   Other eligible non-citizen with an Arrival-Departure Record (I-94) from the Department of Homeland Security showing any one of the following designations: "Refugee," "Asylum Granted," "Indefinite Parole," "Humanitarian Parole," or "Cuban-Haitian Entrant."

√   A citizen of the Republic of Palau (PW), the Republic of the Marshall Islands (MH), or the Federated States of Micronesia (FM).

213

All of these categories of student should have an Alien Registration Number, or ARN, to use the FAFSA. For more information about becoming an eligible non-citizen, or to obtain an ARN, you must contact the Social Security Administration, at *ssa.gov*.

If you're not any of those things, you're officially an international, or foreign, student—a citizen of a country other than the United States—and you won't be eligible for the aid we outlined in Chapter 2 (federal financial aid). You may still have to complete the PROFILE. For you and your family, parts of the college application process will be exactly the same (the merit or academic scholarship part) and other parts (the required forms) will be very different from that of the typical American student.

When a U.S. college or university offers admission to you, it will also send to you the documentation (an I-20 form) you need to obtain a visa to enter the United States for study. By sending an I-20 to you, that school is certifying that you have submitted to it documentation that demonstrates that you have the ability to benefit from your education, that you possess the funding to pay for your education, that you have a residence in another country to which you will return, and that you intend to depart from the United States at the conclusion of your program of study. Whew. Buried in all of this is a very important word: *documentation*. Just as you will have to submit documents that prove your academic ability, such as certified copies of your high school transcript or the final results of your national school leaving exam and TOELF or IELTS exam, you, and your parents, will have to submit *financial* documentation.

As we say throughout this book, the most important thing to remember about college in the United States is that it is very, very expensive. The U.S. Department of State estimates that there are only 1,000 international students each year who receive a "full ride" (aka. a complete scholarship) as an undergraduate to a U.S. college. There are currently more than 274,000 undergraduate international students in the United States. So if 1,000 students per year got a full ride, that means that at most 4,000 out of the 274,000 plus, or .014 percent, get the coveted complete scholarship. So be realistic about your chances. It's doubtful that you will be able to go to college in the United States for free.

What Parts of the Cost-Based College Search Process Are the Same, Regardless of the Color of Your Passport?

The answer is reassuring: most of them. Let's begin with that oh-so-important conversation you've got to have with your parents about money (if you haven't already, take a look at Chapter 4). As an international student, this is *doubly* important, because they'll likely be paying for your costs out of pocket, and you'll also need to document your financial circumstances for each college you apply to. You and your parents will have to submit truthful and accurate information about your financial situation and the resources you have to pay for college. If you're a parent who is reading this chapter for your child, please look at Chapter 5 as well.

The entire process you'll use to figure out what schools might be a good match for you remains the same, regardless of your citizenship status. Chapters 6 and 7 in this book taught you how to look for merit scholarships at schools and how to use the MAP to match your own strengths to schools. The processes colleges use to award merit aid remain the same, regardless of the nationality of the applicant.

Most of the materials you'll need to submit as a part of your application for admission and financial aid will be the same as those required of U.S. citizens. Good writing—the kind you will demonstrate in your essay—is not bound by any national borders. You'll be expected to display the same caliber of fluency and ability to use the English language as any native speaker. Nearly all classes in the United States *are* taught in English, except advanced coursework in foreign languages. Incidentally, if you cannot write well enough in English to submit an application essay, you will likely not succeed as a student.

Strong letters of reference, with certified translations attached if necessary, can speak volumes about personal qualities and abilities regardless of the nationality of the writer.

Making the effort to build a personal relationship with staff responsible at each school for admitting and giving scholarship dollars to foreign students is also something you must do. This is not optional.

Additionally, just like your fellow students who happen to be U.S. citizens, you should be making a dollar-to-dollar cost comparison before making your final choice of school, which we discussed in Chapter 11.

Chapter 12 is possibly even more important for those of you who do not live in the United States. There are more than 4,400 colleges and universities in the United States, and the odds are pretty good that you have never heard of most of them. You'll be tempted to turn to "external" evaluations to determine which are the "best" of them all, and we want to help you make that a useful experience.

WHAT IN THE ADMISSION AND FINANCIAL AID PROCESS WILL BE DIFFERENT FOR YOU?

APPLICATION FOR ADMISSION

It may be that the school in which you are interested has a different application form for use by international students. Part of the difference in this form is that it will be more user-friendly for recording non-U.S. addresses and contact information. If so, this will be *very* evident on the school's website, with a special tab/section labeled for international students. If a school has a form for international students by all means use it, or expect after completing and submitting the form for U.S. students to be asked to also complete the international student form.

SUPPLEMENTARY MATERIALS

If you are not from an English-speaking country, you will need to supply proof of your fluency in English, generally results of either the TOEFL or the IELTS test. Most schools will publish the minimum score required for each of these exams on their website. Go to the appropriate testing website to find information about testing dates and sites in your country: *ets.org* for the TOEFL and *ielts.org* for the IELTS. A few schools will also require you to take the SAT (*collegeboard.com*) or the ACT (*act.org*). If your home country has a national school leaving exam, or if you've completed an IB or EB curriculum, you will need to have your predicted scores (for exams you will sit at the end of the year) included as a part of the school report.

SECONDARY SCHOOL TRANSCRIPTS AND SCHOOL REPORT

You will need to submit official copies of your secondary school transcripts (records of courses taken and grades or scores earned), and perhaps certified translations as well. The school report is to be written by the principal, headmaster or headmistress, or career adviser at your school. And as much information as your school can provide about itself—enrollment, grading system, curriculum, placement of graduates, success with national school leaving exams—can all help to strengthen your application, so attach those to your application if they're available.

FINANCIAL AID

Good news: No FAFSA will be required of you. But you *will* need to submit either a completed institutional financial aid application (from the college itself) or a College Board PROFILE and the International Student Certification of Finances (*collegeboard.com*). The PROFILE is explained in Chapter 2. The Certification of Finances will require a listing of *exact* amounts of assured and projected funding from your own money, your parents, personal sponsors you may have either at home or in the United States (if applicable), or the government of your home country. In addition to listing the amounts of money, you will need to have that amount certified by signature by an officer at your bank, signatures of those providing the money (your parents or sponsor), and a copy of the award letter for any funds from your home government. If you are offered admission, a copy of this form will be attached to your certificate of eligibility (I-20), which is the form you will take to a U.S. consulate or embassy to apply for a visa.

Here's where things become *really* different for you. A U.S. college or university *cannot* and *will not* admit you (and give you a Certificate of Eligibility I-20 form to apply for a visa) unless they have proof that you can not only succeed academically but also can afford to pay for your education. You *cannot* simply be admitted and then figure out how you are going to pay. You have to have either your own money, or money from a sponsor, from the college itself, or from your home government or another agency to pay for your education. And you will have to prove that. There is no U.S. government or state funding for international students. Rather, the sources of financial support for you are:

√ *You and your family.*

√ *The college or university itself.*

√ *Private scholarship programs.*

√ *Your home government for either grants or loans.*

There are a limited number of colleges and universities that offer significant amounts of scholarship aid to international students. Do remember that, even if they say they will fully fund international students, that's only if they choose to admit you. And "fully fund" does not mean that they will simply give you the money. You must demonstrate "need" as well; even though you are not completing the FAFSA you will be submitting other financial information. Whether or not general merit aid programs are available to international students is at the discretion of each individual college.

Student loans from either the U.S. government or most private lenders are not an option for international students. There are a few private lenders that offer student loans to international students. To our knowledge most will require a cosigner who is either a U.S. citizen or permanent resident. A cosigner agrees to take the same responsibility for paying the loan off that you do and if you do not pay, the cosigner has to. This is a huge commitment and not one that someone will enter into lightly. Most of these are relatively expensive loan programs for which the interest rates float (adjusts) to a rate that is tied to the LIBOR (London Inter Bank Offered Rate).

Your home country may have student grant or loan programs that you can apply for and use in the United States. Canadian students may obtain loan funding through CanHELP (*hrsdc.gc.ca*).

Student employment (a job on campus) is a possibility, but the earnings will be minimal—perhaps only $2,000 to $3,000 per year. You cannot assume that a job will provide anything more than limited spending money. A small number of U.S. colleges and universities offer what is called "co-op" learning programs, during which students have the opportunity to work off-campus at a corporation for regular wages. Co-op placements are not available to international students until they have completed two terms of on-campus academic work. Jobs are not guaranteed, and most require strong fluency in English.

The best source for information about college and university study in the U.S. in countries around the world is EducationUSA (*educationusa. state.gov*). This service of the U.S. Department of State is in every country in which the United States has a diplomatic presence, with both brick-and-mortar embassies and offices, and virtual presences. Services from EducationUSA are free and include everything from Internet access, to meeting with an educational advisor, to information about U.S. Higher Education Fairs in your home country.

Once you receive an offer of admission and an I-20, there is still no guarantee of being granted a visa to actually study in the United States. The U.S. consular or embassy officer will interview you, and may ask for additional documentation before issuing a visa. The current fee for a foreign student visa is US $140.

Our single best piece of advice for you is this: Find *your* admission counselor at each school in which you are interested, get in touch, and *stay* in touch. If there is funding for you to study at that school, he or she will help you find it.

THE FINANCIAL AID HANDBOOK'S BEST BETS LIST

SELECTED COLLEGES AND UNIVERSITIES THAT MEET THEIR MISSION AND FUND THEIR FAVORITES

If we had millions of dollars, a team of statisticians, and a few years, our list would be a lot more complicated—but we didn't have those things, so it isn't. It's the best we can do with our combined 70 years of experience and brainpower, and it's not hierarchal. It's alphabetical, and we won't say that any college is "better" than any other. They do vary in terms of how difficult it is to gain admission; some are very, very competitive, and some are not. But no matter how selective they are, every single school we list is a wonderful place to get an education, where a student like you could conceivably get enough financial aid to make it affordable. Period.

We did, however, filter, using the following criteria:

1. Average student loan burdens could not exceed $8K per year.

2. Selectivity must be more than 40 percent.

3. Average grants must exceed average loans.

221

4. *We must know something about them, either through personal experience or reports from colleagues we trust.*

Criteria #1, incidentally, knocked our list down from more than 100 schools—places we have worked with and *loved*—down to just 60. We lost some of our favorites that way.

All of the data we collected for our list is publicly available and free, and came from either IPEDS, Petersen's, or the College Board; specific information about merit aid came from the colleges' own websites.

We have personally worked with, or at, a large number of these colleges, and we believe in them and their missions. For colleges where we haven't worked, we found them through recommendations from colleagues, and then we assessed their data. For each college, we tell you what the top 25 percent of the class—where you'll need to be to get the most need and merit-based aid possible—is, by reporting the top 25 percent of test scores, and we report the *average* GPA. You'll need to look up each college individually at *collegeboard.com* to estimate what its top 25 percent GPA might be. We also report average net price, average annual grants and loans, contact information, and, finally, our own opinion. We're completely open about this: It's our opinion. We're Carol Stack and Ruth Vedvik, and this is what *we* think. Is there enough information to select a college on? Absolutely not—but it's a great jumping-off point.

We don't pretend to be definitive—because we don't think anyone *can* be definitive about rankings—but we do stand by each and every one of our choices, and we hope that you'll look into them when you begin your college search. So without further ado, here are our alphabetical, non-hierarchal, wonderful-and-affordable-places-to-go-to-college "rankings."

AGNES SCOTT COLLEGE

Decatur, GA	*Average Annual Amounts:*
Urban, Very Large City	*$41,955 Sticker Price*
Private, Women's Liberal Arts	*$19,546 Net Price*
842 Students	*$22,409 Grant*
237 First Year	*$5,666 Loan*
41% Out-of-State	

NCAA Division III

www.agnesscott.edu

OFA (404) 471–6395

finaid@agnesscott.edu

If you're feeling a sense of déjà vu as you tour, it's because you've already been to Agnes Scott's campus—in the movies. The campus has been the location for more than 20 films, including *The Blind Side* and *Scream 2*. The young women at Agnes Scott constantly engage with faculty and each other, use their voices, and exercise their minds. Decatur is only a 20-minute ride on the Marta (rapid transit) to downtown Atlanta.

The **Agnes Solution** guarantees at least $63,000 in merit aid over four years ($15,000 per year) plus a $3,000 **Agnes Advantage** travel abroad award. Georgia residents must receive a GA Hope Scholarship to be eligible. Non-Georgia residents must have a 3.6 GPA, 1300 SAT cr + m combined score or a 29 ACT composite.

Top 25%	*Agnes Scott*	YOU
SAT	1200	
ACT	28	
Average		
GPA	3.5	

AUGSBURG COLLEGE

Minneapolis, MN

Urban, Large City

Liberal Arts

3,123 Students

465 First Year

13% Out-of-State

Average Annual Amounts:

$37,812 Sticker Price

$23,070 Net Price

$14,742 Grant

$7,892 Loan

NCAA Division III

www.augsburg.edu

OFA (612) 330–1046 (800) 458–1721

enroll@augsburg.edu

Take a look at the student-run website Homemade Augsburg Uncensored (*augsburg.edu/homemade*) for a slice of the real life at Augsburg. Diverse and committed to global education and faith, Auggies also love their sports. Two ice rinks, intramural broomball, and the first Minnesota women's varsity ice hockey team make the bone-chilling Minneapolis winters fun. Augsburg's Cedar/Riverside location is a young, hip neighborhood, filled with music venues and a short bike ride from the large university district. Students love canoeing through the Boundary Waters up north, and tromping through Africa during their semester abroad.

Augsburg Corporation Scholarship: $1,000 to members of Specific ELCA Synods in Minnesota and Wisconsin. **Augsburg Legacy Scholarship**: Scholarships if you're hooked up to Augsburg by blood or marriage.

Top 25%	Augsburg	YOU
SAT	1218	
ACT	25	
Average		
GPA	3.08	

BAKER UNIVERSITY

Baldwin City, KS

Rural, Small Town

Private Liberal Arts

992 Students

257 First Year

27% Out-of-State

Average Annual Amounts:

$33,680 Sticker Price

$19,519 Net Price

$14,161 Grant

$7,584 Loan

NAIA Division I

www.bakeru.edu

OFA (785) 594-4595

Baker is an incredibly friendly place, with very active student life. If you want to go Greek, you can—an unusual benefit for such a small campus. Check out *thebakerorange.com* to see student media work, including their on-line newspaper.

Harter Scholarship: full tuition, competition is by invitation only. **Bishop Qualye Award**: The college will match a scholarship provided by your church, and you don't have to be Methodist! There's a cool scholarship calculator on the financial aid Web page. Type in your GPA and test score. We typed in a 3.8 and 29 ACT and got a $10,000 Presidential Scholarship! Tuition is $21,000, so that could be nearly half-tuition.

Top 25%	Baker	YOU
SAT	1138	
ACT	26	
Average		
GPA	3.48	

BALL STATE UNIVERSITY

Muncie, IN

Suburban, Small City

Public University

17,737 Students

4,178 First Year

10% Out-of-State

Average Annual Amounts:

Instate

$19,640 Sticker Price

$11,757 Net Price

Outstate

$32,208 Sticker Price

$24,325 Net Price

$7,883 Grant

$6,027 Loan

NCAA Division 1-A

www.bsu.edu

OFA (765) 285–5600 (800) 227–4017

finaid@bsu.edu

Ball State was named after the five brothers of the famed Ball Jar corporation. Ball Staters are true red-blooded kids with a great work-hard-play-hard ethic, which is easy to maintain on this gorgeous campus. Beneficience, aka Bennie, a statue standing tall by Old Main, challenges all students to do good, no matter what. The Colleges of Business and

Architecture dominate the academic scene, and there's a distinctive Honors College for students who want to pay a public price for a private-style education.

Whitinger Scholars: 10 full-ride awards per year to the best and brightest. **Emens Scholarship**: Eight per year up to full (in-state) tuition for leadership. Alumnus David Letterman established a scholarship for communication students, for C average students.

Top 25%	Ball State	YOU
SAT	1150	
ACT	24	
Average		
GPA	3.28	

BELOIT COLLEGE

Beloit, WI

Urban, Large Town

Private Liberal Arts

1,407 Students

332 First Year

79% Out-of-State

Average Annual Amounts:

$41,748 Sticker Price

$23,539 Net Price

$18,209 Grant

$4,884 Loan

NCAA Division III

www.beloit.edu

OFA (608) 363-2663

Beloit is small—*really, really* small. The average class size is 15 students, but more than a third of classes have 10 or fewer. There's no place to hide, but it's a great place to learn—and learn they do. Beloit ranks 20th out of 2,000 colleges and universities for producing future PhDs. Beloit students are interdisciplinary in a huge way: International and applied study, with teaching museums on campus, aren't just a first-year program, but a second-year program as well. The Beloit faculty puts together the Mindset list each year. (Google it, and you'll see why we love Beloit.)

Presidential Scholarships: Three levels, named for three different former presidents, are $13,000 to $17,000 per year for students in the top 10 percent with a 27 ACT with significant extracurricular involvement. Competition required.

Top 25%	Beloit	YOU
SAT	1380	
ACT	30	
Average		
GPA	3.39	

BERRY COLLEGE

Mt. Berry, GA

Suburban, Large town

Private Liberal Arts

1,777 Students

569 First Year

21% Out-of-State

Average Annual Amounts:

$36,080 Sticker Price

$21,061 Net Price

$15,019 Grant

$5,355 Loan

NCAA Division III

www.berry.edu

OFA (706) 236-1714

The tabs on a college's website often give great clues as to what it values, and Berry has a tab we haven't seen *anywhere* else. Called "Meaningful Work," it takes you either to an explanation of the traditional student work program on campus, or to Student-Operated Enterprises. If you like to move around and accomplish practical goals, rather than sit in a classroom, you'll love Berry.

A number of merit scholarships are listed on the website, but we love the **WinShape College Program**, which equips students in the areas of discipleship, community, and leadership. As a part of the program, students receive a yearly scholarship of up to $8,000 per year. Participants will experience a training process that includes exploring their unique strengths while navigating a 30-foot sailing vessel and discovering their life purpose while standing on the steps of the Lincoln Memorial.

Top 25%	Berry College	YOU
SAT	1250	
ACT	28	
Average		
GPA	3.64	

BOISE STATE UNIVERSITY

Boise, ID

Urban, Small City

Public University

16,693 Students

2,194 First Year

12% Out-of-State

Average Annual Amounts:

Instate

$16,668 Sticker Price

$14,375 Net Price

Outstate

$25,672

$23,379

$2,293 Grant

$5,099 Loan

NCAA Division 1-A

www.boisestate.edu

OFA (208) 426–1664

FAquest@boisestate.edu

This might be the most popular public university in Idaho; it's certainly the biggest. To ensure you don't get lost, it offers a "Finish in Four" program to incoming students, where you sign a contract and develop a four-year plan. If you're from Idaho, this might be your best local bet—and you'll stay close to the amazing outdoors opportunities in the Rockies.

Merit scholarships awarded based on GPA and test scores. There are dozens of scholarships available; for example, the **Gem Scholarship** for Non-Residents reduces tuition to the in-state rate. Recent winners have had a GPA of 3.5 and an ACT of 25 or higher. Leadership, civic involvement and extra-curricular activities are considered. Some scholarships require a supplemental application; check the college's website for more details. BSU participates in the WUE program.

Top 25%	Boise State	YOU
SAT	1160	
ACT	25	
Average		
GPA	3.31	

BRADLEY UNIVERSITY

Peoria, IL

Suburban, Large City

Private University

5,061 Students

1,106 First Year

13% Out-of-State

Average Annual Amounts:

$35,200 Sticker Price

$22,959 Net Price

$12,241 Grant

$5,936 Loan

NCAA Division I-AAA

www.bradley.edu

OFA (309) 677–3089

bufinaid@bradley.edu

Bradley caters to the kind of students that want the *options* of a large university, but none of the headaches. Average class size is 23, but Bradley's big enough to have separate career-oriented colleges (business, communications, education, and engineering), Greek life, and Division I sports alongside a classic liberal arts school. It's also tied into the local business community, and the plethora of centers and institutes on campus that provide service to businesses from construction to executive development testifies to Bradley's devotion to the practical and the connected.

Presidential Scholarships: $8,500 per year, for students in the top 10 percent of their high school class, 27 ACT and active in their school or community. **Deans Scholarships**: $6,000 per year for those with a 25 ACT.

Top 25%	Bradley	YOU
SAT	1240	
ACT	27	
Average		
GPA	3.59	

CALIFORNIA STATE UNIVERSITY, SAN MARCOS

San Marcos, CA
Suburban, Large Town
Public University
8,727 Students
1,567 First Year
1% Out-of-State

Average Annual Amounts:
Instate
$20,394 Sticker Price
$14,947 Net Price
Outstate
$31,554 Sticker Price
$26,107 Net Price
$5,447 Grant
$5,007 Loan

NAIA Division I
www.csusm.edu
OFA (760) 750–4850

This Cal State school on a beautiful campus in the southern California hills is just 20 years old, which means you'll have an opportunity to forge some new traditions while you enjoy the benefits of living in the San Diego area. As a small school with big university resources, it's a wonderful value, and you won't need to go out of your way to be heard in class or make personal relationships with professors.

Available scholarships are based on academic achievement, program of study, and community involvement.

Top 25%	San Marcos	YOU
SAT	1080	
ACT	23	
Average		
GPA	3.15	

CENTENARY COLLEGE

Hackettstown, NJ
Suburban, Large Town
Private Liberal Arts
2,140 Students
271 First Year
24% Out-of-State

Average Annual Amounts:
$38,518 Sticker Price
$24,503 Net Price
$14,015 Grant
$5,550 Loan

NCAA Division III
www.centenarycollege.edu
OFA (908) 852–1400, ext. 2350
finaid@centenarycollege.edu

Centenary College describes itself as a provider of a student-centered liberal arts education, with a career focus. It also offers an "Equine Studies" major, and it's located about 50 miles outside of New York City.

All applicants to the College are considered for merit scholarships. Our favorite series of awards are called the **"Freddy" Scholarships**: $10,000 each to students who major in theater and demonstrate excellence in one of 23 different categories, ranging from performance to tech to music.

Top 25%	Centenary	YOU
SAT	1020	
ACT	20	
Average		
GPA	2.72	

CENTRE COLLEGE

Danville, KY

Suburban, Large Town

Private Liberal Arts

1,216 Students

332 First Year

38% Out-of-State

Average Annual Amounts:

$41,400 Sticker Price

$23,413 Net Price

$17,987 Grant

$5,452 Loan

NCAA Division III

www.centre.edu

OFA (859) 238–5365

finaid@centre.edu

Centre College offers a four-year guarantee to students who meet the College's academic and social expectations, including an internship and study abroad. Students are bright (they consistently win national awards including the Rhodes, Fulbright, and Goldwater scholarships), fun-loving, and friendly. Eight-five percent of Centre students study abroad at least once.

Bonner Scholarship: demonstrated need and outstanding financial service. $2,500, plus priority consideration for meeting your full need, compensation for summer service, year-round service/learning programming, up to $7,500 in loan forgiveness, and other benefits. The **Language Scholarship**: up to $7,500 per year (Latin, Hebrew, French, German, Japanese, or Spanish).

Top 25%	Centre	YOU
SAT	1340	
ACT	30	
Average		
GPA	3.58	

CLARK UNIVERSITY

Worcester, MA

Urban, Small City

Private University

2,333 Students

550 First Year

60% Out-of-State

Average Annual Amounts:

$43,720 Sticker Price

$24,861 Net Price

$18,859 Grant

$6,896 Loan

NCAA Division III

www.clarku.edu

OFA (508) 793–7478

finaid@clarku.edu

Clarkies take pride in being part of a liberal arts college that describes its program as one of "active discovery." There's an entire section on its website, the L*IN*K, that is devoted to listing and explaining extracurricular ways to achieve active discovery, and the breadth is remarkable. From Baha'i and Ballroom Dance to Water Watch and Women's Lacrosse, Clark has one of the most active student populations we've ever seen.

To be considered for Clark's generous scholarship program, you *must* apply to the University before January 1st. The **Making A Difference Scholarship** of $15,000 is awarded competitively to students who demonstrate extraordinary commitment to social change. **Presidential Scholarships** of $15,000 and **Achievement Awards** of $12,000 are awarded on the basis of traditional academic credentials and potential.

Top 25%	Clark	YOU
SAT	1290	
ACT	29	
Average		
GPA	3.46	

COLBY-SAWYER COLLEGE

New London, NH

Rural, Small Town

Private Liberal Arts

1,100 Students

352 First Year

67% Out-of-State

Average Annual Amounts:

$43,700 Sticker Price

$25,484 Net Price

$18,216 Grant

$5,671 Loan

NCAA Division III

www.colby-sawyer.edu

OFA (603) 526–3717

cscfinaid@colby-sawyer.edu

A former women's college, Colby-Sawyer was founded in 1837 and is nestled on 200 acres in rural New Hampshire. It's an hour from Boston and three and a half hours from Montreal, and the program focuses on a career-prep liberal arts curriculum.

The competitive **Chargers, Presidential and Founders Scholarships** range from $12,000 to $16,000 per year and reward those with GPAs higher than 3.0. The **Wesson Honor Scholarship** of $17,000 is limited in number, chosen by committee review, and includes direct admission into the Wesson Honors Program. If you know that C-S is the place for you, a $2000 scholarship is awarded to those who apply Early Action and can be "stacked" on top of other awards.

Top 25%	Colby-Sawyer	YOU
SAT	NA	
ACT	NA	
Average		
GPA	3.0	

THE COLLEGE OF IDAHO

Caldwell, ID

Rural, Large Town

Private Liberal Arts

1,002 Students

299 First Year

21% Out-of-State

Annual Average Amounts:

$30,448 Sticker Price

$17,974 Net Price

$12,474 Grant

$5,870 Loan

NAIA Division II

www.collegeofidaho.edu

OFA (208) 459–5307

The C of I Coyotes, known on-campus as the "Howling Yotes," do have one of the weirdest nicknames in college sports—but they love to win (alpine skiing, volleyball, and cross-country). The "First Year Experience" program is there to help you adjust to college, and the school is located about 30 minutes from Boise.

The website has a great online calculator, where you can plug in your GPA and test scores, to determine how much aid you'll qualify for.

Top 25%	College of Idaho	YOU
SAT	1170	
ACT	27	
Average		
GPA	3.59	

COLLEGE OF THE ATLANTIC

Bar Harbor, ME

Rural, Small Town

Private Liberal Arts

336 Students

76 First Year

79% Out-of-State

Average Annual Amounts:

$43,320 Sticker Price

$16,868 Net Price

$26,452 Grant

$4,807 Loan

Intramural athletics

www.coa.edu

OFA (800) 528–0025

The COA is teeny-tiny, is located in a relatively remote area, and only offers one degree: a BA in human ecology. What does that mean? Well, you'll decide. At COA you'll design your own major and curriculum—the only requirements are that it focus heavily on "creativity, critical thinking, community engagement, and integrative thinking," among others. If you want a challenging academic experience that isn't rooted in one department or major, and you love the outdoors, this might be your new home.

Scholarship programs abound, and you might have noticed that their *average* grant is over $26,000. Been an active participant in a FIRST Robotics team? Are you a graduate of the Sierra Club SPROG? COA has these, and other scholarships, starting at $10,000.

Top 25%	COA	YOU
SAT	1310	
ACT	27	
Average		
GPA	3.52	

COLLEGE OF WOOSTER

Wooster, OH

Suburban, Large Town

Private Liberal Arts

1,834 Students

480 First Year

58% Out-of-State

Average Annual Amounts:

$45,500 Sticker Price

$25,190 Net Price

$20,310 Grant

$5,592 Loan

NCAA Division III

www.wooster.edu

OFA (330) 263–2317

financialaid@wooster.edu

Legend has it that if the Kauke Arch can be filled to the top with snow during the night, blocking the main doors, classes will be cancelled the next day. Mischief abounds at this liberal arts college for serious students. The "Scot Pipers," a student bagpipe group, are a campus favorite, and seniors are required to complete the "Capstone Project," a significant independent study project.

The competitive **College Scholar Award** of half to two-thirds tuition requires a separate essay, along with your admissions materials, by January 15th. There's also a **Scottish Arts** scholarship of $2,000 to $8,000, if you play the bagpipe.

Top 25%	Wooster	YOU
SAT	1310	
ACT	29	
Average		
GPA	3.6	

DOANE COLLEGE

Crete, NE

Rural, Small Town

Private Liberal Arts

969 Students

313 First Year

21% Out-of-State

Average Annual Amounts:

$29,860 Sticker Price

$17,002 Net Price

$12,858 Grant

$6,475 Loan

NAIA Division II

www.doane.edu

OFA (402) 826–8260

faoffice@doane.edu

Tucked away on a 300-plus-acre campus outside of Omaha, Doane College is a small liberal arts school with a great reputation. It has an early internship program and a four-year graduation guarantee, with a generous aid program to boot.

All new first year students to Doane are given a $1,000 travel scholarship to use at some point during their study. Doane's website has a chart that will show you, based on your GPA and ACT score, what academic scholarships you will qualify for, from $5,000 to full tuition.

Top 25%	Doane College	YOU
SAT	1130	
ACT	26	
Average		
GPA	3.44	

DREW UNIVERSITY

Madison, NJ

Suburban, Large Town

Private University

1,739 Students

506 First Year

44% Out-of-State

Average Annual Amounts:

$54,043 Sticker Price

$36,550 Net Price

$17,493 Grant

$5,167 Loan

NCAA Division III

www.drew.edu

OFA (973) 408–3112

finaid@drew.edu

Drew's College of Liberal Arts touts itself as being the first liberal arts college in the nation to give every student a computer. That translates into a curriculum in which computers and technology are fully integrated across all disciplines, just 25 miles from New York City, with a student body that's 30.2 percent students of color.

All applicants for admission are considered for the **Drew Merit Based Scholarship**. The **Civic Engagement Scholarship** ($5,000 per year) goes to students who have extensive community service commitments on their resumes.

Top 25%	Drew	YOU
SAT	1250	
ACT	27	
Average		
GPA	3.27	

ECKERD COLLEGE

Saint Petersburg, FL	*Average Annual Amounts:*
Suburban, Large City	*$45,312 Sticker Price*
Liberal Arts	*$31,177 Net Price*
1,863 Students	*$12,135 Grant*
505 First Year	*$7,425 Loan*
80% Out-of-State	

NCAA Division II

www.eckerd.edu

OFA (727) 864–8334

finaid@eckerd.edu

Eckerd is *the* place to study marine life, in the classroom or at the beach. Global and environmental learning are built into the curriculum, and it has a great list of honor societies.

Twenty-five freshmen are selected as research associates and work with faculty in their research, which includes a $1,000 stipend, but the experience is what you want! **Academic Achievement Scholarships** for first-year students range from $9,000 to $14,500, and requirements can be found on the website. **Artistic Achievement** awards for achievement in music, theatre, visual arts, and creative writing are also available.

Top 25%	Eckerd	YOU
SAT	1240	
ACT	28	
Average		
GPA	3.27	

ELON UNIVERSITY

Elon, NC

Suburban, Large Town

Private Liberal Arts

4,995 Students

1,291 First Year

75% Out-of-State

Average Annual Amounts:

$37,225 Sticker Price

$28,746 Net Price

$8,479 Grant

$5,492 Loan

NCAA Division I-AA

www.elon.edu

OFA (336) 278–7640

finaid@elon.edu

Elon's campus looks like a botanical garden, and it's well-known for its high level of student engagement. If you're a serious student who likes to have a "life after the classroom," Elon might be a good fit for you.

The top 25 percent of incoming freshmen receive a $4,000–$4,500 **Presidential Scholarship**, and the **Fellows** program provides $1,000 travel grants, internships, paid research assistantships, and more. **Performing Arts** and **Music** scholarships from $500 to $6,000 are also available.

Top 25%	Elon	YOU
SAT	1310	
ACT	29	
Average		
GPA	4.0	

THE EVERGREEN STATE COLLEGE

Olympia, WA

Rural, Small City

Public Liberal Arts

4,551 Students

578 First Year

43% Out-of-State

Average Annual Amounts:

Instate

$18,199 Sticker Price

$13,267 Net Price

Outstate

$29,277 Sticker Price

$24,345 Net Price

$4,932 Grant

$5,171 Loan

NAIA Division II

www.evergreen.edu

OFA (360) 867–6205

Evergreen was founded in 1971, and has stayed true to its founding identity as a "progressive public liberal arts and sciences college." The Geoducks are a fascinating group of quirky, outdoorsy, creative, and eco-minded students, who are often the first in their generation to attend college. They design their own courses of study, and they don't care about traditional letter grades—just the work itself. The first year class of 578 is half the size of the number of transfer students (more than 1,200) every year.

ESC doesn't make applying for scholarships easy. For each one, you'll have to submit a separate letter of application and other materials. Check the website for specific scholarships and requirements. It'll take some patience, but could be well worth the effort.

Top 25%	Evergreen	YOU
SAT	1230	
ACT	26	
Average		
GPA	3.01	

FORT LEWIS COLLEGE

Durango CO

Rural, Large Town

Public Liberal Arts

3,685 Students

802 First Year

36% Out-of-State

Average Annual Amounts:

Instate

$17,886 Sticker Price

$11,042 Net Price

Outstate

$30,856 Sticker Price

$24,012 Net Price

$6,844 Grant

$4,737 Loan

NCAA Division II

www.fortlewis.edu

OFA (970) 247–7142

Finaid_off@fortlewis.edu

Fort Lewis's goal is to be the finest public liberal arts college in the Western United States, and its sole focus is on undergraduate education, *not* research—which only benefits *you*. Outdoorsy students who love the mountains (Durango is at an elevation of 6800 feet) and reading should look into the college's Common Reading Experience, Co-op Education, and Community Based Learning and Research programs.

President's Scholarship: $2,000 in state, $8,000 out of state. **Native American** Tuition Scholarship: $15,000 for those who are members of a federally recognized tribe. It has an on-line calculator to help you figure out how much aid you could get, and it adjusts for in or out of state residency.

Top 25%	Fort Lewis	YOU
SAT	1145	
ACT	24	
Average		
GPA	3.1	

GEORGIA STATE UNIVERSITY

Atlanta, GA

Urban, Large City

Public Commuter

22,384 Students

2,994 First Year

3% Out-of-State

Average Annual Amounts:

Instate

$22,146 Sticker Price

$15,522 Net Price

Outstate

$40,356 Sticker Price

$33,632 Net Price

$6,724 Grant

$3,807 Loan

NCAA Division I-AAA

www.gsu.edu

OFA (404) 413–2400

scholarships@gsu.edu

This incredibly large and diverse university is located in the heart of Atlanta, and while GSU is predominantly a commuter college, they do offer apartment-style living, and Atlanta-area students ride the Marta (rapid transit) right to campus. It's also a Division I school.

Berner Scholarships are available for students from Troup and Meriwether counties. **Campus Atlanta Scholarships** pay the out-of-state portion of tuition for non-residents who qualify. The **Lanette L. Stuttles Scholarship** helps pay for childcare, based on need and academics.

Top 25%	GSU	YOU
SAT	1170	
ACT	24	
Average		
GPA	3.35	

GUSTAVUS ADOLPHUS COLLEGE

St. Peter, MN

Rural, Small Town

Private Liberal Arts

2,475 Students

630 First Year

19% Out-of-State

Average Annual Amounts:

$41,660 Sticker Price

$23,586 Net Price

$18,074 Grant

$7,738 Loan

NCAA Division III

www.gustavus.edu

OFA (507) 933–7527

finaid@gustavus.edu

Gusties love their hockey, and they're smart, well-rounded students who value a faith-based setting without too much emphasis on formal pedagogy. Their spectacular campus, located on the bluffs of the Minnesota River, was rebuilt in the '90s after a tornado devastated the property. They've got two kinds of core curricula, distributive and integrative, that cater to every type of student.

The **Dean's Scholarship** is $4,000 to $14,000 annually. The **Jussi Bjorling** Music Scholarship is available for any major, $2,000 to $6,000 annually.

Top 25%	Gustavus	YOU
SAT	1370	
ACT	29	
Average		
GPA	3.61	

HARTWICK COLLEGE

Oneonta, NY

Rural, Large Town

Private Liberal Arts

1,473 Students

402 First Year

33% Out-of-State

Average Annual Amounts:

$43,805 Sticker Price

$27,168 Net Price

$16,637 Grant

$7,959 Loan

NCAA Division III

www.hartwick.edu

OFA (607) 431–4130

finaid@hartwick.edu

Located on 425 acres in the foot of the Catskill Mountains, Hartwick has made a real effort to keep its price affordable, using both an aggressive financial aid and scholarship plan and a three-year bachelor's degree program. There's no on-line component, no summer school, and no fine print, but you do have to be motivated and a hard worker. Test score submission for both admission and scholarship consideration is optional.

Hartwick has an on-line scholarship calculator to help you estimate your aid eligibility, as well as a chart that shows, given a GPA and test score level, what scholarship amounts (from $7,000 to $22,000) are a match for your credentials.

Top 25%	Hartwick	YOU
SAT	1200	
ACT	27	
Average		
GPA	3.1	

HENDRIX COLLEGE

Conway, AR

Suburban, Small City

Private Liberal Arts

1,456 Students

412 First Year

52% Out-of-State

Average Annual Amounts:

$42,662 Sticker Price

$24,873 Net Price

$17,789 Grant

$5,906 Loan

NCAA Division III

www.hendrix.edu

OFA (501) 450–1368

adm@hendrix.edu

Hendrix places a *lot* of emphasis on academics, graduate school placement, and student research. The Hendrix Odyssey program will allow you to tackle your education in a nontraditional setting, with experiential and active learning.

The Hendrix website has some great charts that show exactly what credentials you have to present to get what amount of scholarships, as well as any other required materials. Many deadlines are early, so pay attention.

Top 25%	Hendrix	YOU
SAT	1370	
ACT	32	
Average		
GPA	3.83	

HOLLINS UNIVERSITY

Roanoke, VA

Suburban, Small City

Private Women's University

796 Students

198 First Year

48% Out-of-State

Average Annual Amounts:

$40,955 Sticker Price

$24,555 Net Price

$16,400 Grant

$6,943 Loan

NCAA Division III

www.hollins.edu

OFA (540) 362–6332

sfa@hollins.edu

Young women who are serious about transforming themselves into passionate, *brilliant* women will love Hollins. It turns possibilities into probabilities for the next generation of working women. Known for writing, it has an amazing equestrian program as well.

Battan Scholar Award: up to full tuition scholarships for top-ability students. **Hollins Award**: up to $20,000. Separate **Science, Math** and **Creative Talent**, and **Founders** awards are for students with outstanding achievements, and range from $5,000 up to $13,000.

Top 25%	Hollins	YOU
SAT	1230	
ACT	28	
Average		
GPA	3.5	

ILLINOIS COLLEGE

Jacksonville, IL

Rural, Large Town

Private Liberal Arts

895 Students

225 First Year

12% Out-of-State

Average Annual Amounts:

$31,200 Sticker Price

$17,653 Net Price

$13,547 Grant

$6,229 Loan

NCAA Division III

www.ic.edu

OFA (217) 245–3035

finaid@ic.edu

Historically, IC educated most of the profession-bound students in Illinois; now students have a strong liberal arts degree as their foundation, no matter what their goal. IC students are *involved*—in everything. Instead of fraternities or sororities, they have literary societies that are social *and* academic. Beecher Hall, which is depicted on the 19-cent first-class stamp, was part of the Underground Railroad, and IC is the oldest college or university in Illinois.

Trustee Scholarships provide full tuition for top students. Scholarships range from $5,000 to $15,000 including the **Edward Beecher** $8,500 scholarship, named for IC's first president (and brother of Harriet Beecher Stowe). Test score submission is optional.

Top 25%	IC	YOU
SAT	NA	
ACT	26	
Average		
GPA	3.39	

LAWRENCE UNIVERSITY

Appleton, WI

Urban, Small City

Private, Liberal Arts

1,495 Students

352 First Year

65% Out-of-State

Average Annual Amounts:

$43,799 Sticker Price

$26,994 Net Price

$16,805 Grant

$6,084 Loan

NCAA Division III

www.lawrence.edu

OFA (920) 832–6583

financial.aid@lawrence.edu

Lawrence combines a liberal arts college with a fantastic music conservatory, and both are committed solely to undergraduate education. Although their taglines about the "power" of individualized education might seem cheesy, the reality, to put it simply, is awesome. Alumni *love* Lawrence. You'll' use state-of-the-art media during your application process, like Skyping your interview, and Lawrence has its own YouTube channel, in addition to Bjorlunden, its 425-acre retreat center on Lake Michigan.

More Light Scholarships, from $1,000 to $7,000 per year, are for students who have given back to their to local, environmental, or global communities. There are also four academic scholarships, from $7,000 to $15,000 per year, available for the top of their incoming class. Test score submission is optional.

Top 25%	Lawrence	YOU
SAT	1440	
ACT	31	
Average		
GPA	3.63	

LEWIS & CLARK COLLEGE

Portland, OR

Urban, Very Large City

Private Liberal Arts

1,977 Students

498 First Year

91% Out-of-State

Average Annual Amounts:

$47,583 Sticker Price

$30,686 Net Price

$16,897 Grant

$6,500 Loan

NCAA Division III

www.lclark.edu

OFA (503) 768–7090

sfs@lclark.edu

Just southwest of Portland, Lewis & Clark's beautiful campus draws students from all over the country and the world. It describes itself as an "alternative to traditional colleges and universities," and it attracts students who love adventure in—and out—of the classroom.

Barbara Hirschi Neely Scholarships are full tuition and are offered to 10 students with stellar credentials with a GPA of 3.3 or higher. **Trustee Scholarships** are half-tuition and awarded to 15 students with a GPA of 3.3 or higher. Preferred consideration for both is given to students in the sciences and math or those with a special focus on international cultures. Leadership and service awards valued at 25 percent of tuition are offered to 100 students.

Top 25%	Lewis & Clark	YOU
SAT	1390	
ACT	30	
Average		
GPA	3.69	

LOYOLA MARYMOUNT UNIVERSITY

Los Angeles, CA

Suburban, Very Large City

Private Catholic

5,833 Students

1,385 First Year

30% Out-of-State

Average Annual Amounts:

$52,124 Sticker Price

$32,648 Net Price

$19,476 Grant

$7,972 Loan

NCAA Division I-AAA

www.lmu.edu

OFA (310) 338–2700

This Jesuit University blends academics and faith. Perched on bluffs overlooking the Pacific Ocean, students enjoy the tranquility of campus life with fast-paced LA just at their feet. Students who want to combine academic and social opportunities in a Catholic community go to LMU.

Arrupe Scholarship: a minimum of $12,500 awarded to 10 percent of the incoming freshmen based on academic qualifications. **Presidential Scholars** are selected from Arrupe and LMU scholarship recipients after a campus interview. Amounts range from $17,000 to $22,500.

Top 25%	Loyola Marymount	YOU
SAT	1280	
ACT	28	
Average		
GPA	3.66	

LOYOLA UNIVERSITY MARYLAND

Baltimore, MD

Urban, Large City

Private Jesuit University

3,757 Students

968 First Year

84% Out-of-State

$50,320 Sticker Price

$28,153 Net Price

$22,167 Grant

$6,217 Loan

NCAA Division I-AAA

www.loyola.edu

OFA (410) 617–2576

financialaid@loyola.edu

Another Jesuit University, Loyola Maryland offers the best of multiple worlds: the rich Jesuit educational tradition of excellence with a spiritual context at a small university. Students looking for an experience—not just an education—will love this Loyola.

Loyola requires both the CSS PROFILE and the FAFSA. Three levels of Presidential scholarships are offered to top students: $12,500, $18,750, and $25,000. The **Marion Burk Knott Scholarships** are four-year, full-tuition awards available on a competitive basis to Catholic students residing in the Archdiocese of Baltimore.

Top 25%	Loyola Maryland	YOU
SAT	1270	
ACT	28	
Average		
GPA	3.41	

MIDDLE TENNESSEE STATE UNIVERSITY

Murfreesboro, TN

Urban, Small City

Public University

22,299 Students

3,596 First Year

6% Out-of-State Average

Average Annual Amounts:

Instate

$16,878 Sticker Price

$10,428 Net Price

Outstate

$28,806 Sticker Price

$22,356 Net Price

$6,450 Grant

$4,866 Loan

NCAA Division I-A

www.mtsu.edu

OFA (615) 898–2830

It boasts about being the biggest and best university in the state—the number-one destination for Tennessee residents. It has an elite recording program and a fine business school, but it's known for a fabulous teaching program. Blue Raiders want to be where the action is! There's a robust Greek life, as well.

Of the six scholarships available for incoming freshman, the **Buchanan Fellowship** is the only one with a specific application process. Recipients are selected by the Honors College. The **Dream Scholarship** is awarded for academics and diversity.

Top 25%	MTSU	YOU
SAT	1160	
ACT	25	
Average		
GPA	NA	

MILLS COLLEGE

Oakland, CA

Urban, Large City

Liberal Arts Women's College

921 Students

162 First Year

27% Out-of-State

Average Annual Amounts:

$51,112 Sticker Price

$25,615 Net Price

$25,497 Grant

$7,827 Loan

NCAA Division III

www.mills.edu

OFA (510) 430–2000

finaid@mills.edu

A popular t-shirt on the Mills campus reads "Smarter than Barbie, Stronger than Ken." We wouldn't argue the point; smart women are the Mills legacy. Fifty-five percent of the students at this women's college declare themselves as women of color, and Mills is *not* an HBCU. It's on an oasis of safety in Oakland, California, and students can take courses at UC

Berkeley and pull their internships from all around the San Francisco Bay Area.

Few colleges are as generous with financial aid as Mills—so apply, and find out. Full-tuition scholarships are available for students at the top of the incoming class.

Top 25%	Mills	YOU
SAT	1250	
ACT	27	
Average		
GPA	3.7	

MONTANA STATE UNIVERSITY—BOZEMAN

Bozeman, MT

Rural, Large Town

Public University

10,840 Students

2,316 First Year

38% Out-of-State

Average Annual Amounts:

Instate

$17,468 Sticker Price

$9,314 Net Price

Outstate

$29,131 Sticker Price

$20,977 Net Price

$8,154 Grant

$5,387 Loan

NCAA Division I-AA

www.montana.edu

OFA (406) 994–2845

"Mountains and Minds" is the tagline at MSU Bozeman, where students take advantage of the outdoors by constantly skiing, hiking, rafting, and climbing in the nearby Gallatin Range. Academics focus on environmental and global issues.

The unimaginatively named **Non-Resident Freshman Scholarships** give up to $15,000 per year, and the award amounts are determined by ACT/SAT score and delineated on a chart right on the website. Don't meet those criteria? The **Distinction Scholarships** are targeted to you, but will require a separate application and short essay.

Top 25%	MSU Bozeman	YOU
SAT	1250	
ACT	27	
Average		
GPA	3.28	

MUHLENBERG COLLEGE

Allentown, PA

Suburban, Small City

Private Liberal Arts

2,517 Students

577 First Year

72% Out-of-State

Average Annual Amounts:

$48,230 Sticker Price

$31,374 Net Price

$16,856 Grant

$6,661 Loan

NCAA Division III

www.muhlenberg.edu

OFA (484) 664–3175

finaid@muhlenberg.edu

We've got to admit that we're drawn to Muhlenberg—not only for its liberal arts program and successful educational experience—but because it's the only college we know of that *really* explains financial aid on its website. It also has an index of student blogs on its website.

At "Berg," merit scholarships range from $1,000 to $16,000 per year and go to students in the top 10 percent of the class with SAT in excess of 1250. No separate application for scholarship is necessary, but Muhlenberg will require both FAFSA and PROFILE for any need-based aid.

Top 25%	Muhlenberg	YOU
SAT	1310	
ACT	30	
Average		
GPA	3.27	

NORTH DAKOTA STATE UNIVERSITY

Fargo, ND

Urban, Small City

Public University

11,733 Students

2,459 First Year

60% Out-of-State

Average Annual Amounts:

Instate

$16,323 Sticker Price

$12,955 Net Price

Outstate

$25,422 Sticker Price

$22,054 Net Price

$3,368 Grant

$7,637 Loan

NCAA Division 1-AA

www.ndsu.edu

OFA (701) 231–7533

NDSU has a few unusual resources, including a program in agriculture that has so perfected the development of pasta that Italians send their researchers there to learn. Students love their free time—and their Bison: Sports are big, Greek life is bigger, and their fine arts programs are great.

NDSU offers competitive academic scholarships to students with a 26 ACT and a 3.5 GPA.

Top 25%	NDSU	YOU
SAT	1260	
ACT	26	
Average		
GPA	3.37	

OKLAHOMA STATE UNIVERSITY

Stillwater, OK
Suburban, Small City
Public University
17,849 Students
3,148 First Year
26% Out-of-State

Average Annual Amounts:
Instate
$19,082 Sticker Price
$12,881 Net Price
Outstate
$29,436 Sticker Price
$23,235 Net Price
$6,201 Grant
$4,889 Loan

NCAA Division I-A
www.okstate.edu
OFA (405)744–6604
finaid@okstate.edu

Go west, young men and women! The Cowboys embrace the western tradition and flair, and OSU is a charming—and wild—place to hit the books. Oklahoma City and Tulsa aren't far away if you need bigger city excitement once in a while.

Students may choose a tuition lock program, and freeze tuition costs for four years. The **Regent's Distinguished Scholarship** offers $2,500 per year to students with a 30 ACT or 1330 SAT and a 3.0 GPA. The **Cowboy Covenant for Promise Scholars** is a program offered by OSU and the State that provides additional cash for books and fees.

Top 25%	OSU	YOU
SAT	1240	
ACT	27	
Average		
GPA	3.52	

PACIFIC LUTHERAN UNIVERSITY

Tacoma, WA

Suburban, Large City

Private University

3,305 Students

716 First Year

29% Out-of-State

Average Annual Amounts:

$40,279 Sticker Price

$24,620 Net Price

$15,659 Grant

$6,553 Loan

NCAA Division III

www.plu.edu

OFA (253) 535–7134

finaid@plu.edu

What's a Lute? That could be you. These quirky Lutherans (and many others) love their school and its setting in Washington State. On campus and off, Lutes love engagement, with each other and the world. The classroom extends beyond the four walls to the real world.

Full-tuition **Regent's Scholarships** go to highest ability students with strong leadership and service. The **President's Scholarship** and **PLU Scholarship** are available based on academics, leadership, and service.

Top 25%	PLU	YOU
SAT	1220	
ACT	28	
Average		
GPA	3.6	

PACIFIC UNIVERSITY

Forest Grove, OR

Suburban, Large Town

Private University

1,474 Students

333 First Year

51% Out-of-State

Average Annual Amounts:

$40,594 Sticker Price

$26,208 Net Price

$14,386 Grant

$7,744 Loan

NCAA Division III

www.pacificu.edu

OFA (503) 352–2222

financialaid@pacificu.edu

Located in a suburb of Portland, Pacific is not shy about listing its "Firsts, Best and Honors"—ways in which the University shines. One of these ways is in making its liberal arts program financially accessible.

Merit scholarships from $7,500 to $12,000 are awarded on the basis of GPA and test score, and the University keeps a chart delineating the criteria for each level on its website. Have you been a high school forensics jock? If so, Pacific has scholarships for you, if you want to continue participating in college.

Top 25%	PU	YOU
SAT	1220	
ACT	27	
Average		
GPA	3.61	

PRESBYTERIAN COLLEGE

Clinton, SC

Rural, Small Town

Private Liberal Arts

1,221 Students

364 First Year

36% Out-of-State

Average Annual Amounts:

$40,325 Sticker Price

$17,079 Net Price

$23,246 Grant

$5,776 Loan

NCAA Division I-AA

www.presby.edu

OFA (864) 833–8290

finaid@presby.edu

Self-governance, honor, and ethics are at the core of the student commitment to PC, and they permeate all aspects of student life, which is terrifically diverse: Great classroom experience, Greek life, DI athletics, and more abound on this southern campus.

Quattlebaum Honor Scholarship: two full tuition scholarships. Very competitive. **Chinese Scholars**: 30 freshmen are selected each year to take two semesters of Chinese as freshmen and travel to China to study with $1,000 travel stipends from the College. **Presbyterian Church USA Servant Leadership Scholarships:** Eight $5,000 scholarships are awarded each year for demonstrated service to the church and community.

Top 25%	PC	YOU
SAT	1250	
ACT	27	
Average		
GPA	3.43	

RANDOLPH- MACON COLLEGE

Ashland, VA

Suburban, Small Town

Private Liberal Arts

1,246 Students

362 First Year

32% Out-of-State

Average Annual Amounts:

$40,573 Sticker Price

$24,544 Net Price

$16,029 Grant

$,4917 Loan

NAIA Division III

www.rmc.edu

OFA (804) 752–7259

financial-aid@rmc.edu

R-MC offers a distinctive freshman year experience program and committed faculty members. Compared to other East Coast schools, its sticker price is a bargain, and it's been around since 1830—plenty of traditions to choose from.

Half-tuition scholarships are available for students heading to the ministry in an approved denomination. Sibling grants up to $8,000 are available. **Schapiro Research Fellowships** offer experience and $3,000 for travel. Just like in the real world, you'll write proposals for this fellowship.

Top 25%	R-MC	YOU
SAT	1160	
ACT	NA	
Average		
GPA	3.3	

SAINT MARY'S COLLEGE

Notre Dame, IN

Suburban, Small City

Private Women's Liberal Arts

1,664 Students

435 First Year

69% Out-of-State

Average Annual Amounts:

$41,722 Sticker Price

$27,290 Net Price

$14,432 Grant

$7,095 Loan

NCAA Division III

www.saintmarys.edu

OFA (574) 284–4557 (866) 502–7788

finaid@saintmarys.edu

At Saint Mary's, you can join in on all the academic and student life at Notre Dame (including classes, clubs, sporting activities, and more) and still belong to a close-knit community at a private women's college. Saint Mary's also has Centers for Academic Innovation, Spirituality, and Intellectual Leadership, and a competitive women's golf program.

Its generous merit aid program gives $5,000–$17,000 per year to qualified students, and note its *average* grant of more than $14,000 per year.

Top Quartile	Saint Mary's	YOU
SAT	1220	
ACT	28	
Average		
GPA	3.71	

SAM HOUSTON STATE UNIVERSITY

Huntsville, TX

Suburban, Large town

Public University

14,569 Students

2,170 First Year

3% Out-of-State

Average Annual Amounts:

Instate

$17,870 Sticker Price

$10,781 Net Price

Outstate

$26,180 Sticker Price

$19,091 Net Price

$7,089 Grant

$5,271 Loan

NCAA Division I-AA

www.shsu.edu

OFA (936) 294–1774

SHSU, a *very* large public university located about 70 miles outside of Houston, has all the benefits that a huge state school can offer, including 79 degree programs, intercollegiate rodeo, campus television, radio stations, Greek life, and more.

The **Bearkat Promise** covers tuition and fees for Texas residents from families with incomes less than $25,000. All other applicants **must** use the online ScholarX application, available from the SHSU website, to be eligible for scholarship dollars.

Top 25%	SHSU	YOU
SAT	1090	
ACT	22	
Average		
GPA	NA	

SANTA CLARA UNIVERSITY

Santa Clara, CA

Suburban, Small City

Private Jesuit University

5,200 Students

1,085 First Year

41% Out-of-State

Average Annual Amounts:

$52,080 Sticker Price

$36,901 Net Price

$15,179 Grant

$6,774 Loan

NCAA Division I-AAA

www.scu.edu

OFA (408) 554–4505

financialaid@scu.edu

Santa Clara University is the oldest college in California, and boasts the fourth-highest graduation rate of similar schools throughout the United States. It has a strong religious tradition (Jesuit) and a fantastic engineering school, and its location—at the south of the Bay Area and near Stanford and both Apple and Google headquarters—is spectacular.

The **Presidential** Scholarship (upon entry only) offers full tuition for distinguished students, and the **Provost** Scholarship offers half tuition. There's also the **SCU Incentive Grant,** which goes to students (not receiving other scholarships) who will bring some measure of diversity.

Top 25%	SCU	YOU
SAT	1330	
ACT	30	
Average		
GPA	3.55	

SEWANEE: UNIVERSITY OF THE SOUTH

Sewanee, TN

Rural

Private University

1,469 Students

402 First Year

75% Out-of-State

Average Annual Amounts:

$45,832 Sticker Price

$23,985 Net Price

$21,847 Grant

$5,975 Loan

NCAA Division III

www.sewanee.edu

OFA (931) 598–1312

finaid@sewanee.edu

"The Domain" is the local nickname for this 13,000 acre campus on the Cumberland Plateau, and although the student population is small, it's filled with *really* bright students who love nature. Tigers are drawn to this remote area to focus on their studies *and* the environment. For example, you can go rock climbing—on real rocks, not walls—after class year-round. Sewanee is tied to the Episcopal Church, and Greek life abounds on campus.

Academic scholarships based on achievement with consideration of intellectual promise, leadership ability, and potential for service are awarded to incoming students.

Top 25%	Sewanee	YOU
SAT	1360	
ACT	30	
Average		
GPA	3.6	

SOUTHERN METHODIST UNIVERSITY

Dallas, TX

Suburban, Large Town

Private University

6,228 Students

1,329 First Year

56% Out-of-State

Average Annual Amounts:

$49,920 Sticker Price

$31,227 Net Price

$18,693 Grant

$7,661 Loan

NCAA Division I-A

www.smu.edu

OFA (214) 768–2068

enrol_serv@smu.edu

Home of the Mustangs, SMU offers more than 100 majors for under-graduates, and if you're from Texas, you've probably already considered going here. It's just as big as you think it is—and it claim its merit aid program is one of the largest in the country.

SMU says it has one of the most "substantial commitments" to merit and leadership scholarships in the United States, but it doesn't publish the criteria, and you must apply by January 15th to be eligible for consideration.

Top 25%	SMU	YOU
SAT	1340	
ACT	30	
Average		
GPA	3.57	

SPRING HILL COLLEGE

Mobile, AL

Suburban, Large City

Private Jesuit Liberal Arts

1,310 Students

356 First Year

57% Out-of-State

Average Annual Amounts:

$38,980 Sticker Price

$20,291 Net Price

$18,689 Grant

$6,461 Loan

NAIA Division I

www.shc.edu

OFA (251) 380–3460

SHC bills itself as "the Jesuit College of the South," and seeks to remind us that Jesuits try to be synonymous with educational excellence, and commitment to service. The curriculum, and the experience, are rigorous.

All applicants for admission are considered for academic scholarships, which run from $7,000 to $16,000 per year.

Top 25%	SHC	YOU
SAT	1170	
ACT	26	
Average		
GPA	3.49	

ST. ANDREWS PRESBYTERIAN COLLEGE

Laurinburg, NC	*Average Annual Amounts:*
Rural Large Town	*$35,500 Sticker Price*
Private Liberal Arts	*$24,541 Net Price*
600 Students	*$10,959 Grant*
147 First Year	*$4,464 Loan*
63% Out-of-State	

NCAA Division II

www.saca.edu

OFA (910) 277–5560

If you love the country, outdoor sports, and the liberal arts, SAPC (30 miles outside of Pinehurst, North Carolina) could be a wonderful fit for you. Its 640-acre campus has its own lake, and an additional 300 acres for its equestrian center. Although the college is church-related, it doesn't identify as a religious institution.

The **Vardell Award** is up to $8,500 per year, or $34,000 for all four years, and is awarded to incoming freshman with an SAT of 1300 or higher, and/or and ACT of 29 or higher, and a GPA higher than 3.7. Scholarships for theatre, choir, English and Western horseback riding, and bagpipes are also available.

Top 25%	SAPC	YOU
SAT	1070	
ACT	NA	
Average		
GPA	3.04	

St. Olaf College

Northfield, MN

Rural, Large Town

Private Liberal Arts

3,099 Students

778 First Year

51% Out-of-State

Average Annual Amounts:

$45,600 Sticker Price

$27,319 Net Price

$18,281 Grant

$5,600 Loan

NCAA Division III

www.stolaf.edu

OFA (509) 786–3019

finaid@stolaf.edu

Um! Yah! Yah! Oles are brilliant, engaged, curious, and committed to music, athletics, or service (and more often than not, all three). Since 1996, St. Olaf has produced more Rhodes scholars than any other liberal arts college in the nation, and more than 700 Oles go on study abroad each year (roughly one quarter of the student body). If your credentials are competitive enough to put you into St. Olaf's top 25 percent, make sure you check out the website, and arrange a visit if you can.

The **Buntrock Scholarship** of $16,000 is renewable annually, and the **Service Leadership Scholarship** of $6,000 annually is for students who participate in church, community, or service.

Top 25%	St. Olaf	YOU
SAT	1400	
ACT	31	
Average		
GPA	3.63	

UNIVERSITY OF DENVER

Denver, CO

Urban, Very Large City

Private University

5,343 Students

1,207 First Year

53% Out-of-State

Average Annual Amounts:

$49,185 Sticker Price

$32,612 Net Price

$16,573 Grant

$5,992 Loan

NCAA Division I-AAA

www.du.edu

OFA (303) 871–4020

finaid@du.edu

DU's admission process includes the "Ammi Hyde Interview," where each applicant meets with a three-person group for a 20-minute conversation to bring your personal goals and values alive. Its vision is to be a "great private university, dedicated to the public good," and we think it's really succeeded. The location, campus, and academic programs are all amazing, and don't let UC Boulder, the larger, public school to the north, distract you from DU.

All admitted students are considered for merit scholarships from $3,000 to $18,000 per year, and talent awards are first-come, first-serve.

Top 25%	DU	YOU
SAT	1290	
ACT	29	
Average		
GPA	3.68	

UNIVERSITY OF MINNESOTA—MORRIS

Morris MN

Rural, Small Town

Public Liberal Arts

1,705 Students

492 First Year

13% Out-of-State

Average Annual Amounts:

$21,122 Sticker Price

$14,781 Net Price

$6,341 Grant

$6,105 Loan

NCAA Division III

www.morris.umn.edu

OFA (800) 992–8863

morrisfa@morris.umn.edu

Its motto is "a renewable, sustainable education." UMM is a public liberal arts college with a career focus, and we think it lives up to the challenge. It's very committed to green and local practices, and produces its own renewable and sustainable energy on campus. The UMM Academic Center for Enrichment is kind of a one-stop shop for all things academic—study abroad, honors work, research, and more—and the Center for Small Towns is a community outreach program that connects Morris students with local businesses, government, and projects.

Automatic academic scholarships are available, and UMM publishes a chart on its website to show you what your specific credentials could net you, before you apply. **National Merit Scholarships** are accepted here, and **Prairie Scholars** (a competitive award) receive full tuition.

Top 25%	UMM	YOU
SAT	1420	
ACT	28	
Average		
GPA	3.28	

UNIVERSITY OF THE OZARKS

Clarksville, AR

Rural, Small Town

Private Liberal Arts

625 Students

152 First Year

36% Out-of-State

Average Annual Amounts:

$29,712 Sticker Price

$15,623 Net Price

$14,089 Grant

$5,993 Loan

NCAA Division III

www.ozarks.edu

OFA (479) 979–1221

Ozark's tiny, and it's not a good fit for anyone who wants to hide in the back row, but it is a fantastic—and *affordable*—choice for anyone who wants to know, and be known. The Jones Learning Center is staffed with professionals to assist students with AD/HD or any other learning disability, but beware the extra fees.

Scholarship opportunities range from those that are purely test score–based and GPA-based to one for siblings, with a priority application deadline of March 1st.

Top 25%	Ozarks	YOU
SAT	1090	
ACT	25	
Average		
GPA	3.35	

UNIVERSITY OF PUGET SOUND

Tacoma, WA

Suburban, Small City

Private Liberal Arts

2,608 Students

721 First Year

76% Out-of-State

Average Annual Amounts:

$48,125 Sticker Price

$31,628 Net Price

$16,497 Grant

$7,504 Loan

NCAA Division III

www.pugetsound.edu

OFA (253) 879–3214

sfs@pugetsound.edu

Eco-friendly Tacoma is in striking distance of Mount Rainier, Seattle, and the San Juan islands, but Puget Sound is more than its neighborhood. It has rigorous academics, creative faculty, and a great sense of humor (Go Loggers!). Puget Sound students aren't afraid of rain or hard work, and they're from all over. Only 24 percent hail from Washington State, and Puget Sound offers a nine-month Pacific Rim/Asia study-and-travel program once every three years.

Trustee Scholarships are $12,000 renewable annually, and **President's Scholarships** are $9,000 renewable annually. Neither requires a separate application.

Top 25%	UPS	YOU
SAT	1340	
ACT	30	
Average		
GPA	3.5	

UNIVERSITY OF TULSA

Tulsa, OK

Urban, Large City

Private University

3,084 Students

690 First Year

48% Out-of-State

Average Annual Amounts:

$41,295 Sticker Price

$24,451 Net Price

$16,844 Grant

$7,891 Loan

NCAA Division I-A

www.utulsa.edu

OFA (918) 631–2526

Like many of the campuses in this part of the United States, much of Tulsa's strength comes from the oil and gas industries. Combine those resources with the ambitious student body (one out of every 10 TU undergraduates is a National Merit Scholar), and you'll find a university committed to on-campus energy research work for undergraduates (and with a huge endowment to back it up). You might also be amazed at what Tulsa and Oklahoma have to offer.

If you are a National Merit finalist, consider the highly competitive **Presidential Scholarship** competition, which provides full tuition and basic room and board for four years. All admitted students are considered for **University Scholarships** of up to $12,000 annually.

Top 25%	TU	YOU
SAT	1390	
ACT	32	
Average		
GPA	3.75	

WARREN WILSON COLLEGE

Asheville, NC

Rural, Small City

Liberal Arts

946 Students

249 First Year

80% Out-of-State

Average Annual Amounts:

$35,814 Sticker Price

$25,871 Net Price

$9,943 Grant

$5,171 Loan

NAIA Division II

www.warren-wilson.edu

OFA (828) 771–2082

Warren Wilson takes a truly unique approach to education: Students join a "Triad," or a small community of students with similar interests, and combine their academic program with work crew and service participation. They grow their own food, clean out their own stables, and march to their own drummers. It doesn't get much prettier than the Blue Ridge

Mountains, and students who want to invest in their academics, work for the common good, and provide service to others will thrive here.

Scholarships of $4,000 per year are available for students who graduate first or second in their high school class, **National Merit Scholarship Finalists,** and residents of North Carolina who are in the top 20 percent of their class, with an SAT higher than 1100 and/or ACT higher than 24. Scholarships of $2,000 annually are also available for students who display a commitment to **Work**, **Service**, or **Sustainability**.

Top 25%	WW	YOU
SAT	1270	
ACT	27	
Average		
GPA	3.2	

WEST VIRGINIA UNIVERSITY

Morgantown, WV

Suburban, Small City

Public University

21,720 Students

4,589 First Year

51% Out-of-State

Average Annual Amounts:

Instate

$16,034 Sticker Price

$10,542 Net Price

Outstate

$27,132 Sticker Price

$21,640 Net Price

$5,492 Grant

$4,958 Loan

NCAA Division I-A

www.wvu.edu

OFA (800) 344–9881

finaid@mail.wvu.edu

On the homepage of WVU's website, there's a link to its "Brockumentary," *Born to be a Mountaineer*. It's funny, a little edgy, unpretentious, and full of WVU pride—which, in a nutshell, also describes its students. This is absolutely a campus for "doers," which means extroverts—athletes, musicians, volunteers, and anyone who loves DI sports. Morgantown doesn't offer much in the way of alternatives to campus life.

West Virginia residents may use the **PROMISE Scholarship** (assuming you qualify) here, but the WVU website lists a slew of other merit scholarships for all other students. There are five levels of merit scholarships neatly arranged on a matrix on the website, from $3,000 to $17,500 per year, depending on your credentials.

Top 25%	WVU	YOU
SAT	1140	
ACT	26	
Average		
GPA	3.3	

WILLIAM JEWELL COLLEGE

Liberty, MO

Suburban, Large Town

Private Liberal Arts

1,083 Students

282 First Year

36% Out-of-State

Average Annual Amounts:

$36,240 Sticker Price

$21,733 Net Price

$14,507 Grant

$6,360 Loan

NCAA Division II

www.jewell.edu

OFA (816) 415–5975

finaid@william.jewell.edu

William Jewell is a wonderful (but very small) college with a series of academic experiences that rely on an intimate environment to be successful, and it has a four-year graduation guarantee. Jewell students want a rigorous academic program, but they're still pretty mainstream; you won't see a lot of tattoos or piercings here. The Oxbridge Honors Program combines British teaching methods on-campus with a year at Oxford or Cambridge.

William Jewell has a ton of merit aid available, including but not limited to the following: **Jewell Scholarships** offer $15,000, $17,000 or full tuition for student in the top 20 percent of their class rank, 27 ACT, 3.5 GPA. **Oxbridge Honor Scholarships** offer $15,000 per year, for students in the top 10 percent of their class rank, 28 ACT, 3.75 GPA, and an Oxbridge essay.

Top 25%	William Jewell	YOU
SAT	1290	
ACT	29	
Average		
GPA	3.68	

WILLAMETTE UNIVERSITY

Salem, Oregon

Urban, Small City

Private Liberal Arts

1,997 Students

541 First Year

71% Out-of-State

Average Annual Amounts:

$46,000 Sticker Price

$28,602 Net Price

$17,398 Grant

$6,908 Loan

NCAA Division III

www.willamette.edu

OFA (503) 370–6273

finaid@willamette.edu

Willamette, which dates itself back to 1834, has a complicated history—but it doesn't shy away from it, and you can read all about it (primarily the subjugation of the native peoples) on its website. That's why we like Willamette: It's a no-nonsense kind of place, and its students aren't afraid of anything. Most Bearcats are strong academically *and* have a strong sense of social responsibility; its motto is "Not unto ourselves alone are we born."

Willamette is home to five Centers for Excellence (Ancient Studies and Archaeology, Asian Studies, Governance and Public Policy Research,

Study of Religion, Law and Democracy, and Sustainable Communities), all of which provide public programming, support research by faculty and students, develop partnerships with external groups, and more.

The **Mark Q. Hatfield Scholarship** offers full tuition for four years, and is available to freshman only, with an extensive record of public service and a 3.25 GPA or higher. Other merit-based scholarships range from $3,000 to $15,000 per year.

Top 25%	Willamette	YOU
SAT	1320	
ACT	30	
Average		
GPA	3.72	

XAVIER UNIVERSITY OF LOUISIANA

New Orleans, LA

Urban, Very Large City

Private Catholic University

2,666 Students

765 First Year

36% Out-of-State

Average Annual Amounts:

$26,319 Sticker Price

$19,517 Net Price

$6,802 Grant

$5,343 Loan

NAIA Division I

www.xula.edu

OFA (504) 520–7517

finaid@xula.edu

Xavier, the only historically black *and* Catholic university in the country, is a spirited and faith-based place that isn't just nominally Catholic. If you're looking for a faith-based education (in one of the most distinctive and vibrant cities in the United States), Xavier may be a good fit for you. Although Katrina did major damage in 2005, New Orleans is rebuilding at an amazing pace, and it could be a fantastic professional environment for you upon graduation.

All incoming freshman are considered for merit scholarships, and no supplementary applications or materials are required.

Top 25%	Xavier	YOU
SAT	1060	
ACT	24	
Average		
GPA	3.16	

NOTES

CHAPTER 1

1. Mary Pilon, "Earnings Gap Between College and High School Grads Small," The Wall Street Journal, February 2, 2010.

2. Paul Krugman, "Graduates Versus Oligarchs," The New York Times, February 27, 2006.

3. Trends in College Pricing 2010, The College Board, www.thecollegeboard.org.

4. Mark Krantrowitz, "Ask Kanthro," Fastweb. com, September 22, 2009.

5. Digest of Education Statistics 2009, "Table 331," National Center for Education Statistics, U.S. Department of Education, nces.ed.gov.

CHAPTER 2

1. Alexander W. Astin, What Matters in College: Four Critical Years Revisited, page 388. Jossey-Bass Inc., San Francisco, Calif.: 1993.

CHAPTER 3

1. Annual NACE Salary Survey, 2009 (19%) and 2010 (24%), nace.org.

2. Peter Coy, "The Lost Generation," *Business Week*, October 11, 2009.

3. Anthony Carnevale, Nicole Smith, and Jeff Strohl, *Help Wanted: Projecting Jobs and Education Requirements Through 2018*, Center on Education and the Workforce, Georgetown University, June 2010, *www9.georgetown. edu/grad/gppi/hpi/cew/pdfs/FellReport.pdf.*

4. *Annual NACE Salary Survey 2010*, Nace.org.

5. "Contexts of Postsecondary Education," U.S. Department of Education, 2009, nces.ed.gov.

CHAPTER 6

1. *Digest of Education Statistics*, 2009, "Table 349: Percentage of full-time, full-year postbaccalaureate students receiving aid, by type of aid, level of study, and control and type of institution: Selected years, 1992–93 through 2007–08," National Center for Education Statistics, U.S. Department of Education, nces.gov. (Numbers cited are from 2008, the most recent year for which such data is available.)

2. COAs mentioned here come from the colleges' own websites. Acceptance and enrollment data comes from the College Board, collegeboard.com.

3. From the College Board (collegeboard.com) and College Navigator (nces.ed.gov).

CHAPTER 7

1. Tamar Lewin, "Senator Calls for New Rules for For-Profit Colleges," *The New York Times*, June 24, 2010.

2. "For Profit Colleges," GAO 10-948T, August 4, 2010, gao.gov.

INDEX

ABOUT THE AUTHORS

Carol Stack and **Ruth Vedvik** have each worked for 35 years in the college admission and financial aid industry and for the past 14 and nine years, respectively, as principals at Hardwick-Day, an enrollment consulting firm that works with the admission and financial aid offices of private colleges and universities. Both have held cabinet-level positions at private colleges as directors of admission, with full responsibility for the recruitment, selection, and funding of the annual freshman class. Carol has worked in secondary school guidance offices at two international schools, and began her career working in the admission office at Macalester College, where she eventually became director of admission. Ruth has extensive experience in the public sector, as the director of admission at Ball State University, the University of Illinois at Urbana-Champaign, and Agnes Scott College. She began her career as an admission counselor at Gustavus Adolphus College.

In their extensive consulting practice, Carol and Ruth have assisted colleges and universities with recruitment, selection, communication, and the development and implementation of financial aid policy. Among the client colleges and universities with which they have worked with or are working are: Mills College, St. Mary's College, the College of Wooster, Webster University, American University, Grinnell College, Randolph Macon College, Oberlin College, Whittier College, Reed College, St. Olaf College, the University of Portland, and Xavier University. Their expertise on all aspects of financial aid is gained from daily work with a multiplicity of colleges and universities: watching the college recruitment and selection process at work, listening to the kinds of phone calls that come in to college financial aid and admission offices, seeing the data—the results of real-time decisions that students and parents are making.

We're not finished yet! For even more information, go online to *the-financialaidhandbook.com*. We agreed with our publisher that the information we proposed for this section of the book changes annually and in order to keep it current, we need to have it online. What is so important that you must absolutely know the most current version? The federal and state procedures, rules, regulations, and dollar amounts of funding that are available for you.

At *thefinancialaidhandbook.com* you'll find a section for every state in the United States. We'll link you to your state's financial assistance organization and other important state agencies that will provide information about state loan and savings programs—if your state has them. We've done the research so you can just follow the links.

We'll have other information available as well. Some sections will have short refreshers about important information from the book; other sections will have new information that wasn't available when we wrote the book or wasn't important enough at the time to be included. Things change rapidly in the financial aid world, and we want you armed with the good stuff—the latest word on all things related to college funding.

You will also find PDFs of the tables we've created for you so you may print them out and go at creating your MAP!

We may have an occasional surprise on the Website—a contribution from an admission dean or financial aid director with tips about getting in and getting money at their schools.

So off you go to *thefinancialaidhandbook.com*. Enjoy!